FAITH AND FRATRICIDE

The Theological Roots
of Anti-Semitism

FAITH AND FRATRICIDE

The Theological Roots of Anti-Semitism

Rosemary Radford Ruether

The Seabury Press

5 4 3 2 1

Winston Press, Inc.
430 Oak Grove
Minneapolis, Minnesota 55403

Copyright © 1974 by The Seabury Press, Inc.
Designed by Paula Wiener
Printed in the United States of America

LIBRARY OF CONGRESS CATALOGING IN PUBLICATION DATA

Ruether, Rosemary Radford.
    Faith and fratricide: the theological roots of anti-Semitism.

    1. Christianity and antisemitism—History.
I. Title.
BM535.R8   268.8'34'51924   74-11341
ISBN 0-8164-2263-X

This study
is dedicated to my uncle,
DAVID SANDOW

Acknowledgments

I wish to thank Camilla Ream of the Divinity School of Harvard University, who typed this manuscript and whose editorial and linguistic skills were most helpful. I also wish to thank Yosef Yerushalmi of Harvard University and Dr. Sidney Hoenig of Yeshiva University and Dr. Jacob Neusner of Brown University who read and criticized parts or all of the manuscript. Dr. Gregory Baum of St. Michael's College and Dr. Emil Fackenheim of the University of Toronto have seen this manuscript through from the beginning. Dr. Eva Fleischner of Montclair College also read and gave helpful criticism of chapters in this work. I wish to thank Rabbi Ben Zion Gold at Harvard-Hillel, who read this work and promoted discussion of its contents at Harvard. Finally I wish to thank Rabbi Solomon Bernards of the Anti-Defamation League of B'nai B'rith for his constant support and help in developing this work for publication. Rabbi Bernards gave me the opportunity to present the contents to a critical audience at the Jewish-Christian Academic Seminar at Princeton Theological Seminary, February, 1973. He also contacted Dr. Sidney Hoenig, who did a careful reading of the manuscript for points of tension in Jewish and Christian scholarship. Finally Rabbi Bernards assisted me in the preparation of indices for the work in its final stages.

Contents

✓Chapter 5

THEOLOGICAL CRITIQUE OF
THE CHRISTIAN ANTI-JUDAIC MYTH   226

Introduction

Gregory Baum

The injustices and pogroms inflicted over the centuries on the Jews by Christian nations, often in the name of Christian principles, did not stir the conscience of theologians until fairly recently. It was the advent of Hitler's anti-Semitism that produced uneasiness in some Church circles and made theologians take a new look at their Christian past. Was the refutation of Judaism that was implicit in the Christian religion and in the Christian polemics against the unbelieving Jews in any way connected with the anti-Semitism prevalent in Western history and its culmination in the racial anti-Semitism of the Nazis? Some Christian thinkers began to speak out in favor of the Jews on theological grounds. They abhorred anti-Semitism: they came to recognize that the Church's anti-Jewish polemics have created anti-Jewish feelings in the past, but they trusted that the Church's central message, namely the love of God and neighbor, would be able to overcome the prejudices and antipathies generated by the ancient polemics. The Catholic names that come to mind in this connection are Jacques Maritain, Charles Journet, Henri de Lubac. These and some other authors sought a Christian manner of speaking of Judaism that would not produce contempt for the Jews; they searched for scriptural promises that applied to Christians and Jews alike; and they tried to acknowledge an abiding vocation for the Jewish people.[1] These authors were convinced that the anti-Jewish trends were peripheral to the Church's teaching, that they were in fact deformations of the gospel introduced at a later point in history, and that it would consequently be comparatively easy to purify the Church's life and message from anti-Jewish prejudices and the expressions of contempt. Little did these authors realize, despite their generosity, how deeply the anti-Jewish trends were woven into the significant documents of the Christian religion and how closely these trends were connected with the Church's expression of its faith.

The publication in 1948 of *Jésus et Israel*,[2] written by a French historian, Jules Isaac, himself a Jew, brought out, as no study had done before, how closely the contempt for the Jewish people and the vilification of Jewish religion were linked to Christian preaching from the New Testament on. In particular, Jules Isaac showed that even the sacred books of the Gospels contained much polemical material that drew an unfaithful picture of Jewish religion and created disdain for Jews and Judaism. *Jésus et Israel* raised the frightful question whether the Christian Church could ever separate itself from its anti-Semitic heritage.

Jules Isaac's book moved me very deeply. When in the late fifties I tried to give a partial response to Jules Isaac in a book entitled *The Jews and the Gospel*,[3] I readily acknowledged the anti-Jewish trends present in Christian preaching, but I then thought that it was my religious duty as a Christian theologian to defend the New Testament itself from the accusation of prejudice and falsification. At that time I thought that the anti-Jewish trends were later developments in Christian history. In my apologia for the New Testament, I interpreted the passages hostile to Jews and Jewish religion according to three principles. There were passages, first of all, that were specifically addressed to the generation of Jerusalem to which Jesus himself belonged. These Jews were the unfaithful ones; they had rejected Jesus' preaching; they were under God's judgment. I argued that it was only the malevolent interpretation of Christians of a later period that extended these condemnations to the entire Jewish people. Secondly, I argued that many passages in the New Testament accusing the Jews of blindness and hardheartedness were prophetic utterances made by Christians belonging to Israel to touch the hearts of their own people and convert them to the Christian way. These derogatory passages were not intended as descriptions of first-century Judaism; they were exhortatory sermons, partly prophetic and partly polemical, pronounced by men who still identified themselves with the Jewish people and who sought to lead their compatriots to the gospel. These passages, I then argued, acquired their anti-Semitic meaning only when they were repeated by gentile Christians as judgments on Jewish religion made by outsiders. Finally I proposed that many passages in the New Testament which present a negative picture of the scribes and Pharisees as well as the other opponents of Jesus were not meant to convey an historical account of these groups: these passages intended to reveal the deformations and pathologies to which religion remains ever vulnerable and to initiate the Christian Church itself into critical self-examination. The conflict of Jesus with the various groups and parties in his own people symbolized the ongoing conflict between authentic and inauthentic religion within the Christian Church, and it was precisely the unwillingness on the part of Christians to recognize this and to come to critical self-knowledge that made them project the harsh criticism of these groups and parties onto the entire religion of Judaism. In this way the Church tried to escape the judgment of the gospel on its own life and practices.

Yet my apology for the New Testament led me to a contradiction: for I had to admit in the course of my study that many biblical passages reflected the conflict between Church and Synagogue in the first century.[4] While I was bound to acknowledge that already the New Testament proclaimed the Christian message with a polemical edge against the religion of Israel, I refused to draw the consequences from this. I was still convinced that the anti-Jewish trends in Christianity were peripheral and accidental, not grounded in the New Testament itself but due to later developments, and that it would consequently be fairly easy to purify the preaching of the Church from anti-Jewish bias. Since then, especially under the influence of Rosemary Ruether's writings, I have had to change my mind. Writing this introduction gives me the opportunity to declare that the book I wrote in the late fifties and published in 1961 no longer represents my position on the relationship between Church and Synagogue.

This early stage of Catholic self-criticism, worked out and shared by a good number of exegetes and theologians, found expression in the declaration on Jewish-Christian relations (more correctly, the "Declaration on the Church's Attitude to Non-Christians")[5] which Pope John XXIII, probably inspired by a visit of Jules Isaac, had asked the Second Vatican Council to prepare and publish. While this declaration has been greatly criticized for not going far enough in admitting Christian responsibility for modern anti-Semitism and in rethinking and reformulating Christian teaching regarding the Jews, the conciliar document did make a number of significant points.

In the first place, the Vatican II declaration asked Catholics to engage in dialogue and cooperation with Jews. "Since the spiritual patrimony common to Christians and Jews is thus so great, this sacred Synod wishes to foster and recommend that mutual understanding and respect which is the fruit above all of biblical and theological studies, and of brotherly dialogues."[6] By thus recognizing Judaism as a religion in its own right and an equal partner in dialogue, Vatican II abandoned, at least implicitly, the Church's missionary stance toward the Jews. This move was paralleled by the open attitude of the Council to the other world religions: God's saving truth, we were told, is operative also in them. "The Catholic Church looks with sincere respect upon those ways of conduct and of life, those rules and teachings which, though differing in many particulars from what she holds and sets forth, nevertheless often reflect a ray of that Truth which enlightens all men."[7] Secondly, the Vatican declaration asked Catholic preachers and teachers to eliminate the various evil myths that have been projected upon the Jews in the Christian tradition, especially the myth that they are a rejected people, a people abandoned by God, condemned for their unbelief. "Although the Church is the new people of God, the Jews should not be presented as repudiated or cursed by God, as if such views followed from the Holy Scriptures. All should take pains, then, lest in catechetical instruction and in the preaching of God's Word they teach anything out of harmony with the truth of the gospel and the spirit of Christ."[8] Far from being repudiated, the Jews, according to the teaching of Vatican II, continue to be God's chosen people, *populus secundum electionem carissimus*.[9] Thirdly, the conciliar declaration gives expression to the common hope, shared by Christians and Jews, that God's ultimate victory will eventually overcome the powers of evil and liberate the human family from all the enemies of life. "In company with the [ancient] prophets and the apostle Paul, the Church awaits that day, known to God alone, on which all peoples will address the Lord in a single voice and 'serve him with one accord' [Zeph. 3:9; cf. Isa. 66:23; Ps. 65:4; Rom. 11:11–32]."[10]

Since Vatican II, great efforts have been made to integrate the new attitude and the new teaching in catechisms and other instruments of religious education. The men and women involved in the catechetical renewal have been much more sensitive to the Church's anti-Jewish heritage than theologians and preachers. Yet despite the goodwill of the catechists, the success of this new education has been quite limited. The conciliar directives to respect Judaism as a religion in its own right, to acknowledge the continued election of the Jewish people, and to stress the common hope of Christians and Jews, cannot be successfully inserted into Christian education because they seem to contradict the more central presentation of the Christian gospel.

This takes us to a second stage of Christian self-examination, one that transcends the theological efforts that led to the declaration of Vatican II. Under the impact of the holocaust that destroyed six million Jews, some Christian theologians have been ready to submit Christianity to a radical ideological critique. They have been willing to face the possibility that the anti-Jewish trends in Christianity are not simply peripheral and accidental, but woven into the core of the message. As long as the Christian Church regards itself as the successor of Israel, as the new people of God substituted in the place of the old, and as long as the Church proclaims Jesus as the one mediator without whom there is no salvation, no theological space is left for other religions, and, in particular, no theological validity is left for Jewish religion. The central Christian affirmation seems to negate the possibility of a living Judaism. It is for this reason that marginal corrections, worked out by theologians and adopted by Vatican II, have next to no effect on Christian preaching and teaching: for they seem to be in contradiction to the central Christian claims. If the Church completes its christological and ecclesiological teaching without reflecting on its relation to Israel, and only afterward, when its basic teaching is defined, introduces the acknowledgment that the Jews remain God's chosen people and that therefore their religion has an abiding significance before God, this late recognition can no longer be integrated into the central Christian doctrines: it will remain marginal and ineffectual.

This contradiction between the Church's central teaching and the new approach of Vatican II was brought up by conservative Christians who, for various reasons, religious and political, opposed the Church's new openness to Judaism. They recognized—correctly, I now feel—that the acknowledgment of the Jews as *populus secundum electionem carissimus* and hence as spiritually alive was against the teaching of Christian Scripture and tradition.

In particular Paul himself, from whom Vatican II has taken its language about Israel's ongoing election, had no intention whatever of recognizing Jewish religion as a way of grace. Israel had become blind, according to Paul; it was a way of death, of spiritual slavery. Despite this blindness, the apostle taught, God did not permit Israel to disappear; the election remained with it, not however as a source of present grace, but as a divine promise guaranteeing the conversion of the Jews at the end of time and their integration into the Christian Church, the one true Israel. All attempts of Christian theologians to derive a more positive conclusion from Paul's teaching in Romans 9–11 (and I have done this as much as others) are grounded in wishful thinking. What Paul and the entire Christian tradition taught is unmistakeably negative: the religion of Israel is now superseded, the Torah abrogated, the promises fulfilled in the Christian Church, the Jews struck with blindness, and whatever remains of the election to Israel rests as a burden upon them in the present age.

If the Church wants to clear itself of the anti-Jewish trends built into its teaching, a few marginal correctives will not do. It must examine the very center of its proclamation and reinterpret the meaning of the gospel for our times. Is such a reinterpretation possible?

It was not until the holocaust of six million Jewish victims that some Christian theologians have been willing to face this question in a radical way. In his *Voice of Illness*,[11] Aarne Siirala tells us that his visit to the death camps in eastern Europe after the war overwhelmed him with shock and revealed to him that something was gravely sick at the very heart of our spiritual tradition. He felt that it would not do to look upon the extermination of the Jews as an unfortunate crime committed by wicked people, a dreadful accident of history, with no relation to the cultural and religious past of Western society. The holocaust may not be reduced to a monstrous criminal act to be deplored and then forgotten. Auschwitz has a message that must be heard: it reveals an illness operative not on the margin of our civilization but at the heart of it, in the very best we have inherited. The holocaust challenges the foundations of Western society. It summons us to face up to the negative side of our religious and cultural heritage. Since the time of his death camp visit, Aarne Siirala has understood his theological quest as an effort to diagnose and confront this illness alive in the Christian tradition.

A few theologians have been willing to listen to the message of the death camps. While it would be historically untruthful to blame the Christian Church for Hitler's anti-Semitism and the monstrous crimes committed by him and his followers, what is true, alas, is that the Church has produced an abiding contempt among Christians for Jews and all things Jewish, a contempt that aided Hitler's purposes. The Church made the Jewish people a symbol of unredeemed humanity; it painted a picture of the Jews as a blind, stubborn, carnal, and perverse people, an image that was fundamental in Hitler's choice of the Jews as the scapegoat. What the encounter of Auschwitz demands of Christian theologians, therefore, is that they submit Christian teaching to a radical ideological critique. Their task is to discern the trends in the Church's teaching that legitimate Christian power over others and have destructive effects on

Jews (and other groups of men and women). Is such a radical reinterpretation of the gospel possible? Is it possible to purify the Christian message of its anti-Jewish ideology without invalidating the Christian claims altogether? This is the frightening question.

If a theologian places himself on the ground of Scripture and past tradition alone, such a radical critique may be impossible. But what if God is addressing the Church anew through the awful event of the holocaust? What if a message is revealed there, in the light of which we must examine the entire Christian religion? The holocaust teaches the Church that any monopolistic claim to divine truth or any form of ecclesiastical self-elevation will eventually translate itself—because Christianity has achieved cultural dominance, even if its membership should diminish—into social attitudes and political action and hence generate grave injustices that eventually accumulate to become major crimes. Christian love—the subjective factor—is unable to stop the harmful effects of the symbols of power and domination—the objective factor—woven into Christian preaching and teaching. This, I hold, is the message of Auschwitz addressed to the Church. Why? Because here the theological negation of Judaism and the vilification of the Jewish people that were part of the Christian tradition were translated into genocidal action of monstrous proportions, not indeed by Christians themselves, but by a political party that used for its own purposes a heritage built up by Christianity and counted on a good deal of Christian cooperation.

Christian theologians are able to submit the gospel to a radical critique if they hold that the authentic handing-on of the Christian message in history does not consist in the simple repetition of previous teaching, biblical or ecclesiastical, but rather is a creative process in which past Christian teaching, in obedience to God's Word in the present, is reinterpreted and reformulated as the good news for the present age. God's Word, addressed to the Church in the present, provides a focus, in the light of which biblical and traditional teaching may be reinterpreted and, in this sense, changed. "Brothers" in the New Testament stands only for fellow Christians; but under the impact of contemporary religious experience, Vatican Council

II, following the teaching of modern theologians, applied the title of "brothers" to all men wherever they are, for they are all summoned by divine grace—in this they do not differ from Christians—to become a single, reconciled humanity. Listening to God's judgment on the Auschwitz holocaust, Christian theologians are summoned to remove the elements of death from the Christian message of life and to reinterpret, if need be in a radical way, the self-understanding of the Christian Church.

It is here that we must place the theological achievement of Rosemary Ruether.

Before introducing the thought of Rosemary Ruether, I wish to refer to a few theologians who, after the holocaust, have tried to rethink the Church's self-understanding in an original way so as to make theological room for Jewish religion. Two Catholic thinkers, Karl Thieme and Paul Démann,[12] have proposed and defended the viewpoint that the coming of Jesus produced a tragic schism in God's people, a schism between Church and Synagogue, leaving both communities slightly damaged. The Church, according to this viewpoint, may not regard itself as the heir of the people of Israel. What has taken place, rather, is a thwarting of God's plan, a harmful rift within his people, and as long as the Jewish tradition remains apart from the Church, it is not as one, holy, catholic, and apostolic as it was meant to be. The absence of the older sister, the Synagogue, has left the Church estranged from the Jewish environment of its foundation: this estrangement, in turn, introduces tensions in the Church's life that lead to further schisms and weakens the fidelity of the Christian community to the original message. While according to these authors, Jewish religion remains incomplete without Jesus, the Christian religion remains incomplete without the Jewish tradition. Grace and healing are available at this time through the ongoing interaction between Church and Synagogue; the final overcoming of the schism is promised for the eschatological fulfillment at the end of time.

Some Protestant thinkers have proposed the view that the Synagogue and the Church actually represent the same biblical faith, even if they have been created by distinct though interrelated covenants. The ancient covenant made with Israel remains valid for the Jews until today; the new covenant, brought by Jesus, extends the ancient promises to the Gentiles, but it in no way replaces the ancient covenant made with Israel. The Jews have access to divine grace through fidelity to the original covenant, while the Gentiles find faith in the one God and deliverance from idolatry through their faithful acceptance of the new covenant. There are two ways, then, within the one biblical faith, one for the Jews and one for the Gentiles, ways that remain in some tension and are meant to test and encourage one another. This view was expounded by James Parkes, the courageous British theologian who began to deal with the anti-Jewish trends in Christian teaching in the mid-thirties, before other theologians had given them much attention.[13] But even in the more developed theological thought of Reinhold Niebuhr and Paul Tillich, we find the theory of the two covenants. Both Niebuhr and Tillich insisted, especially after the holocaust, that the Jews do not need Christianity to be faithful to the biblical promises.[14]

An interesting theory has been proposed by Coert Rylaarsdam,[15] who sees the tension in biblical religion not so much between old and new covenant (i.e., between Jewish people and Christian Church) as between *two types* of covenants, found in the Old as well as in the New Testament, which affect the very nature of biblical religion, whether Jewish or Christian. Rylaarsdam distinguishes between the covenant with Israel, made at Shekem, which was forward-looking, democratic, loosely structured, and charismatic, and the covenant with David, at Mount Zion, which was commemorative of the past, institutional, hierarchical, and cosmic. The tension between Shekem and Zion pervades biblical religion, Jewish or Christian, at times making people put emphasis on the transformation of life within history, or at other times making them stress the overcoming of history in the age to come. Jews and Christians are engaged in an everlasting conversation on how they deal (each in their own religious community) with these two paradoxical covenants, neither of which can be dissolved into the other.

Rylaarsdam's theological effort to make room for Judaism, as well as the theories proposed by the other theologians, Catholic and Protestant, mentioned above, dealt mainly with a renewed understanding of the believing community, in other words with ecclesiology. But it is first of all the Christology of the Christian Church that determines whether Christians can leave room for Jewish religion or whether they must regard Judaism as a religion destined to disappear by conversion to, or transmutation into, Christianity. It is here that Rosemary Ruether's original work begins.

The first task which Rosemary Ruether has set for herself in *Faith and Fratricide* is to detect the source and origin of the anti-Jewish trends in the Christian tradition. It is only after this wound has been detected and its effects on later developments analyzed that Christian theologians will be able to affirm the Christian message without simultaneously negating Jewish existence. Is it possible, we ask ourselves, that the anti-Jewish virus is an integral part of the Christian message so that by removing the virus we destroy the message? Will the attempt to purify the gospel from the anti-Jewish ideology leave the gospel itself intact or will it be pulled out by its root? Christian theologians may not know the answer to this question beforehand; at the same time they hold it is impossible to defend the message of Jesus by protecting it from an ideological critique. The gospel needs no false protection: if the Christian message were in need of being shielded from a critique of its destructive implications, it would not be God's word of salvation.

In *Faith and Fratricide*, Rosemary Ruether shows that the anti-Jewish trends in Christianity are not due to late developments; they go back to the earliest times. They were, almost from the beginning, linked to the Church's proclamation of Jesus as the Christ. The affirmation of Jesus as the promised Messiah, and hence as the fulfillment of the promises made to Israel in the past, brought with it a special way of reading the ancient Scriptures. The faith in Jesus as the Christ provided a new key for understanding the biblical books, the books which the Church later designated as Old Testament. In the early years, prior to the formation of the New Testament, the Jewish Synagogue and the Christian Church based their existence on the same Scriptures, but they read them in different ways: for the Jews the promises were still awaiting fulfillment; for the

Christians they were already fulfilled in the kingdom inaugurated by Jesus Christ. It was, therefore, almost from the beginning that the Christian affirmation of Jesus as the Christ was accompanied by a refutation of the synagogal reading of the Scriptures. This accompanying refutation, which Rosemary Ruether calls "the left hand of Christology," is the source and origin of Christian anti-Semitism.

The Christian community had to demonstrate in a persuasive way that the Jewish interpretation of the Scriptures was wrong. Only the Church had the true hermeneutical key for the Scriptures; the Synagogue read the Scriptures without understanding their true meaning. The Jews read the Scriptures literally, yet their true meaning was not in the letter but in the spirit. The Jews, according to this Christian refutation, were attached to the letter, to externals, to the shell, while the Christians were open to the spirit, the inward content, the deeper meaning of God's promises. The Christians, troubled by the Jewish refusal, tried to find in the Scriptures the prediction of "the blindness" of Israel. They read the history of Israel as a series of failures and infidelities, which had now climaxed in the rejection of Jesus as the one who fulfilled the scriptural promises. The Jews had always been blind, the argument went; they never understood the meaning of the Scriptures; they never listened to and knew the God who spoke to them. Christian preaching, extending the left hand of Christology, began to split the religion of Israel into two distinct sections, the law and the promises. The Jews, it was said, were attached only to the law; they mistook the outward dress for the inner substance; they were blind to the promises of grace announced in the Scriptures, which culminated in Jesus and found their fulfillment in the Christian community. The substance of the Scriptures was available only in the Church. The Christians were the true Israel.

It was this left hand of Christology that generated, almost from the beginning and with growing intensity as time went on, the radical distinction between the believing Church and the blind Synagogue, between the Israel of the spirit and the Israel of the flesh, between the heavenly and the earthly Jerusalem. Eventually all the dichotomies of salvation between spirit and flesh, light and darkness, truth and falsehood, grace and damnation, life and death, trust and self-righteousness, were projected on the opposition between Church and Synagogue until the Jewish people became the embodiment of all that is unredeemed, perverse, stubborn, evil, and demonic in this world.

The left hand of Christology, already present in the New Testament, was further elaborated, under various historical circumstances, by the writers of Christian antiquity. The fathers of the Church made use of this christological perspective to create a wide *adversus Judaeos* tradition, which presented the Jews as an unfaithful people and the worship of the Synagogue as devoid of meaning. The Jews were wicked; Judaism was an empty house. While the Jews were still reciting the ancient Scriptures, they did not understand what they were saying. They had no faith: there was no place for them before God. The Church's theological stance toward the Jewish people was eventually, after Christianity had become the official religion of the Roman Empire, translated into an imperial legislation that excluded the Jews from the body of society and placed them in a situation of legal oppression. The Church's spiritual negation of Jewish existence thus found expression in social and political terms. The faithless Jews received their due.

Only after the Enlightenment and the subsequent secularization did the lot of the Jews begin to change in some countries—even though the Enlightenment thinkers, unwilling to face the repressed side of their Christian past, carried forward the traditional anti-Semitism in a new form. In Russia and Poland, where the great majority of Jews lived (after they had been chased out of the German-speaking lands in the fourteenth century), the legal structure inherited from the Constantinian past remained operative right into the early twentieth century. When Hitler came, armed with an anti-Semitism that translated the older antipathy to the Jews into racist form, he turned the negation of Jewish existence into brutal fact and executed—something the Christian Church had never done—the ancient death-wish against the Jews with the technology of genocide.

If the Christian Church wants to purify its message and its life from the anti-Jewish virus, it will have to remove this left hand of Christology. This means that the Church must be willing to leave room for a Jewish reading of the ancient Scriptures. This, as I see it, is the conclusion of Rosemary Ruether's research. But is such rethinking of Christology possible? Is not Jesus the fulfillment of all the promises made in the Scriptures? Is he not the one mediator between God and man? Is it possible for the Church to relativize Jesus as the Christ?

This question is asked today not only as the result of the theologians' anguished reflection on the holocaust and the recognition that the Christian proclamation must be freed from its anti-Jewish impact; it is also asked by theologians who have reflected on the white man's hegemony in the world. How was it possible, theologians ask themselves, that the white man of Europe felt justified in invading the other continents—the Americas, Asia, and Africa—conquering the territory where other peoples lived, and imposing political and/or economic structures that eventually brought the greater part of the world's resources under his own control? The impulse for this invasion was not religious; it was built into the political and economic structure of Europe. But this invasion was legitimated by the Christian Church with reference to its missionary call. Jesus had wanted his message preached to all the nations of the earth. He was the way of salvation for all men; apart from him there was only darkness. For this reason, then, the Christian Church regarded as providential the expansion of Western power and was ready to send missionaries to follow, or even to accompany, the conquerors and soldiers. The Western domination of the globe, which is being challenged in our time, is therefore not unrelated to the Christian message.

What does this mean in sociological terms? When a Church that has become culturally dominant proclaims Jesus as the one mediator between God and man and regards him as the one way, invalidating all other ways of salvation, it creates a symbolic imperialism that no amount of personal love and generosity can prevent in the long run from being translated into social and political realities. The symbols of exclusiveness belonging to a religion that has become culturally successful are objective factors that will affect the consciousness of a people and promote their cultural and/or political domination, a trend that no subjective factors, such as love and generosity, can overcome. A religion that has achieved cultural success, there-fore, must be willing to submit itself to an ideological critique. Here too then, in connection with the white man's domination over other races, theologians have asked themselves if it is possible to relativize Jesus. Can Christians make theological room for other religions? Or must they desire that the whole world be Christian? Can Christians acknowledge the existence of several world religions as a divine dispensation, or must they look upon the other religions as preparations for Christianity and hence as entities like Judaism that are destined to disappear?

Confronted with this question, theologians may be tempted to choose the "liberal" solution by abandoning the gospel's claim to absolute truth altogether. However, if we propose Christian teaching as one truth among many, we lose all powers of discernment. If we claim that the gospel is true for us while other religions are for their followers, we have no universal norm by which to judge human history and discern the direc-tion of life which we must follow. If the gospel is only true for Christians, then we have nothing to say to others, then our religion has no relevance to the liberation of people from the many forms of personal and social oppression. If we simply abandon a universal norm, we are unable to detect the power of evil in the human world and unite with others in a common struggle against it. The "liberal" view of religious pluralism underestimates this power of evil. Yet the gospel is radical: it applies as critique and promise to the whole of human life.

A responsible relativizing of Jesus, therefore, must protect an aspect of absolute and universal significance. This transcend-ent element does not invalidate other religions but, instead, offers a critique of all religions, including the Christian one. This transcendent element submits all cultural patterns and political movements to a test. This transcendent element con-fronts each person, in the Church and outside, with a principle of self-knowledge leading to transformation of awareness. While Christian theologians wish to create theological space for other religions on God's earth, they do not speak of religious pluralism unless they simultaneously mention liberation from evil and injustice.

In recent Christian theology we find principally two ways of relativizing the Christian claims. The first way removes Christianity's monopoly of divine grace by regarding Jesus as the visible embodiment of a divine principle operative, in a hidden way, in the entire history of men. This approach is a version of the ancient Logos Christology: Jesus is identified with the divine Logos that is creating the cosmos and redeeming the history of men. Thanks to the omnipresence of the Logos, divine grace is available to people wherever they are; even the world religions may become mediators of salvation, even though this grace is fully and completely embodied only in the man Jesus. This theology of universal grace, developed by Protestant thinkers in the nineteenth century and by Catholic thinkers such as Maurice Blondel and Karl Rahner in the twentieth, was able to influence the teaching of Vatican II and create the doctrinal basis for the Catholic Church's new openness to the world religions and to secular culture in general. According to this new approach, grace is as universal in human life as sin, and more abounding.

While this teaching dissolves the Church's monopoly of salvation and relativizes Christianity in a certain way, it continues to link the fullness of grace to Jesus Christ and hence to consider Christianity as the complete and full manifestation of divine religion. While this theology enables Christians to be open to God's grace operative in other religions and in secular human history, it still makes them look upon graced men and women as Christians without knowing it, as "anonymous Christians" (Karl Rahner) or "implicit Christians" (Schillebeeckx), as people alive by a grace that flows from Jesus Christ and is oriented toward its fullness in the profession of his name. This christological approach, therefore, cannot be considered as an adequate doctrinal basis of religious pluralism: according to this theology, other religions inasmuch as they are authentic are implicit Christianities destined to be superseded by explicit Christianity. They are provisional and partial, and the further they move along the way of divine grace, the closer they come to their displacement by the Christian Church. Karl Rahner makes this quite clear in his theology of religious pluralism: he likens the world religions to the religion of Israel.[16] Like

Israel they anticipate the grace of Christ and prepare his total manifestation in the Christian Church. We are back, then, to the theory of substitution. We are left with a theology which, in a more refined form, negates Jewish existence as an abiding historical reality. Judaism and the other world religions are stages on the way to the Church. If Jews were faithful to their divine call, they would cease to exist as Jews.

There is, however, a second way in which theologians have tried to relativize Christianity so as to leave room for other religions, and in particular for Judaism, before God. This way stresses the incompleteness of present redemption. Jesus is a significant beginning, an irreversible turning point, and a promise for future fulfillment. Rosemary Ruether follows this line of thought.

The early Christians had a special vocabulary for speaking about the unfinished character of present redemption: they spoke of the Second Coming. They expressed their hope in the return of Christ at the end of time. While this language was used in the ancient creeds, it did not receive adequate attention in traditional theology. A purely literal understanding of this language even embarrassed many modern Christians. Does it make sense today to speak of the kingdom of glory promised for the last day? Yet by making the Second Coming a central affirmation of Christian teaching, contemporary theologians have been able to interpret the absolute affirmation regarding Jesus as statements that will be true only at the end of time. Krister Stendahl has developed this idea in his beautiful articles on the meaning of Jesus.[17] Rosemary Ruether follows this eschatological perspective.

God's revelation in Jesus remains incomplete, unfinished, oriented toward the final manifestation. The redemption brought by Jesus to mankind in the present is proleptic or anticipatory of the future glory: it is a token, a pledge, a first installment of the complete redemption promised in the Scriptures. Present salvation is an aperitif (Rubem Alves) preceding the banquet of the last days, making us impatient with the bread of tears offered us in these days of injustice. The absolute claims the Church has made for Jesus and its own historical existence must be translated into eschatological terms, announcing what life will be like rather than what it is at present. In Jesus, then, we have the symbol of flesh and blood of what will happen in the future, revealing the destiny of the human race, and making known the transformation by which men shall enter into their destiny. But since divine redemption is not finished in Jesus, except by way of anticipation, the Church is not the unique vehicle of grace: room remains in world history for other ways of grace, for many religions, and in particular for the other biblical faith, for Judaism.

The Christology which Rosemary Ruether presupposes in her *Faith and Fratricide*, without spelling it out in detail, is worked out by her with great brilliance in a large manuscript, as yet unpublished, entitled *Messiah of Israel and Cosmic Christ*. The Christian reader of *Faith and Fratricide* may regret that the book only alludes to the foundations of Christology, without fully establishing them from the Scriptures. He may even feel that the positive content of the gospel does not get its full share. But what Rosemary Ruether has tried to do in *Faith and Fratricide* is to expose the ideological deformation of the Christian religion in a thoroughgoing way. We first must let the negation stand and only afterward reclaim the life that survives under it. If we interrupt the negative critique too soon, if we take refuge in the positive elements of our tradition, we actually evade the kind of conversion or raising of consciousness that is required to redeem Christianity from its anti-Jewish virus and its absolutizing trend.

The Christian reader may feel that the author of *Faith and Fratricide* has paid too little attention to the resurrection of Jesus, the central event grounding the Christian religion, and hence has left herself in a situation where she could be accused of having abandoned the center of the gospel, i.e., of no longer being a Christian theologian. However, what Rosemary Ruether wants to do in her book is to use a language about the Resurrection which clearly reveals that the facticity of this event is different in kind from the facticity of Israel's Exodus from the land of bondage, which was visible to all participants as well as to their oppressors. The Resurrection does have a weaker kind of visibility. It is a different kind of event, one that is real only when seen in a certain faith perspective. Outside of this faith perspective, it is not a recognizable event; and hence it is impossible to accuse the Synagogue of blindness when it lives out of a faith perspective in which this event cannot be assimilated. Precisely because the Jews expected the coming of the messianic age to have the same visibility-beyond-argument that had the ancient Exodus, they rejected the Christian claim that after Jesus' death on the cross the final age of the world had arrived. The messianic age is not with us as long as human misery prevails.

We touch here upon the vulnerable point of the Christian message. Can we seriously affirm that we live in the messianic age while suffering, injustices, and evil abound, unless we choose to give such a spiritual interpretation to this age of fulfillment that we remove ourselves from the expectations of Israel's faith? Can Christians affirm that Jesus is already the Christ?

This question takes us to the important distinction, introduced by Rosemary Ruether, between fulfilled and unfulfilled messianism. Fulfilled messianism is preached by the Church whenever it forgets the meaning of the Second Coming and teaches that the promises contained in the Scriptures are already fulfilled in Jesus. This fulfilled messianism has made the Church regard itself as the manifestation of the absolute in history and hence as beyond the need of an ongoing self-criticism. Here is the root of the monopolistic and absolutizing bent that has produced so much oppression and so easily led the Church to make exaggerated claims of power.

Fulfilled messianism is the cause of religious imperialism. Unfulfilled messianism, on the other hand, is the good news preached by the Church when it remembers that Jesus will be the Christ in the fullest sense only at the end of time. Jesus is the Christ *now* only in the sense that he anticipated the divine victory at the end, exemplified the structure of the radical transformation promised for the whole of history, and incarnated the breakthrough by which the kingdom enters into history and moves it forward toward the final fulfillment. "If Jesus is to serve as our paradigm of man," Rosemary Ruether writes, "then he must not be seen simply as a finalization of an ideal, but one who reveals to us the structure of human existence as it stands in that point of tension between what is and what ought to be. We might say that Jesus is our paradigm of hoping, aspiring man, venturing his life in expectation of the kingdom, and Christ stands as the symbol of the fulfillment of that hope."[18] Christianity is a messianism that is unfulfilled. The Christian faith does not look back to events in the past that have ushered in the new age once and for all; it rather looks forward to the promises that are made for the transformation of history, typified and guaranteed by the life and message of Jesus.

What follows from this is that Christians stand together with Jews looking for the fulfillment of the promises in the future, restless in this world, ever discerning the injustices and the evil in the present, and open to the victorious coming of God's power to renew human life on this earth. Because Christianity proclaims an unfulfilled messianism, the Church is not the only instrument that serves the coming of the final kingdom: there is room for other vehicles of grace. The Synagogue also discerns present evil and looks forward to God's victory on the basis of her own scriptural foundation, in particular the story of the Exodus. She stands with the Church in the midst of history, trusting and relying on the coming kingdom as the foundation for the present struggle to overcome evil.

For Rosemary Ruether, the Jewish refusal to accept the Christian message has a positive role in creating the Christian self-understanding.[19] For the Jewish "No" to any claim that the messianic age has come as long as suffering and misery prevail could be a constant reminder to Christians not to understand their faith as a fulfilled messianism. The Jewish "No" could prevent Christians from making absolute claims about truth and salvation that either blind them to the evidence of history or make them interpret their religion in such a spiritual way as to void the biblical promises. What has actually happened, however, is that the Church's unspoken and unacknowledged malaise with the claim that with Jesus the final, messianic age had arrived (overlooking its own teaching on the *parousia*) produced the vehement Christian anger with the Jewish "No" and the ardent desire to negate and abolish Judaism.

Faith and Fratricide is a brilliant book. It is also very disturbing. For here the Christian tradition is examined by a

Christian theologian who is willing to let the documents of the past say what they have to say, without softening their meaning to make them a little more acceptable to modern ears. The learned author tries to raise to consciousness the repressed side of Christianity that has affected language, theology, and cultural attitudes of Christians over the centuries and that is still, because repressed and unacknowledged, perpetuated by the Church's doctrine and operative in the Church's collective unconscious.

One consequence of this is the Christian ignorance of living Judaism. Christians have tended to identify Jews and Judaism with the pre-Christian religion of the Bible: for some, Judaism is the Old Testament religion; for others, it is the supposedly legalized religion of the Jews after their return from the Babylonian exile. In either case, the Jews have been superseded; they represent the past over against which Christianity defines itself. Christians have not looked at Judaism as a living religion that has developed over the centuries from its biblical foundation. Until recently universities and seminaries did not provide facilities for studying Judaism at all. Judging from seminary curricula, Christians prefer to go on speaking of "the Jews" and the Church's relationship to "the Jewish people" without encountering Judaism as a complex, historical reality that has revealed its creativity from the beginning to the present day.

Facing the repressed side of one's own history causes pain and demands a great deal of rethinking. Since Christian biblical scholars like to speak of the Jews the way the New Testament does, define the Christian faith in terms of opposition to Jewish religion, and read the Hebrew Scriptures from a perspective that takes for granted that their entire meaning is the preparation of Christianity, it may demand a great deal of rethinking on the part of such scholars to become aware of the constant negation of a living people implicit in their approach. Christian theologians use the traditional language about Jesus and his Church, the true Israel, without asking themselves to what extent this language suppresses a living people and excludes from the face of God other religious traditions. Listening to God's judgment on the Jewish holocaust and the tradition out of which it arose, they will look for a formulation of the Christian faith that does not negate Jewish existence. I wish to quote a sentence from Vatican Council II that has here an authentic, even if unexpected, application: "Christ summons the Church, as she goes its pilgrim way, to that continual reformation of which it always has need, insofar as it is an institution of men here on earth. Therefore, if the influence of events or of the times has led to deficiencies in conduct, in church discipline, or even in the formulation of doctrine (which must be carefully distinguished from the revealed gospel), these should be appropriately rectified at the proper moment."[20]

GREGORY BAUM

St. Michael's College
University of Toronto

Chapter 1

The Greek and Jewish Roots of
The Negative Myth of the Jews

I. *Pagan Anti-Judaism as a Factor*
in Christian Anti-Judaism

It has sometimes been said that anti-Semitism is essentially pagan, not Christian. This view would have it that the Christian opposition to the Jews was benignly theological. Virulent anti-Semitism entered the picture only when the Christian community was assimilated into the gentile world and took over a preexisting, non-Christian "pagan hate" for the Jews.[1] This thesis is misleading (especially since it is based on a theological stereotype of the "pagan"). For this reason, it would be well to give a summary of the character of pagan anti-Judaism in order to establish its relationship to the development of the Christian polemic against the Jews.

As Marcel Simon has pointed out, classical anti-Semitism was not economic. The Jews were not identified with special economic roles that incited jealousy. There was none of that special identification of Jews with money or banking such as has been typical of anti-Semitism built on the traditions of medieval Christendom. Nor was classical anti-Semitism racial, strictly speaking. The Greeks and Romans did regard Orientals with a certain contempt and looked on them as a degenerating influence. But this prejudice was cultural, rather than strictly racial. That is to say, it disappeared as the Oriental assimilated into Greco-Roman culture. Rather, the special polemic against the Jews was a consequence of religious sociology; that is, it was a reaction caused by the special social consequences of Jewish religious law.[2]

The more generalized polemic against Jews in classical authors should, however, be distinguished from a special strain of anti-Judaism that has a specifically Egyptian provenance. The Jews had long had a special tension with Egypt, and this took a new form in Hellenistic times. They were settled in Alexandria in large numbers by the Ptolemaic rulers as a privileged minority and were used, as such immigrant groups are often used in colonial societies, as middlemen between the rulers and the subject population. This situation gradually inflamed a resentment against the Jews in Egyptian society that worsened in late Hellenistic and Roman times.[3]

Moreover, Egyptian native intellectuals realized that Egypt was the butt of the negative side of the Jewish salvation story. In the Exodus, the Jews were saved at the expense of the Egyptians. The plagues upon the Egyptians were signs of God's favor upon his people. So the Egyptians are the negative side of the Jewish salvation drama, a fact which one pagan critic was not slow to point out.[4] These areas of tension between Jews and Egyptians produced anti-Jewish riots in Alexandria and a literary tradition of Egyptian anti-Jewish polemic. This latter took the form of counter-myths to the story of Exodus. It was said, for example, that while in Egypt the Jews had actually been a sordid and disease-ridden people who intermarried with the slave population. Far from a miraculous delivery, their departure from Egypt was forced by the Egyptians themselves, who drove them out to rid themselves of a leprous element in the population. The Sabbath was no honorable commemoration but a memento of the same disease-ridden condition characteristic of the Jews. The Jews, in fleeing from Egypt, could only travel six days at a time because they were afflicted with syphilis. Their sabbatical rest reflects this shameful malady. These sorts of anti-Exodus stories were gathered together by the Egyptian priest Manetho in the third century

B.C.E. and were refuted by Hellenistic Jewish writers, such as Josephus.[5] They were repeated in various forms by Hellenistic historians, such as Cheremona and Lysimachus of Alexandria, and Apollonius Molon and Pompeius of Trogus, and thus passed into the general tradition of Hellenistic anthropological and geographical lore.[6]

As distinct from this Egyptian tradition, there is a more generalized tradition of anti-Jewish attitudes in Hellenistic society, which expressed the popular reaction to the religiously sanctioned exclusivity of the Jews. This reaction was not racial, since it would disappear as soon as a Jew gave up his life under Jewish law. It was the spontaneous reaction to a social group that lived in the midst of Hellenistic cities according to a religious law that set it apart from the cultural manners of others. It was a reaction specifically to the social consequences of Jewish religion. Since Hellenistic society regarded Greek culture as the standard for humane existence, that such a group of "barbarians" would refuse assimilation into Hellenistic culture on the grounds that its gods were false and its manners "unclean" was a cultural affront of no small proportions. The stage was set for a *Kulturkampf* between Jewish and Greek society that took the form of forced attempts at Hellenization, such as that under Antiochus Epiphanes, and the struggle for Palestinian independence from the Maccabees to the Jewish Wars.

Given the depth of this cultural and political confrontation, some degree of negativity toward Jews in Greek society is not surprising. However, there were several factors that blunted the collision between Jews and the dominant culture. The Jews had an alliance with Rome, stemming from their struggle against the Seleucids. Jewish writers and leaders continued to trade on this historic friendship to blunt the edge of the hostility that might have developed as a consequence of the Palestinian liberation struggles of the first and early second centuries C.E.[7] In addition, Jewish religious thought in the Diaspora and even in Palestine appropriated many Hellenistic elements, and Jewish Hellenistic apologists, such as the author of Aristeas' letter, Josephus, and Philo, went far in the direction of presenting Judaism in the dress of Greek philosophy.

The Greeks, in turn, cultivated a certain curiosity about ancient Oriental peoples and played their own role in Greco-Oriental assimilation by regarding ancient Eastern wisdom as a kind of "natural philosophy" that predated Plato. The Jews, along with the Egyptians and the Hindu "gymnosophists," were imagined to have an ancient version of this original philosophical religion. The Jewish apologists, in turn, could appropriate this Greek tradition and use it to argue that Plato had learned his philosophy from Moses.[8] Jewish monotheism and ethics attracted those Greek thinkers who were seeking a purer and less anthropomorphic religion, and thus Jewish diatribes against polytheism and idolatry could be fused with the diatribes of Greek philosophy against ancient myth and cult.[9]

So the Jewish reaction to its Greek environment was not merely one of antipathy, but a complex dialectic of assimilation of the best elements and transformation of these into Jewish terms. Judaism could thus present itself to the Hellenistic world as the original version of that higher philosophy for which the Gentiles were seeking. This took the form of an active and highly successful missionary stance of the synagogue within Hellenistic cities. Judaism in the Greco-Roman period was an evangelical religion that was in the process of breaking its ethnic boundaries to become a universal faith. The Septuagint, the Greek translation of the Scriptures created in Alexandria in the third century B.C.E., is the sole example in Jewish history of a scriptural translation that was allowed (for a time) to enjoy the same status as an inspired text as the Hebrew Bible.[10] The doctrine of the Noachian laws gave Judaism a rationale for accepting the "righteous pagan" as a child of God who had a place in the promised Kingdom.[11] Rabbinic teaching urged the full equality of the proselyte with the born Jew and indeed a special solicitousness for the proselyte, since his faith was presumed to be weaker than that of the born Jew.[12] This missionary period of Judaism created around the Hellenistic synagogue a circle of "God-fearers" who were attracted to Jewish monotheism and ethics. It was this universal dimension of Judaism, created by the Jewish mission to Gentiles in the Diaspora, that the Christian Church took over and appropriated. It is impossible to understand the rapid spread of the Church in the Diaspora without recognizing that it built upon and fell heir to this work of Jewish mission and Hellenistic Jewish apologetic.

The political confrontation between Palestinian Jewry and Rome, with its messianically inspired feeling, ended in the disastrous wars of 66–73 C.E. and 133–136 C.E. This struggle generated the suspicion that the Jews were a disloyal and rebellious group. However, these wars did not result in anything like a full-fledged persecution of the Jewish people, such as were later to afflict the Christians. This appears to have been partly due to the fact that the messianic tradition, with its virulent antipathy to the "empires," was not well known to the Greeks and Romans. It was an inner tradition of Jewish hope, and mention of it was typically concealed from Gentiles by Hellenistic Jewish apologists,[13] who stressed the loyalty of the Jews and the tradition of friendship between the Jews and the Romans. The Romans, in turn, had no desire to enter into a campaign of total confrontation with the Jews. Their purpose was the practical task of placing each ethnic group in a workable administrative relationship to the governing apparatus. When Jewish religious prejudices forbade expressions of loyalty to the empire that were tainted by paganism, Jews were allowed to substitute other expressions of loyalty which were more acceptable. Even after the Jewish Wars, the Roman attitude was one of pacification rather than annihilation of Jewry. The temple was destroyed, and Jerusalem razed, because they were the rallying ground for Jewish revolutionary struggle. But the Romans simultaneously entered into relationship with the Pharisees, who exodused to Jamnia and were ready to cooperate with the Romans, to find formulae of mutual cooperation that would respect Jewish religious distinctiveness.

So the reaction of the Greco-Roman world to the Jews was an ambivalent one. On the one hand, their exclusiveness was decried as an absurd misanthropy and a pretension to superiority in a foreign people whom the educated Greek regarded as superstitious "barbarians." Their various customs, such as circumcision, abstinence from pork, and Sabbath leisure, were regarded with amused contempt, rather than hatred. On the other hand, there was the traditional Greek philosophical curiosity and Roman political practicality that created cultural assimilation and administrative accommodation. Jewish laws were recognized by the Romans as the legitimate national customs of a protected people, and a special place was made in Roman law to accommodate these peculiarities within a framework that would not jeopardize Roman dominance. Jewish leaders in Palestine and the Diaspora cooperated to find formulae of coexistence between the Jews and Rome. This special privileged status of the Jews in Roman society began to be rescinded only after Christianity became the official religion of the Roman empire and a Christian anti-Semitism began to express itself in anti-Jewish legislation. This development will be discussed more fully in the fourth section of this study. At this time, however, we will merely note that it was a pagan Rome that found formulae of special accommodation of Jewish ways within Greco-Roman society, while it was Christian Rome that gradually repealed this protected status of the Jews and began to create the legal instruments of the ghetto. This fact alone must lead us to question the thesis that it was pagan anti-Semitism, wrongly assimilated by Christians, that resulted in the embitterment of relations between Christians and Jews in Christendom. Historically, the relation is somewhat the reverse.

Rather, we must recognize Christian anti-Semitism as a uniquely new factor in the picture of antique anti-Semitism.[13] Its source lies in the theological dispute between Christianity and Judaism over the messiahship of Jesus, and so it strikes at the heart of the Christian gospel. It was this theological root and its growth into a distinctively Christian type of anti-Semitism that were responsible for reversing the tradition of tolerance for Jews in Roman law.

There was little in the pagan tradition of anti-Semitism which the Church could take over untransformed. Since the Christians shared with the Jews the biblical Exodus story and also used the word *Egypt* as a negative religious term, they could not appropriate the native Egyptian anti-Exodus polemics without transforming them into a wholly different framework and motivation. Christianity shared fully with Judaism the negative judgment upon polytheism, pagan myths, and cults and continued the Jewish tradition of anti-pagan polemic, so they could not absorb a pagan answer to this biblical intolerance. Christianity, as much as Judaism, was charged by Hellenistic society with unsociability, misanthropy, and disloyalty, and the privacy of its rites suspected of dark and immoral purposes. Since the pagans objected to Judaism primarily because of its exclusiveness and its condemnation of all other religions as idolatry, these objections could not be taken over by a Christianity which shared the same Jewish attitudes of intolerance.

This does not mean that traces of pagan anti-Semitism cannot be glimpsed behind the Christian *adversus Judaeos* tradition. The notion that the Jews were a peculiarly degenerate people in Egypt, used by the Church Fathers to give a negative value to the giving of the Mosaic laws, may owe something to the Egyptian tradition. But its main emphasis is the biblical charge of idolatry, not the Egyptian one of disease. A certain repulsion against circumcision among the Greeks may add fuel to the negative interpretation of this rite by the Church Fathers, although the main source for this is Paul's view that circumcision is not a sign of election. The notion that the Sabbath is an excuse for laziness, found in the Church Fathers, echoes pagan polemic. The idea that Jewish misfortune shows that God is not on their side was a commonplace of all ancient religions that equated good fortune with divine favor. The Christian use of this idea is primarily that of a Christian interpretation of the biblical link between misfortune and divine wrath.[14] A ritual murder charge against the temple cult is found in Greek writers, but this charge is not taken up by the Church Fathers, who only recently had to refute the same charge against themselves.[15] This idea arose quite independently of pagan tradition in the Middle Ages. The head tax (*fiscus Judaicus*), the prohibition against circumcizing non-Jews, and the exclusion of Jews from Jerusalem—marks of punishment of the Jews after the Jewish Wars—were to find their reaffirmation in Christian anti-Judaic legislation.[16]

But even though these traces of pagan anti-Semitism may add power to the Christian argument, the motives of pagan dislike were not assimilable by the Church. Essentially, Christian anti-Judaism grew from a quite separate and distinct motivation, rooted in the interreligious antagonism between Judaism and Christianity over the messiahship of Jesus, whereas the motivations of pagan anti-Judaism were found in their reaction to Jewish anti-paganism, an anti-paganism and exclusive monotheism which Christianity fully shared. Therefore, insofar as these traces of pagan polemic were taken over and used by the Church Fathers, they must be transformed and incorporated into a framework that expressed the Christian, not the pagan, motivation. Indeed, traces of anti-Semitic material that clearly have a pagan rather than a Christian basis form a very small part of the total tradition of Christian anti-Judaism.

In sum we might say that pagan anti-Semitism provided a certain seed bed of cultural antipathy to the Jews in Greco-Roman society, which Christianity inherited in inheriting that world. But this antipathy had been kept in check and balanced by Roman practicality and Hellenistic Jewish cultural apologetics. It was only when Christianity, with its distinctively religious type of anti-Semitism, based on profound theological cleavage within the fraternity of biblical religion, entered the picture that we begin to have that special translation of religious hatred into social hatred that is to become characteristic of Christendom. Hatred between groups who have no stake in a common stock of religiously sanctioned identity symbols can scarcely be as virulent as hatred between groups whose relations express a religious form of "sibling rivalry." The pagan might regard the Jew with puzzlement or contempt, but the polytheism of pagan culture did not lend itself to fanatical hatred of the Jew. The sad truth of religious history is that one finds that special virulence, which translates itself into diabolizing and damnation, only between groups which pose rival claims to exclusive truth within the same religious symbol system. It is for this reason that I have titled this study *Faith and Fratricide*. In my judgment, the special virulence of Christian anti-Semitism can be understood only from its source in a religious fraternity in exclusive faith turned rivalrous. Pagan anti-Semitism, at most, provides a fertile soil for Christian polemics and legislation against the Jews. Many Gentiles had already been prepared to hear such views with willing ears. But other Gentiles, who belonged to that group that became Christian through the Judaizing direction of pagan culture, remained unable to understand that Judaism and Christianity were not part of a single community of faith. But it was the distinctively religious hostility of Christianity to Judaism that provided the constant drive behind a polemic that was to transform itself in Christian civilization into social anti-Semitism.

2. Universalizing and Spiritualizing Tensions in Hellenistic Judaism

We have seen that Judaism, in the Hellenistic and early Roman periods, was subject to an intense challenge to its religious identity. This took the form of a sharp *Kulturkampf* between Judaism and Hellenistic culture. In Palestine this was also translated into continual waves of armed struggle for national liberation from the Greek and Roman empires, culminating in the Jewish Wars of 66–73 C.E. and 133–136 C.E. This struggle fed, religiously, on Jewish messianism. Its literature was the apocalypses of the intertestamental period. In the third section of this chapter, we will discuss some of the sectarian movements that expressed this messianically-inspired national struggle in the period from the Maccabees to the Jewish Wars.

However, there also developed a tradition of accommodation and apologetic toward Hellenism, especially in the Western Diaspora. The Septuagint translation of the Bible was accorded the status of an inspired text in the Hellenistic synagogue. A succession of Hellenistic Jewish midrashists sought to present the Jewish faith to Jews as well as Gentiles in the dress of a Greek philosophical religion. Jewish missionaries saw in the conversion of Gentiles the fulfillment of the divine promise to bring all nations to faith in the God of Zion. Hellenistic Judaism was by no means a capitulation to Hellenism, however. Rather, it was a highly creative effort to protect Jewish religious identity by translating into Jewish terms those elements of Hellenism most compatible with Hebrew ethics and monotheism. It was a broad-based effort to create a universalized and spiritualized Judaism which could offer itself to Gentiles (and in the eyes of its own Hellenized members) as that higher, universal faith to which God called all men. Therefore, we have not followed the common practice of calling Hellenistic Judaism "sectarian," on the analogy of Palestinian separatist groups.[17] Hellenistic Judaism must be seen as an effort by a philosophical school in the Hellenistic synagogue to redefine the mainstream character of Judaism in denationalized and spiritualized terms.

This does not mean, however, that it was the accepted school of midrash of all in the Hellenistic synagogue, by any means. A strong party influenced by the Pharisaic tradition of interpretation kept constant contact with the Hellenistic synagogue. More recent immigrants from the East often reacted unfavorably to the assimilated ways of Hellenistic Jewry in the great cities of the Western Diaspora.[18] Hellenistic and Pharisaic traditions of midrash must have coexisted in a struggle to control the Hellenistic synagogue, with the Pharisaic tradition gradually winning out after the Church had drawn the Hellenistic mode (and probably much of its clientele) to itself.

On the other hand, there were many Hellenized Jews, such as Josephus, in Palestine. The Palestinian sects, such as the Essenes and Samaritans, were particularly open to Greek Gnosticizing influence. Even the Rabbis were not immune to some prudential use of Greek ideas and language.[19] Thus the issue of rabbinic versus Hellenistic midrash does not divide on geography, much less on reverence for the Torah and the temple. Rather, it is a question of two schools of midrashists: one which developed on native biblical soil, with some admixture of Iranian elements, and was centered on halakic commentary (the spelling out of ritual and ethical observances); and a Hellenistic school of interpretation that sought to translate the Bible into a symbolic code for a philosophical faith. The Hellenistic school, as much as the Pharisaic school, sought to be the definers of the normative Judaism of the future. If the rabbinic school won out, as far as Judaism is concerned, it is largely because the rise of Christianity itself appropriated the fruits of the mission of the Diaspora and its Hellenistic midrash and so made them unacceptable to a Judaism now in a posture of defensive self-consolidation after the Jewish Wars.

The division between Christianity and Judaism was founded on this earlier division between Hellenistic and rabbinic midrash. Christianity, however, also inherited a form of Jewish messianic midrash, grown on the soil of Palestinian sectarianism, and fused this with Hellenistic midrash as it moved out into the Diaspora. It is these two traditions, the Hellenistic and the sectarian, which we will examine in the following two sections of this chapter. We will then take a brief look at the fringe movement of Jewish Gnosticism, as a symptom of an extreme form of Jewish alienation in a Gnosticizing milieu. Finally, we will summarize the Pharisaic reaction to these Hellenistic and sectarian developments after the Jewish Wars, at a time when these were being taken over by an aggressive Church which regarded itself as the true heir of Jewish messianic hope and the Diaspora mission of Judaism.

The two central symbols of first-century Jewish faith were the Torah and the temple: the traditional compilation of the Jewish "Way" and the cultic center of Jewish national life. The interpretation of the Torah and the temple in Hellenistic midrash will illustrate the full scope of this effort to translate Judaism into a universal spiritual religion. The main spokesman for this school was Philo (50 B.C.E.–20 C.E.). The sheer bulk of his writings overshadows what few remnants of this school survive from other hands. But Philo was not the creator of this school. Rather, he was the culminating creative expression of a tradition that goes back at least to the third century B.C.E. The Septuagint itself was as much a Hellenistic midrash on the Hebrew Scriptures as it was a literal translation.[20]

Philo interpreted the Jewish Torah (which the Septuagint translated as *Nomos*, or "Law") as an allegory of that Natural Law which the Stoics saw as the ruling "world soul" of the universe. This world soul, in turn, was an immanent manifestation of the transcendent Logos, or Divine Mind. In Philo's Stoic-Platonic philosophy, the creative Power of God first radiates forth in a spiritual or intellectual world which is both the spiritual "blueprint" and the Demiurgos (or mediator) through which the world was created. Philo calls this the Logos, or Word of God, an idea which combined the biblical Word of God with the middle Platonic concepts of the Ideal World and the creative and ruling Divine Mind. Natural Law was the immanent expression of this transcendent Logos, ruling the cosmos as its guiding principle and expressing itself in the guiding principles and "essential nature" of every created thing, including man, who mirrored the macrocosm in his nature. Torah, therefore, was no particularistic and parochial set of customs of an embattled Semitic tribe. On the contrary, it was universal in its application and accorded with the true traditions of righteousness of all men. For each of these express, as best they can, this same guiding power of the divine Logos-Nomos.

Yet the Torah expressed these aspirations of righteousness of all men with that fullness which manifested its character as a special revelation by God to his chosen people, who thereby acted as a "light to the Gentiles," bringing all men to that universal truth which each religion and philosophy seeks. Hellenistic midrash dissolved Torah into a universal ethic that was declared to be identical with that which is universally human and, in the highest sense, "natural." Yet it also held up Torah as a special concretization of this same universal Way which all men seek, but which the Jews alone possess in its fullest manifestation. This double side of Hellenistic midrash must not be overlooked, on the assumption that the direction of spiritualizing allegory is merely from the particular to the universal. For there is also the sense that the universal is declared uniquely "incarnate" in the particular (in this case, the Torah). This same doublesidedness will appear also in the parallel Christian interpretation of Christ as the incarnation of the universal Logos.

This universalizing of Torah made it necessary to read many of the more particularistic and ritual commandments as allegories of inward ethical principles. For Philo, the Sabbath was the commemoration of the birthday of the universe. It was not merely the culminating day of Creation, but the unitive day, on which the divine Logos emanated from the Father and which provided the divine pattern for the whole of subsequent creation. Therefore, it is the day appropriately set aside from all work and dedicated to the pursuit of that spiritual wisdom whose font is that same Logos-Nomos through whom the world was created and who is manifested in the Torah.[21]

Likewise, the food laws that discriminated between clean and unclean animals were seen as ethical allegories. Their purpose is to remind men of those characteristics of gentleness, justice, cleanliness, and mutuality which God commands, and to forbid the contrary traits of sordidness, rapaciousness, bloodthirstiness, and violence, by proscribing the eating of those animals which express the second type of characteristics, while enjoining a communing with those animals which express the first characteristics. The source of this idea apparently lies in an early adaptation of Greek zoological lore, which compared various animals to particular human virtues and vices. A Jewish adaptation of this Greek allegory on animals as an apology for Jewish food laws was a well-developed tradition two centuries before Philo. It appears in the speech which the author of Aristeas' romance on the origin of the Septuagint puts in the mouth of the high priest Eleazar (composed about 130 B.C.E.).[22] Philo also repeats Aristeas' allegorizing of the laws enjoining the eating of animals that part the hoof and chew the cud as a commandment of the mental attitudes of discrimination and reflectiveness.[23] Circumcision was read as an allegory of God's commandment to cut away all pleasures that bewitch the mind and to excise that idolatrous vainglory that would attribute to man creative power that belongs to God alone, an interpretation that harks back to the prophetic call to circumcize the heart rather than (merely) the flesh.[24]

For Philo and other Hellenistic midrashists, the temple, its priesthood, and sacrifices also became cosmic and spiritual symbols. The contradiction between a local national temple and a universal God was a scandal which Greek philosophy had already attacked and to which Hellenistic Jews felt compelled to respond. They did so by reaching back to the most ancient tradition of temple building, which made the national temple of a people a mythopoetic expression of the universe.[25] Here we see an important characteristic of ancient spiritualizing allegory. Allegory was not built on fortuitous links alone. Quite often it was a reversal of that mythopoetic process whereby the universal is seen as incarnate in the cult and symbols of particular religions. Allegory, in effect, was the philosophical reverse of this process, whereby the particularities of the local traditions of myth and cult could now be read as symbols of universal truths. Yet this philosophical demythologizing of the sanctities of particular religions retained some of the religious force of the myth in seeing the concrete as an embodiment and special presence of the universal. This interaction between the mythological and the philosophical is found in Philo's interpretation of the temple, as well as in the Christian interpretation of Christ as the unique incarnation of the universal Logos.

For Philo, every aspect of the temple was intended to be an allegory of the cosmos. The temple was, so to speak, a "sacrament" of the universe. Its colors and furniture reflected the basic elements of earth, air, fire, and water; its sacrifices and libations, the fruits and animals of the earth; its candles, the astral bodies of the heavens.[26] A similar cosmic symbolism of the temple, drawn from natural philosophy, is found also in Josephus.[27] This doctrine rested on a Greek cosmos piety which saw the universe as "God's temple." Not in temples built with hands, but in the cosmos itself do we find the true dwelling place of God. But Philo carries this symbolism of the temple back to a deeper level, because for him the cosmos itself is only a shadow of that higher spiritual realm of the divine Logos whose spiritual universe is the inner "sanctuary of God."[28] Here not only the universe but also the human body can be seen as the "temple of God." The same High Priest, God's divine Logos, mediates in the temple of the universe and in the temple of the human soul.[29] This doctrine of the Logos as the cosmic and personal High Priest was to be taken over into New Testament Christology, especially in the Epistle to the Hebrews.[30]

The literal, magical character of temple sacrifice provided another scandal to the universalizing and spiritualizing temper. Here too was a theme that went back to the prophets, who decried sacrifices which were divorced from an ethical commitment. In Judaism in general at this time it became normal to interpret sacrifice as valuable only as an expression of the inner disposition of self-offering to God. The real sacrifice is the sacrifice of every wrong desire of the heart, the offering of the will in obedience to God. The real incense that ascends to heaven is the prayer of the contrite man. The inner meaning of sacrifice is prayer and penitence.[31] Philo is at pains to stress the moral and cosmic symbolism of the sacrifices and the fact that they are offered not merely on behalf of Israel, but for all mankind.[32]

These ethical and spiritualized interpretations would seem to do away with any necessity for the temple, the sacrificial system, and even much of the Law. If one observed the inner dispositions, which were the "real meanings" of these things, why bother to continue with an outward observance which appeared, at best, a rather strained way of pointing to these inward truths? But Hellenistic midrash had no intention of abandoning the letter of the Law. It sought rather to invest the letter with a spiritual and ethical significance that would make it meaningful to those who had learned to think of truth in philosophical terms. Philo complains just as bitterly against those left-wing Hellenizers or "Allegorists," who disregard the letter of the Law for its "purely spiritual" meaning, as he does against those "literalists" who see only the outer command and demand that it be obeyed solely because God commands it and not because one has derived from it a higher meaning.[33] Philo's struggle against the Allegorists reveals the true position of the school of Alexandrian midrashists, not as "radicals" in practice, but as spiritualizing conservatives who sought to rescue the meaningfulness of the cultic and legal practices of Judaism in the midst of a cosmopolitan, intellectual culture, by pouring into them a philosophical meaning. They sought, thereby, to establish an essential, sacramental link between the outer ordinance and the inner meaning, so that the outer practice took on the character of God-given, efficacious embodiments of these inner meanings. For Philo, it is as wrong to abandon the letter of the Torah for a "purely spiritual religion" that imagines it can dispense with the outward observance, as it would be for a man to imagine that he can live purely in the soul while abandoning the body:

It follows that, exactly as we take thought for the body because it is the abode of the soul, so we must pay heed to the letter of the laws.[34]

The ordinances are the body which incarnates and expresses the spiritual meaning, just as the Torah as a whole is the embodiment of that cosmic Law which manifests the divine Logos. Philo's allegorical midrash does not seek merely to remove us from the visible image to its spiritual essence, but also to pour the spiritual essence into the visible image in a way that shows the ordinances of God as the revealed and efficacious expressions of a universal, spiritual religion. The reversal of Platonism in Philo was also to be taken over by Church Fathers, such as Irenaeus, and was to lay the basis for the Christian understanding of the sacramentality of creation. Yet Philo's attempt to establish a necessary connection between outer law and inner meaning was in jeopardy in his own life time. There were some on the left wing of his own circle who would take the relationship between outer law and inner meaning as accidental and discardable. It remained for Christianity to take up the same spiritualizing midrash and to interpret the relation of spirit and law as antithetical, and even as divinely abrogated by the "coming" of the inner spiritual meaning of that which was "foreshadowed" in the outer law and history. But this development waited upon the fusion of Hellenistic with messianic, sectarian midrash.

The tenuousness of Philo's unity between outer ordinances and inner meaning can be seen in his interpretation of patriarchal religion. It was common in rabbinic thought to claim that the patriarchs observed the whole Torah, including the whole of the oral Law, before it was actually given. This is a way of pushing back to the time of the patriarchs the basic standard of rabbinic righteousness, which takes not only the written Torah, but the whole of rabbinic commentary as having been revealed on Sinai.[35] For Hellenistic midrash, however, the distinction between patriarchal and Mosaic religion was interpreted along the lines of the distinction between the spiritual principles which were later to be expressed in the outer ordinances. Abraham and the patriarchs are spoken of by Philo in this sense as "living Law"; meaning that Abraham was the living embodiment of that universal Natural Law which the Torah was later to express in concrete ordinances, but which is also identical with the universal law of conscience engraved on the souls of all righteous men.[36] In this interpretation Philo intended to draw back the spiritual and cosmic meaning of Torah to the patriarchs. But, in the process, he also suggested the priority of an unwritten and universal "Law of Nature" that might be practiced without regard for the actual ordinances of Torah. Christian midrash was to take up this distinction in an antithetical manner.

It is perhaps important at this point to define the difference between Hellenistic midrash and Palestinian midrash, both the rabbinic and sectarian. Hellenistic midrash is cosmic and spiritual. It takes Jewish stories and practices as symbols of the cosmos and, through the cosmos, of the spiritual principles which the cosmos embodies. It proceeds from the visible to the spiritual; from body to soul; from the phenomenal to the noumenal world; from the visible cosmos to that spiritual, intellectual world which emanates from and expresses the Mind of God. Its salvation myth is cosmogonic, rather than messianic. That is to say, it leads men upward from the body and the cosmos to the soul and the immanent Nomos, which radiates from that transcendent Word through which God created man and the universe. Salvation is a journey to God that travels back through the same path which God took in creating the world.

Palestinian midrash, on the other hand, is typological rather than allegorical. It does not evacuate the historical for a higher, "spiritual" meaning, but rather moves from historical "types" in the past to later and fuller historical expressions and ultimately their final fulfillment in a messianic future. Its line of analogy is historical and its fulfillment lies in a messianic Kingdom of future history, rather than in a spiritual world from which the physical world "devolved" in the beginning. For the Rabbis, this more often took the form of interpreting details of ancient history as allegories of God's commandments in the Torah read through the rabbinic developments. For example, the Rabbis might interpret the phrase "to feed in the garden" as meaning to nourish the soul in the study of Scripture in the rabbinic schools of learning. The analogy moves from past images to present concrete realities of religious life. The literal text itself is never abandoned, nor is it suggested that it exists on a lower level of meaning and value. Indeed, in reaction to the Christian use of allegory christologically, the Rabbis come to insist on the literal meaning of the text and its past historical reference.[37]

The Palestinian sects cultivated particularly a messianic or *pesher* interpretation of Scripture. Unlike both Philo and the Rabbis, they more often used the books of the Prophets as their text, rather than concentrating primarily on the Pentateuch. The prophetic utterances, as well as the stories of Israel's salvation in the Pentateuch, were read as "types" of that messianic fulfillment that was already appearing in their midst and was unfolding in the history of their own sect. Messianic typology was also well known and utilized by the Rabbis. For the Rabbis every detail of the Exodus, the giving of the Torah, and the other great salvation stories would be repeated in a fulfilled form in the messianic age. Yet the Rabbis would part company with sectarian *pesher* commentary,[38] in that they would believe that these fulfillments of the types of salvation of the past still lie in the future. They would vehemently resist the suggestion that they are already beginning to happen in the special history and separatist observances of the sect. Since, as we have noted, the earliest Christian midrash was built upon this kind of sectarian messianic midrash and was later fused with Hellenistic spiritualizing midrash, it would be well to examine this sectarian viewpoint.

3. *Prophetic and Messianic Tensions in Sectarian Judaism*

The search for the "true Israel" can be traced back to the religious impulse generated by the eighth-century prophets. It was the prophets who translated the Jewish tribal doctrines of election, covenant, and national promise into a religion of ethical demand, and so raised up the possibility of a distinction between ethnic Israel and that "true Israel" whose repentance and obedience qualifies it to be the recipient of that divine favor which the rest of Israel has lost through its apostasy. One finds in the prophets the view that Israel's election does not confer automatic favor, but rather it spells out a demand for obedience and a special liability to divine chastisement upon her failure to live up to this standard. The disasters upon the people are read as indications of the people's apostasy and of God's wrath. On the other side of this chastisement, however, there is the hope that a remnant will be preserved (a term borrowed from the experience of military conquest, which swept a people away but sometimes left a "remnant" from which a tribe might be "reborn").[39] It is hoped that this remnant, which will remain after God's chastisement, will learn thereby to turn back in obedience to God. God will make this remnant into the root from which the nation will be reborn in a new and purified form. The religious search of Israel can be seen as a search for the right way to institutionalize and inculcate this obedience demanded by God to assure that divine favor which waited upon Israel's repentance. The priestly sacrificial movement, the rabbinic development of the oral Law, and the call to repentance issued by the messianic sects can each be seen as variant answers to this same religious quest for the true and obedient Israel who would become worthy of God's promise.

In the period of Antiochus Epiphanes a hasidic movement arose in response to the threat of apostasy posed by Hellenism. It called the nation to a rededication to traditional legal and ritual observance and to resistance to the conquerors. Both the Pharisees and the Essenes appear to be later expressions of this Maccabean hasidic movement, while the Zealot movement and the various prophetic and baptist movements, whose shapes move obscurely behind the references in Josephus and the Church Fathers, appear to be popular responses to the twin calls of Maccabean Judaism to resist the enemy by armed struggle and to prepare the way of the Lord by raising up a purified and obedient Israel. Although it is hard to discern the exact relation of the Pharisees to apocalyptic thought before 70 C.E., there is no doubt that the literature of the Essenes and the Zealots was apocalyptic.[40] Both saw themselves as preparing the way for God's messianic triumph by gathering the community of true filial devotion to God's commandments. As one moves from prophetic to apocalyptic literature, it becomes apparent that the existential stress of Israel's nonfulfillment according to the patterns of ancient national hope and her continued oppression by larger and larger imperial powers were creating a world view of violent and cataclysmic dualism quite different from prophetic, historical future hope. Some of the language for this, such as the battle of angels and demons and the war between the powers of light and the powers of darkness, may have been borrowed from Persian dualism. But the experience itself was that of Jewish history. The result of this experience of oppression, as it clashed with Israel's national hope, was a world view characterized by extreme alienation from present history and from the present world—a demonization of the present "era" of world history. The world of the present era was seen as one from which God's sovereignty had fled. It was an era occupied and ruled by the powers of evil. But this reign of the evil powers is fast coming to an end. Soon God will come to overthrow the world system dominated by the minions of Belial and to establish his reign. Those who wish to be on the side of God and his angels at this coming cataclysm of world history must repent now and be gathered into the community of true obedience. All others, whether Jew or Gentile, will be ranked with the forces of Belial and will perish. It is in this mood of apocalyptic crisis and as the penultimate community of Israel, anticipating the apocalyptic cataclysm, that the sect gathers its community of the "true Israel."

It is characteristic of the Palestinian sectarian movements that they are also, in one form or another, "old believer" movements. That is to say, they regard themselves as the representatives of that original and unfallen Israel who have preserved the faith from its foundations. They are the true line of the covenant from which official Israel has fallen away. For this reason they alone are qualified to represent that ultimate Israel upon whom the promises of God's favor will be bestowed in the messianic restoration. This bipolar relationship between God's establishment of his People and their messianic fulfillment is typical of biblical religion and was the basis of messianic typology.

The claim to be the line of the original covenant from which official Judaism had fallen away had a precedent in the great schism between Ephraim and Judah. The antiquity of the separation of the Samaritans from the Judaists is uncertain. Judaism itself claimed that the Samaritans were not true Israelites, but a paganized population settled by the Assyrians. But the Samaritans themselves claimed to be the representatives of the original covenant of Israel from which the Judaists had deviated at the end of the period of the Judges by separating from the true Aaronic-Zadokite priesthood descended from Phinehas and by setting up a rival sanctuary at Shiloh under the false priest Eli. The Samaritans clung to their mountain sanctuary at Gerizim against the Judaist effort to consolidate national worship at Jerusalem. They preserved an ancient Pentateuchal religion, over against what they saw as a falsely interpolated Torah of the Judaists. They lacked any of the later writings of the Hebrew Bible. For them, Moses was the sole prophet, and they alone possessed his original dispensation on Sinai. They looked for the return of Moses as a messianic prophet-king to restore Israel to favor. As they interacted with Gnostic and Platonic currents in the Hellenistic period and finally with Christianity itself, their doctrine of Moses took on a form closely resembling Johannine Christology. Like the Essenes, they regarded themselves as the keepers of the true Torah and Sanctuary of the Exodus, and representatives of the true Israel during the present Time of Wrath. All Israel must be gathered into their fold in order to participate in the Era of Favor that would follow the return of the Mosaic Christ.[41]

Such old-believer sects evidently were not uncommon at this period. Epiphanius tells us of a group called the Nazaraioi who dwelt along the Jordan and claimed to represent the true religion of patriarchal times against a false Judaism which arose with a spurious version of the Mosaic Law. These Nazaraioi were ascetics who spurned animal flesh and the temple sacrifices at Jerusalem, although they kept the Sabbath, circumcision, and other feasts.[42] The Samaritans, however, were clearly a tribal schism, while the Essenes, and probably the other sects of whom we know little beside their names, were voluntary societies entered through conversion.

It is significant that the Essenes also were an old-believer sect. They claimed to have the true Zadokite priesthood and to preserve the true calendar for festal observances, over against official Judaism, whose temple and priesthood had become corrupt at the time of the slaying of the Teacher of Righteousness by the Evil Priest[43] (probably one of the Hasmoneans during the second century B.C.E.).[44] Their messianic doctrine was complex. They appear to have looked for both a Davidic and an Aaronic Messiah to reign over the kingly and priestly functions of the restored Israel, as well as the coming of a Mosaic Prophet who would be the forerunner of these messianic figures. Like the Samaritans, they saw the present age as an age of darkness dominated by the forces of Belial. They vilified official Judaism as an apostate people who had lost the covenant and had been reduced to the status of the *goyim*: indeed, they were even to be ranked with the forces of Satan.

Since the Pharisees were also known as "purists" and, in some sense, "separatists," it might be well to define the difference between the Pharisaic and the sectarian spirit of prophetic renewal. The Pharisees were probably also descended from the Maccabean Hasidim and appear historically about the same time as the Essenes (in the reign of John Hyrcanus, 135–105 B.C.E.).[45] They, like the Essenes, sought perfection by adopting the standards of purity of the temple priesthood. They separated out into fellowships where they could observe the minute regulations of total Torah observance. They raised themselves above the ordinary Jews, or *'am ha'aretz*, who followed only the general rules of cleanliness and the temple festivals. But they did not cut themselves off from the rest of the nation or anathematize either the ordinary Jew or the priesthood as apostate. Rather, they sought to set the standard for the whole nation to follow and to become the leaven of the whole lump. They saw themselves as the teachers of the nation.[46] Although their milieu was the synagogue and its schools of learning, they also sought to penetrate the priesthood and even the court of the Hasmonean kings with their standards of righteousness. It was these characteristics which fitted the Pharisees to become the consolidators of Judaism after the disasters of the Jewish Wars. It was from them that the normative Judaism of the future was to be descended, whose final expression is the Talmud.

The difference between the Pharisaic and the sectarian manner of relating the prophetic community of renewal to unreformed Israel is strikingly illustrated by the sectarian development of the practice of baptism. The practice of baptism in the sects appears to have been drawn from the use of ritual immersion, which the convert to Judaism must undergo in order to symbolize his renunciation of his former unclean way of life among the *goyim*.[47] To preach a mission of renewal to Israel itself and to offer baptism to Jews as the symbol of their repentance was, in effect, to say that all Jewry, both ordinary Jews and the official leadership, were so totally apostate as to have lost the covenant and to have been reduced to the status of the *goyim*. In order to enter the covenant, they must pass through a proselyte baptism, just like a Gentile who was converted to Judaism. No practice could have been a clearer symbol of the sectarian self-understanding that the rest of Israel was apostate and "gentilized." The sect alone holds title to be the true Israel of the covenant and the heir of its messianic promise.

For the Pharisees, the question was one of calling the people to a more total commitment to those laws of the covenant under which they already presently lived. To the sects, the nation had lost the covenant, had become apostate, "goyish," and even diabolic. Those who wished to become believing Jews had to be converted and gathered anew into the wilderness to become again God's Exodus people and the heirs to the promise of the covenant. All the titles of Israel were transferred to the sect, which alone possessed them legitimately. They alone were the Congregation (*'edah*) of Israel, the Assembly (*qahal*) of Israel, the People of the Covenant (*berit*) and the Community (*yahad*) of God, whereas the Judaism of the temple and of ordinary believers was to be ranked with the "nations" and counted among the hosts of Belial. The sect, therefore, proposed a new definition of Israel, based no longer on birth, but on conversion, baptism, and gathering into a separatist, voluntarist community, whose purified way of life gave them claim to the titles of the "true Israel" and heirship of its future.[48]

In these last days of the era of wickedness, it is the Zadokite brotherhood which represents the place of repentance and righteousness which God has appointed as the final opportunity for the salvation of Israel. The covenanters assume an evangelical stance, as well as a separatist stance, toward other Jews. Those who hear their call and repent of their wickedness are to be purified in the waters and enter into the covenant and discipline of the brotherhood. The water does not effect purification by itself. It is to be seen as a testimony of those who have repented and wish to turn from their evil ways. It seals and witnesses to their repentance. Somewhat like the later Christian use of holy water at the entrance to the church, it seems to have been repeated continuously as a sign of the members' continual renewal of their decision of penitence. Those who spurn these waters of repentance God will not permit to live.[49]

These Sons of Zadok are the elect of Israel who "will go on functioning in the last days." All who turn from this renewed covenant and who turn from the "well of living water will not be reckoned as of the communion of the people nor inscribed in the roster of it throughout the period from the time when the Teacher of the community is gathered to his rest until the time in which the lay and priestly Messiah assume their office."[50] The covenanters speak of themselves as the ones who are preparing the "way for the Lord in the wilderness" during this last epoch of wickedness. Forty years are to elapse from the death of the Teacher of Righteousness "until the men who relapse into the company of the Man of Falsehood [ordinary Judaism following the temple priesthood in Jerusalem] are brought to an end." Then God will "punish to extinction all who have refused to enter the covenant." But those who have repented and have kept the covenant will see salvation revealed to them. The Qumran community looked forward to a period of forty years of warfare in this final apocalyptic struggle between God and the powers of wickedness. The battle is between the true and the apostate Israel, which is ranked with the armies of the "nations." But behind each army lie the heavenly and demonic hosts of God and Belial. This final apocalyptic battle between the "Sons of Light" and the "Sons of Darkness" concludes with the triumph of the army of God, assembled under the banner of Israel's patron angel Michael, and the establishment of the messianic Reign.

This will be the time of Salvation for the People of God, the critical moment when those who have cast their lot with Him will come to dominion, whereas those who have cast their lot with Belial will be doomed to eternal extinction. . . . Streaks of lightning will flash from one end of the world to the other, growing ever brighter until the era of Darkness is brought utterly to an end. Then, in the era of God, His exalted grandeur will give light forevermore, shedding on all the Sons of Light peace and blessing, gladness and length of days.[51]

We might say that the essential characteristics of the sectarian viewpoint are an antithetical distinction between the true and apostate Israel; a definition of the true Israel as a spiritual, voluntarist community of personal conversion, rather than a tribal community; and a vilification of official Judaism and its rank-and-file members as apostate. Official Judaism is to be regarded no longer as part of the covenant (i.e., reduced to the status of the *goyim*) and finally, like the *goyim* in much of the apocalyptic writings, to be seen as satanic in character. The sects at this period typically come to birth in a mood of intense apocalyptic crisis. They regard themselves as the messianic community of the "last days," who have already tasted the definitive transformation from unrighteousness to righteousness and are awaiting their vindication in the final acts of world history which will bring the era of wickedness to an end and inaugurate the Reign of God. It was in this milieu of Jewish messianic sectarianism that Christianity was originally born in Palestine. But, unlike the other messianic sects, such as the Essenes, Christians believed that their teacher of righteousness actually was the Messiah long awaited by the Jewish world. He had been crucified by the forces of apostate Israel. But he had been vindicated by God in the Resurrection and caught up to heaven for a brief period wherein the community might announce the message of salvation based on belief in his name.

Apostate Israel was thus given a last chance of repentance before his return on clouds of glory as Son of man to inaugurate the final apocalyptic revolution of world history.[52]

4. *The Diabolizing of the Jewish God in Jewish Gnosticism*

The tension created in the Jewish cultural soul by the struggle to resist or assimilate Hellenism, amid the pressure of the successive empires of antiquity, was profound. While this struggle generated extraordinarily creative responses in the Hellenistic, Pharisaic, and messianic movements, it also found expression in a kind of psychic breaking point where the group personality seemed to lose its ability to bring conflicting elements into a total perspective and fell into vilification and diabolizing of the alienated pole of the conflict. We have seen this psychic distortion as it made its appearance in Jewish apocalyptic sectarianism. Not only the "nations" but even official Judaism was diabolized, the two becoming fused as the "enemy" in the struggle for that perfection that would win God's favor.

In the Diaspora the struggle to assimilate Hellenism on Jewish terms seems to have generated a similar psychic breaking point. A segment of those of Jewish background crossed over to the Hellenistic side, claiming a "purely spiritual" meaning for an ancestral faith which now appeared mean and superstitious by contrast to that glorious vision of an inner transcendent world opened up through philosophical speculation. We have seen Philo struggling against this extreme in his criticism of the Allegorists. A Jewish group, alienated from their ancestral tradition, met and mingled with an uprooted intelligentsia of Egyptian, Syrian, and Greek background, who had experienced a similar collapse of the symbols of their ancestral faith and culture. A pervasive sense of the demonization of existing perceptible reality, including all of the religious symbols which formerly had mediated meaning to the universe, colored their view of the world. The eclectic movement generated out of this experience of profound malaise in ancient culture is called "Gnosticism." It drew its symbols freely from Greek philosophy, ancient Oriental religions, and the Jewish Bible. But its religious experience was new and foreign to all these ancient faiths and had the effect of turning them all upside down, so that what was formerly revelatory and sacred now became negative and demonic. Indeed the very word *demonic* (originally a Greek word for "divinity") is itself a testimony to the influence of Gnosticism upon Christian language.

According to an oversimplistic division between Palestinian and Hellenistic Judaism, it has been common to see Jewish messianism (including apocalypticism) and Gnosticism as poles apart; the former as part of the "good ancestry" of Christianity, and the latter as the false and spurious "acute Hellenism" which Christianity rightly repudiated. But this division can no longer be sustained, not only because both a Gnostic and an apocalyptic pattern exerted a formative influence on early Christian thinking, but also because it becomes apparent that apocalyptic and Gnostic modes of thinking spring from a similar experience of acute alienation. Both regard the existing universe as demonic. In Jewish sectarianism these two strains were mingled. Several of the sects of Palestinian Judaism which survived, such as the Mandaeans and the Samaritans, developed a markedly Gnostic theology sometime between the first and third centuries C.E. Even mainstream Pharisaic Judaism was never immune to these developments. In the late apocalyptic book, Third Enoch, we can see the process whereby Jewish apocalypticism is subtly transmuted into a Jewish mysticism[53] of the kind that was to flow, as an underground esoteric tradition among some of the Rabbis themselves, until it emerged again in the medieval Kabbalah.[54]

However, that Jewish mysticism of the type of Third Enoch, or the "Throne Mysticism" of the early Christian period which Gershom Scholem examines,[55] remained orthodox. Its God, however removed from this earth by many levels of angelic spheres, nevertheless was the creator of this world. The light stream of Being which passed from heaven to earth was a continuous one. But that which we will call "Jewish Gnosticism," as distinct from Jewish mysticism (following Hans Jonas's definition of Gnosticism),[56] breaks the continuity of this relationship between God and the world. For Jewish Gnosticism, the God of the Bible is not a revelatory or redemptive figure, but the expression of ignorance and evil. Far above this diabolic god there exist the true divinity and true heaven. But this transcendent divinity is not responsible for creating the universe and is only antithetically related to all those mistakes through which the present evil universe came into existence. It is this radical break between the evil god who is the creator of "this world," and the transcendent God who is our true origin and goal, the radical break between creation and redemption, that is characteristic of Gnosticism. This viewpoint was as foreign and distasteful to Greek cosmos piety as it was to the biblical view of creation. Hans Jonas perhaps hits on the right solution when he guesses that Gnosticism arose from the ranks of alienated intellectuals in the Near East, all of whose national cultures had been submerged by the march of Roman imperialism. Gnosticism expresses the profound malaise of their common experience of suppressed identity.[57] Gnosticism draws on the language of all the religious cultures of the Greco-Oriental East, but uses them to express a world alienation which turns all traditional religious symbols upside down. All the present religious symbols mediating meaning to the universe are felt to have failed. One looks beyond these to some radically new and hitherto unrevealed God whose revelation will replace the revelations which have grown dark and opaque.

Until recently one could only guess at the possibility of a Jewish contribution to this Gnostic mixture from the heavy use of Hebrew words on Gnostic amulets and magical papyri. The Jewish background of that Christian Gnosticism which appears so early in the Church among the opponents of Paul could only be surmised.[58] But with the discovery of the Gnostic library at Nag-Hamadi in upper Egypt, we now have a corpus of Jewish Gnostic works which probably served as the original form of a Gnostic tradition which was then Christianized in the postapostolic period and achieved developed expression in the great Christian Gnostic theologians of the second century C.E., Valentinus and Marcion.[59]

The affinity between Marcionite and Pauline thinking has long been a subject alternatively frightening and fascinating to

Christian theologians. Lutherans especially have had a tendency to look kindly in the direction of this radical disciple of Paul who took to an extreme the Pauline antithesis between Torah and Gospel.[60] Marcionism reveals its source in Gnostic anti-Judaism when it converts the Hebrew Creator God into a blustering Demiurgos of crude and ignorant might who is to be contrasted to the true God of love who is the Father of the Redeemer and not responsible for this evil universe.

But is it possible to imagine that such an alienated view of Judaism could actually have arisen among Jews? The texts of Sethian Gnosticism from Nag-Hamadi have suggested that this was the case. The mythic structure of these texts is built on Genesis. The divine Wisdom (Sophia); the biblical Sabaoth who declares, "I am the Lord thy God; I shall have no other Gods beside me"; the story of the garden and the fall of Adam and Eve and the Noachian flood; even the cherubim throne of Ezekiel, which was the pinnacle of the ecstatic vision in contemporary Jewish mysticism—all this is present, but it has been turned on its head. God's Wisdom is a foolish Aeon who is responsible for the fall of the transcendent world and the generation of the Demiurge and the evil world. Sabaoth is an ignorant Power whose cherubim throne and self-proclamation are expressions of arrogant ignorance. The state of Adam and Eve in the garden is one of enslavement to the domain of ignorance of this demonic Power. Their disobedience to his command is no longer the root of sin, but rather the beginning of human enlightenment! All the biblical symbols of divine revelation have been demonized, while the symbols of the Fall—the snake, the woman, and the flood—have become symbols of liberation from this lower universe and return to that transcendent heavenly home far beyond the domain of the ignorant Sabaoth.[61]

What kind of community could have produced such a point of view? Their authors must be either extremely alienated Jews on the left wing of Jewish Hellenism, or else Gentiles on the fringes of the Jewish proselytizing movement who have adopted Jewish symbols into a Gnostic system. The answer perhaps lies in a combination of these two. But it is primarily from Jewish religious language that the community is alienated and against which it sets its Gnostic dialectic. This suggests that, however marginally, it was a community for whom Judaism was the normative faith of a religious past which they have now "surpassed" in a search for a higher Savior in whose transcendent light Jewish religious language takes on an antithetical and diabolic tone. In a not dissimilar way, Saint Paul, having accepted the faith in the transcendent Christ, now feels that he has a superior revelation in whose light the Jewish Torah becomes reduced to a demonized revelation and negative power on the level of those evil Powers and Principalities which reign over the imprisoned cosmos.[62]

In Jewish Gnosticism, therefore, we find a third potential source of anti-Judaism in an alienated Judaism that resulted from the struggle to respond to the threat of cultural imperialism. Certainly the kind of anti-Judaism which we have uncovered in Jewish Gnosticism was to be repudiated as heartily in the New Testament and the Church Fathers as it was by Jewish orthodoxy. Yet it must be reckoned as lying on the left wing of that same ambit within which Christianity itself developed. It was drawn from much the same Jewish sectarian and syncretistic philosophical materials as Christianity drew upon to formulate its theology, and it arose about the same time and in many of the same circles to which the Church's mission was appealing. The rapidity of the appearance of a Christian Gnosticism in full-blown theological systems, paralleling, even antedating, the earliest orthodox Christian canons and systematic theology, points to a similar cultural mix in which the two were growing together from the earliest days of the Church's mission. The earliest Christianity in Alexandria as well as the Palestinian Church, which was to spread eastward, were Gnostic-Essenic in coloring. Although repudiated by the Great Church in the West in the second century, this Gnostic-Essenic ascetic type of Christianity gradually penetrated into Western Christianity. By the end of the fourth century its point of view had become the prevailing spirituality, despite its contradiction of the continued affirmation in orthodox Christianity of the goodness of material creation.

5. *The Pharisaic Reaction to Hellenistic and Sectarian Judaism after the Fall of the Second Temple*

The nature of the Pharisaic response to Hellenism, to the messianic sects, and to the fall of the temple is obscure. This is partially because the Pharisees themselves concealed the innovative aspects of their program under a rubric of conservative fidelity to the past. But, more importantly, the Christian myth of "obsolete Judaism" as a spiritually sterile religion has added an impenetrable mystery to the matter, so that, for most Christians, Ellis Rivkin's chapter title "The Pharisaic Revolution" would appear a contradiction in terms.[63] Yet revolution it was.

The heart of the Pharisaic revolution, a revolution which was in preparation for two centuries before the fall of the temple (70 C.E.), was the proclamation of the *oral Torah*. The development of the oral Torah allowed Judaism to emancipate itself from the Aaronite priesthood and its temple cultus. No longer did the individual Jew need a priestly caste or a sacrificial system to intervene for him with God. Long before the temple actually fell, the Pharisees had been enunciating the way of prayer and study, declaring that acts of repentance, thanksgiving, and loving-kindness were equivalent to, perhaps even better than, the temple sacrifices.[64]

The existence of the oral Torah was a Pharisaic creation, as the Sadducean guardians of the old temple cultus knew. There is little basis for it in the Pentateuch, which the Pharisees claimed to follow faithfully.[65] Rather, the oral Torah was a way of freeing Judaism from the apparatus of a system of atonement based on the priesthood, the temple, and the national fortunes of Israel in its ancestral homeland. Through the device of the oral Torah, the Pharisees were able to free Israel from the letter of the past and to find an open way into new futures, while simultaneously making it their intention to preserve every jot and tittle of that past itself. The oral Torah was intended to remain oral, to be embodied in the living stream of a people, not in a document, even though it eventually was given written form. The Mishnah, moreover, is not generally a midrash on the Scriptures. It makes no textual references to the written Law as its necessary basis. It is a free deduction of ethical principles that adapts custom to the practical needs of daily life in the light of an ideal of obedience. Its deductive principles are self-validating, rather than being based on a biblical hermeneutic. Indeed, the oral Torah is not seen as a commentary on the written Torah, but a parallel and independent stream, going back to Moses. Thus it allowed the Pharisees to innovate freely, subject only to that authority which was theirs as the rightful successors of a line of oral tradition that runs back through the *Sopherim* and the prophets to Moses through Joshua (bypassing Aaron!). From this line of tradition (created by themselves) the Pharisees were able to spin those "mountains hanging by a hair" which were their souls' delight.

The Pharisaic revolution is one which took over the heart of the internalizing revolution of Jewish Hellenism, while firmly resisting its doctrinaire tendencies and its temptation toward a disjunction of spirit and flesh. Except for a few fundamentals, Judaism eschewed doctrinal formulation and philosophized systematics (except where it had to defend itself against Christianity). So it remained surprisingly open to a free theological imagination that is not frozen as dogma.[66] But the ingenuity of the Pharisaic mind was directed primarily at *halakah*, at spelling out the "Way" of obedience to God's will.

The Pharisees took over something of the internalization of Jewish Hellenism, without its spiritualizing and philosophizing, and in a way that transmuted it into the distinctively Jewish viewpoint. The Hellenism it used, indeed, was probably more that of the rhetors and statesmen of the Greek polis than that of the Platonic school. The Pharisees translated this Greek idea of the constitution of the *politeia* into a form that could be carried by the people wherever they went and amid whatever political system they lived; something which could subsist within and yet apart from these political systems, without contradicting them or needing to be recognized as the dominant political system of the land.[67] In short, Pharisaism gave Judaism a way of surviving in the midst of unfulfillment under dominant imperial powers, insulated from some of the anxiety and identity crisis that characterized the period of the Second Temple.

The Rabbis also had a definition of the "spiritual Jew," but it was a "both-and" definition, rather than the "either-or" definition of the messianic sects. To be born a Jew was an opportunity to become a Jew after the spirit, to adopt the religious consciousness and the regulated life of a son of the covenant. This was the true Israel, as distinct from the "natural Jew." But it was a mandate laid on each Jew, by reason of birth, whereas for Gentiles it was an open possibility, but not a mandate. For the Pharisees, the way from the birthright to the observant Jew was through education, not by a baptismal conversion (characteristic of the messianic sects) that regarded all other Jews as outside the true covenant. Yet Pharisaic Judaism was also an option open to all men. The successors of the Pharisees, the *Tannaim*, indeed prided themselves on the fact that some of the most notable of the Teachers were of proselyte background. The synagogue was a place for the gathering of those Jews who had adopted this Pharisaic definition of the true Israel and came to be educated in its practice. Thus Judaism, after the fall of the temple, did not retreat into ethnocentrism, but continued to proselytize. It was the laws of the Christian empire, not the dicta of the Pharisees, that brought to an end the era of Jewish proselytism. But the proselyte must show his goodwill by adopting the full Jewish praxis. There could be no halfway converts. Any proselyte who wanted to abrogate part of the Torah proved his lack of good intent. Yet for the true proselyte, no praise was too high. Abraham himself was said to have been the first proselyte and the father of proselytes. The proselyte was fully the equal of the born Jew and indeed especially dear to God's heart.[68]

It is essential to understand this union yet distinction of the birthright and the observant Jew in the Pharisaic view of Israel. For the Christian dichotomizing of the "Israel after the flesh" and "Israel after the spirit" was foreign to it. Every Jew is called to be a religious Jew. Yet the Jew who declines to accept the religious consciousness of Israel remains within the people and its covenant until such time as he definitively puts himself outside of it by adopting an antithetical identity. Becoming a

Christian was the adoption of such an antithetical identity. Yet even here the medieval Rabbis insisted on regarding the Christian convert as a son of the covenant, although a reprobate one. A Jewish Christianity which did not define itself as a new covenant, superseding the historical covenant of Abraham and Moses, but as a renewal standing within the *one* covenant, adding only the belief that it will be Jesus who will return as the Christ, might have remained as a form of Judaism. Judaism might discipline a Jewish Christian if he tried to make his midrash normative in the ordinary synagogue, but it would not define him as outside the covenant. Such a Jewish Christianity might have coexisted with Pharisaic Judaism, but with its own synagogues, midrash, and halakah, even as Essenic Judaism coexisted with Pharisaic Judaism, or as Orthodox, Reformed, and Conservative Judaism coexist today. It was the raising up of faith in Messiah Jesus as a supersessionary covenantal principle—the view that one was not within the true people of God unless one adopted the faith in this form—that caused the break between the Church and Israel. But this, in turn, caused a dichotomizing of "carnal Israel" and "spiritual Israel" in Christianity foreign to the spirit of Judaism. This is not because Judaism lacks its own possibility for being the spiritual Israel. Rather, it was because it knew itself to have and to continue to have its *own* possibility for being the spiritual Israel, a power which Christianity denied.

But this Christian view of carnal Israel, as the supposed identity of Judaism *coram Deo*, becomes then an externalization of the Christian unwillingness to connect faith in Jesus within the one, ongoing covenant of Israel. Once outside of Judaism, this becomes an obscurantism which expresses a fixed inability to penetrate the continuing Jewish religious principle of life, that very principle which caused the religious Jew so firmly to resist the Christian message. Out of this inability of the Church to fathom the spiritual principle behind this Jewish "obduracy," there was fabricated the myth of the "purely carnal Israel," without any spiritual principle at all, which was to be mysteriously preserved in a physical way as a witness to God's wrath upon Jewish "unbelief." Although this is not itself racism, but a mystification of nondialogue, it is easy to see how this Christian myth of the carnal Israel could be translated into anti-Semitic racism under the influence of nineteenth-century secularization.[69] Such a view of Judaism, of course, lacks any inkling of the interior ethic of the Pharisaic revolution. Indeed, it dogmatically declines to learn anything about the rabbinic tradition of Judaism after the time of Jesus, so that it can preserve its myth intact.

But Judaism, as much as Christianity, made its way into the future from the dissolution of Hebrew national religion by absorbing the Hellenistic attitudes of spiritualization, universalism, and individualism. Indeed, in some respects, it surpassed the Church, since it taught that the righteous pagan, who kept the natural law, would be saved *in his own faith*.[70] And so it opens up that parochialism of the doctrine of Election which Christianity was to reaffirm in a more absolute form. Pharisaism also emancipated the Jew from the need for priestly mediatorship and for historical vindication, whereas the Church continued to be tied to the latter through its messianic heritage, and redeveloped the former in a revived priesthood and vicarious sacrificial system. The Pharisaic Jew, by contrast, carried his temple with him whereever he went. He needed no priest, for he was his own high priest, making acceptable offerings to God through prayer, penitence, and deeds of lovingkindness. Each man made his own decision to incorporate himself into the way of salvation. Rabbinic learning was a pathway open to all men.

One surprising characteristic of Pharisaism is its a-historicism. It is a commonplace to speak of Judaism as a historical religion, uniquely characterized by the idea of salvation history. But there is a sense in which Pharisaism sought to emancipate the Jew from the tyranny of history, as much as from the tyranny of tribe and national homeland. Just as the spiritual Jew can be a Jew without the land, the temple, or political autonomy to vindicate God's love for him, so he no longer should read history with too much anxiety to be sure that it is going his way, or even that it is very clearly going any place at all. Rabbinic Judaism makes little effort to distinguish history from myth. The story created out of free religious imagination can stand alongside the story of Moses as a revelation of God's

Word. What is important is not exactly what happened then, but the spiritual point that is revealed apropos of the present situation. As one contemporary Jewish philosopher has put it, "No *Midrash* wants to be taken literally. Every *Midrash* wants to be taken seriously."[71]

The Pharisaic revolution gave Judaism a way into the future from the national religion of the past that sought to protect the Jew from historical misfortune. As Arthur Cohen has put it, "The Jew is an expert at unfulfilled time."[72] But this Jew who is the expert at unfulfilled time was preeminently a Pharisaic creation. Rabbinic Judaism, significantly, was shaped first in the Babylonian exile, and so from the first, the synagogue was tailored to handle the indefinite reality of exile, even though it nurtured these developments in Palestine for several centuries thereafter. It is symbolic of its locus that the final expression of the oral Torah, the Talmud, was issued from Babylonia.

What, then, was the response of the Pharisees to the fall of the temple and to those messianic movements which were the expression of the volatile expectation that led finally to the Jewish Wars? It is important to ask these two questions together (the response of Pharisaism both to messianism and to the fall of the temple), for Christianity was to create a myth that firmly fixed a connection between the fall of the temple and the rejection of Jesus as the Christ. The Pharisaic response to Christianity is explicable only from the side of its reaction to messianic activism of this period generally.

To say that official Judaism, specifically the Pharisees, literally *rejected Jesus as the Christ* is to confound several things which need to be distinguished. There was probably no such "meeting" between Jesus and the Pharisees in a manner that one can say literally that the Pharisees, as a school, evaluated and rejected Jesus' teachings in his own lifetime. The importation of the Pharisees into the controversy stories, as well as the concern in the Gospels that Jesus is rejected by the *teaching tradition on religious grounds,* was primarily a creation of the Church out of its later conflict with this teaching tradition.[73] The messianic claims of Jesus existed in the inner history and experience of the small group of disciples around Jesus, who later communicated their experience to many followers. But o these claims and the reaction of rabbinic Judaism to them in Jesus' lifetime not a line is discernible in the rabbinic traditions. Perhaps mention of this confrontation in its *Sitz im Leben Jesu* has been repressed in the tradition. But it is hard to find the reason for this, since negative comments on Jesus were added to the rabbinic tradition in reaction to that Christian Christ with which the Church was to confront Jewish religious consciousness. How much better to have been able to state the official judgment of the tradition upon Jesus in his own lifetime, if such had existed.[74]

Rather, Christians must reckon with the paradox that what is, for them, the great revelatory and salvic event, dominating the center of world history, is, for Judaism's own historical consciousness, a buried footnote in a curious side-path of Jewish religious history, which ended, as far as rabbinic Judaism was concerned, in a dead end. Although the Pharisees apparently did not take such note of Jesus in his own lifetime that one can say, literally, that they rejected *him,* they did reject him retroactively, in the sense that they rejected the Christ presented to them by the Church. They did so in the same spirit in which they turned their back on all the messianic activism of this period. For them this development had revealed itself as a false direction, destructive alike to the nation and to the individual religious personality.

The Pharisaic relation to messianism was one of continuity *in theory* and discontinuity *in practice.* The Pharisees are responsible for preserving the main doctrinal developments of the apocalypses: the resurrection from the dead and the eternal world beyond history. But they repressed the apocalyptic writings, which, along with Philo's works, were preserved by the Church, not by Judaism. The Pharisees maintained the idea of the messianic age, including a hope for the restoration of all the symbols of the national religion: the Davidic king, the great Prophet, the true priesthood, the rebuilt Jerusalem and temple. But they abrogated any religious dependency on these hopes in practice. They set their face against messianic praxis, especially after one of their own leaders, Rabbi Akiba, lapsed into messianic activism during the Bar Kokhba war of 133–136 C.E.[75] Messianic faith was preserved as ultimate hope. The resurrection from the dead and eternal life were taken into Pharisaism, but now as the final reward for following the Pharisaic way. But the Pharisees sought to foreclose indefinitely the possibility that Israel should ever again stake her life on the expectation of imminent fulfillment of these hopes. Henceforth, the Jew could remain faithful to God and sure of his election in any time or place, good fortune or bad, in the midst of a history whose ups and downs revealed no clear line of progress and whose salvic direction had become illegible.

The fall of the temple in 70 C.E. was, then, for the Pharisees, the opportunity to complete a spiritualizing and universalizing revolution which they had been developing before, in conflict with the Hasmonean dynasty and the Sadducean temple priesthood. They did not express themselves consciously in this manner. They, like all Jews, were stunned by the tragic events and deeply mourned the disaster. The Pharisees carefully preserved all the laws of the temple cultus as a part of their study and enshrined the hope that all this would eventually be restored. But, stunned though they were, they were hardly stunned out of their senses. For they, of all the Jewish movements of this time, had an answer to this event that could carry Israel into the future. The whole apparatus of priesthood and temple cult was now out of the way. With its fall the Sadducees and the Essenes withered and died. There remained only Pharisaism, with its synagogue and its portable *politeuma,* lodged in the heart of each observant Jew, that could survive the fall of national religion without these foundations.

Even the traditions about the tragic loss of the temple are given the typical Pharisaic turn. It is said that God himself is so distressed by the loss of the temple that his *Shekinah* ("Presence") has followed his people into exile.[76] But this means that God is not localized in the temple, nor has he broken his bond with Israel with its fall. Rather, God is available throughout the Diaspora in every house of prayer and wherever the Jew makes the oblation of his heart to his heavenly Father. According to one rabbinic tradition, since the fall of the temple, God's *Shekinah* is present in two places: in the schools of learning and when a man embraces his wife. The synagogue and the family were henceforth to be the twin pillars of Jewish life.[77]

The Pharisees also created the tradition that the temple had been destroyed because Israel had sinned. This judgment appears, at first, to echo the Christian one. But, in actuality, this Pharisaic tradition is intended to cancel out the Christian viewpoint. The Pharisees declared that the temple fell because Israel was disobedient and went astray from God's commandments, a generalization which might be applied to almost any misfortune. But the Pharisees certainly did not mean by this what the Church meant by it: that Israel was punished for its failure to believe in Christ. On the contrary, what they implied was that God had punished Israel for *too much believing* in the imminent advent of the Messiah, for too much dependence on the lively expectation of a historical redemption which had kept Palestinian Jewry at a fever pitch for three centuries, instead of sober attention to the path of salvation which God had commanded through his Torah. Therefore, God had punished Israel by removing it from the homeland and national shrine which fed these hopes. Israel was to learn thereby to turn away from apocalyptic frenzy and to attend to the Pharisaic way of life wherein alone lay its salvation.[78]

The behavior of the Pharisaic leadership during the great Jewish Wars reveals their readiness for such a disaster. The tradition has it that, no sooner had Jerusalem become occupied by messianic Zealots and the disastrous course of the war become evident, even before the city actually fell, Rabban Yohanan ben Zakkai had his two disciples smuggle him out of the city in a coffin. He then proceeded straightway to the general of the besieging Roman army, Vespasian, and petitioned to reconstitute the teaching Sanhedrin at Jamnia, greeting the general with a prophecy that he would be victorious in the war and would thence be elevated to the imperial purple. The future emperor acceded to his request, and henceforth the Romans recognized the Pharisees as the legitimate leaders of Jews with whom they would deal in the future.[79] For the Pharisees, the fall of the temple and the city were distressing events, but they also seized upon them as opportunities to put into full effect that alternative mode of Judaism which they had been preparing in the womb of Palestinian Judaism for three centuries and which they could now bring forth full-born and ready for growth.

The myth that the early Church confronted an obsolete and sterile Judaism, which had lost its spiritual power, derives from the Christian ideological need to put Judaism behind itself. But this myth actually conceals and makes incomprehensible the real historical *Sitz im Leben* of the conflict. For the Judaism which rejected Jesus as the Christ and which resisted Christian preaching was not the Judaism of the temple priesthood of Jesus' lifetime, but the Judaism of the Pharisees, which brought to full development at Jamnia that alternative to the temple which also excluded the Christian answer. This was the Judaism with which Christianity was in conflict during its early mission. If Christianity regards Judaism as "obsolete" and its continued existence as a "mystery," now that it has "rejected" its own future in Christ, it might be equally true that Judaism regards Christianity as "obsolete," a holdover from the heady apocalypticism of Jewish Palestine from the time of the Maccabees to the Sicarii of the Jewish Wars. This, from the Pharisaic perspective, had already been proven a false line of development. That Christianity could actually survive such a birth and continue to grow, not merely to adulthood but into a kind of giant, is, from the Jewish perspective, an enigma, given the self-contradiction of its religious starting point. That Christians could through the ages continue to assert that the Messiah has come, when evil demonstrably continues to reign—and, still more, to do such evil "in his name"—is, from a Jewish perspective, an unfathomable self-contradiction.

Thus, Church and Synagogue, like the two brothers of Rebekah's womb, were born with the younger holding on to the heel of the elder—and claiming to be the rightful heir. The Church, elaborating its theology between the second and fifth centuries, and Judaism, codifying its oral Torah into the Talmud in the same period, stand as parallel but mutually exclusive answers to the same question of how Hebrew national faith finds its way into a postnational future. As Arthur Cohen has stated, the "Judaeo-Christian tradition" is a Christian myth which forecloses any real dialogue between Judaism and Christianity, since it reduces Judaism to the Scriptures of Hebrew national religion which stand as the "Old Testament" to the Christian "New Testament," declared to be its universal and spiritual fulfillment. But a Judaism so defined makes incomprehensible that real Judaism of the synagogue which the Church confronted in its mission and which was the object of that negativity toward "the Jews" in the New Testament and in the anti-Judaic literature of the Church Fathers. The Church was at enmity with *this* Judaism, not because it was obsolete, but because it refused to be obsolete and threatened, again and again, to become compellingly relevant in a way that could call into question the very foundations of the Christian claim. This Judaism was dangerous to the Church because it possessed a viable alternative to the Christian New Testament, and regarded itself as the true and legitimate successor and fulfillment of the Hebrew Scriptures.

Chapter 2

The Growing Estrangement:
The Rejection of the Jews
In the New Testament

1. *The "True People of God" and the Rejection
of "the Jews" in the Synoptics and Acts*

In the synoptic tradition, messianic and anti-Judaic midrashim
arose as two sides of the same development. The character of
anti-Judaic thinking in the Christian tradition cannot be correctly evaluated until it is seen as the negative side of its
christological hermeneutic. This reciprocal relationship between
messianic and anti-Judaic midrashim was rooted in the
Church's evangelical experience. As the Church developed its
christological exegesis and found this opposed by the traditional
midrash of the priestly and scribal classes, and especially by
the Pharisees, who were the new leaders of the scribal tradition,
an anti-Judaic midrash grew up to negate this negation given
to the Church's messianic interpretation of the Scriptures by
official Judaism.

It is important to note that Christology and anti-Judaism
were both exegetical traditions in early Christianity—or rather,
two sides of the same exegetical tradition. That is to say, they
both took the form of an interpretation of the books of Moses,
the Psalms, and the Prophets, which was for the Church, as
much as for its rivals, the sole Bible. Upon this common Scrip-

ture the scribes and Pharisees were developing their oral Torah
of halakic midrash, based mostly on the Pentateuch, while the
Church developed its oral New Testament upon a messianic
midrash of the Psalms and Prophets. Since the Sadducean class
rejected this whole development of an oral tradition, it was the
Pharisees that were the primary rivals of the Church's claim to
have the true interpretation. Hostility toward the Pharisees
tended to grow during the Church's early mission and the word
"Pharisee" was now added to controversy stories where previously there had been unnamed or earlier opponents.[1] The
strong rejection of the Church's interpretation by the schools of
the Law evoked an anti-Judaic midrash from the Church designed to negate the teaching authority of this class, in order to
prove that only the Church knew the true meaning of the
Scriptures.

   This midrashic character of anti-Judaic writings continued to
be true down through the patristic period. The *adversus
Judaeos* literature of the Church Fathers continually takes the
form of a collection of testimonies from the "Old Testament"
to which were added one or two New Testament texts. The
testimonies form was the earliest type of Christian theological
reflection. That there was a "book of testimonies," as a written
text, behind this tradition in the New Testament is now generally disputed.[2] But certainly the first Christian theology took
the form of christological midrashim on the Jewish Scriptures.
The anti-Judaic tradition exists as the negative side of this
christological-testimonies tradition and continues to remain in
this form down through the patristic period. What we have here
are two sides of the same argument. On the one hand, the
Church argues that the true meaning of the Scriptures is that
of a prophecy of Jesus as the Christ. And, on the other hand, it
developed a collection of texts "against the Jews" to show why
the authority of the official Jewish tradition should be dis-
counted when it refutes this christological midrash of its own
Scriptures.

   Having pointed out both the midrashic and also the archaic
character of the Church's anti-Judaic tradition and its interdependence with Christology, let us try to reconstruct the setting
of the first development of this tradition. How did the first

development of the Church's christological hermeneutic evoke, alongside of it, this anti-Judaic "negative side"? The crucial experience that generated the Church's Christology was the crucifixion itself or, rather, the decision of faith made by the circle of Jesus' disciples in response to the trauma of the crucifixion. This decision of faith was a refusal to see this event as "proof" that Jesus' messianic mission had failed, and a determination to understand the crucifixion as a "necessary test" through which the messianic prophet is intended to pass in order to fulfill his salvic mission.

Jesus' own teachings probably are reflected in the spiritualizing halakah of the synoptics. His ethical teachings took a somewhat more radical, but not entirely different, form from that of the contemporary school of Hillel. It was the school of Hillel that declared, for example, that the whole of the Law can be summed up in the command to love one's neighbor.[3] Jesus' teachings on divorce were in accord with the strict interpretation of the school of Shammi, however (Mishnah, *Gittin* 9, 10). That the Sabbath was made for man and not man for the Sabbath was also a familiar Pharisaic principle, which recognized the need to modify Sabbath law to accommodate basic human needs.[4] So, too, was the principle that it is the inner motivation that determines the righteousness of an act, and not just the external form.[5] But while there was a similarity in content, there was a difference in style between Jesus and the scribal schools that led to an overestimation of the difference between them. Jesus was an itinerant prophet preaching to the 'am ha'aretz on the roads and hillsides in a way that rejected the barrier between the observant and the unwashed. While the Pharisees conducted their ethical interpretation in a carefully conservative manner that preserved the outer form, Jesus' spiritualizing of the halakah was iconoclastic toward the outward form. Doubtless this was the setting of the controversies between himself and the scribal class.

More importantly, however, Jesus set his demand for righteousness in the context of messianic proclamation. The heart of his teaching was a proclamation of repentance in relation to the imminent advent of the Reign of God. This proclamation implied his own divinely designated role as the proclaimer of repentance in the light of this coming Kingdom, so that those who responded to or rejected his proclamation were making a decision equivalent to inclusion in, or separation from, that Kingdom shortly to be established by divine action. Jesus probably did not identify himself originally with the Messiah. This would actually have been meaningless prior to the messianic revolution itself. Rather, he declared that he was the definitive prophet of a coming Son of man whose Kingdom was soon to be established by God (Mark 8:38; Luke 9:26; 12:8–9). Inclusion in this Kingdom *then* rests on how people respond to Jesus' word *now*. This would raise the question in the minds of the hearers as to "who he was." Was he the Elijah who was to come before the Messiah, or was he the Mosaic prophet who was to give the definitive interpretation of the Law and convert the hearts of the people to prepare for God's Advent? Or was he the Davidic Messiah who would free Israel by taking up the sword to lead the hosts of God against the minions of Belial? Or was he perhaps the mysterious Son of man who would burst open the heavens to reveal the power of God? Since Jewish messianic thought was very fluid, both mystical and practical, it was possible to fluctuate back and forth amid all these positions, according to the "signs of the times."

It is probable that Jesus' own self-understanding came increasingly to approximate that of the Messiah at the end of his life, when he turned his steps toward Jerusalem in the belief that his proclamation of the Kingdom there would be the definitive act that would bring about the divine revolution in history. His use of the symbolism of the advent of the Davidic king into Jerusalem from the ancient New Year's ritual suggests a willingness to identify his role with that of the kingly Messiah.[6] His final Jerusalem mission, therefore, created a swiftly mounting élan of ecstatic expectation that this act would coincide with God's dramatic incursion into history, overthrowing the reign of evil powers and establishing the reign of blessedness for God's elect. But this élan resulted instead in the rapid denouement of his own death. When, instead of the expected miracle, Jesus was hustled away from the Mount of Olives where he was encamped with his followers, quickly tried by the political Sanhedrin and the Roman powers, and executed in the common death by crucifixion of an insurrectionist, the disciples were faced with a decisive choice about the truth of that expectation which they had followed with mounting hope up to the point of this reversal. Either Jesus was not the vehicle of the messianic Advent of God, and they and he had been wrong, or else his rejection by the Roman powers, with the cooperation of the Jewish colonial leaders, was a hostile assault by the "enemies of God" which did not cancel Jesus' messianic identity.

Until the actual moment of Jesus' death, one cannot really speak of a trauma of rejection as fundamentally conditioning the attitude of the disciples toward the official Jewish tradition. But this is only to say that, prior to this trauma of Jesus' death, one cannot speak of Christian faith at all, but only of those preconditions that prepared for its revelatory moment. There was nonresponse in Jesus' lifetime, to be sure. The scribes were hostile to certain aspects of his view of halakah. But most of all they were hostile to his declared role as the definitive prophet of God's Kingdom. But that is simply to say that, before the fact, they were unconvinced that God's Kingdom was actually imminent and so were not convinced that Jesus was its definitive prophet. There were, of course, the "crowds who heard him gladly." They did believe that the Kingdom was imminent and so, by implication, accepted his role as its definitive prophet. But these were disappointingly small and fickle compared to that conversion of all Israel which, for Jesus and his disciples, was necessary before God's Advent. Finally, in Jerusalem, instead of meeting an overwhelming turn of heart, they encountered the hostile cooperation of the Sadducean aristocracy with the Romans in the quick arrest and execution of the messianic agitator.

But even these negative factors did not constitute a traumatic conflict with the tradition and its official spokesmen until Jesus' actual death. Up until that moment, there was always the possibility (for the disciples, for the "crowds," and even for the official leadership) of a miracle. If he were really the Messiah, God would rescue him from impending disaster, overthrow his enemies, and vindicate His prophet in some miraculous intervention that would show that Jesus' word was an intrinsic part of God's plan for the coming of the Kingdom. But instead, Jesus died, was buried in a borrowed grave, and to most eyes, no miracle occurred.

For the dominant Jewish religious consciousness, including those "crowds who heard him gladly"—i.e., hoped that he was to be the one who would establish the Kingdom—this settled the matter. Jesus was not the Messiah. For Judaism had never heard anything about a dying Messiah. True, there was the idea of the suffering prophet, but this was not identified with the Messiah.[7] There was also the minor tradition of the Messiah ben Joseph who would die prior to the establishment of God's Reign, but he was supposed to die gloriously in battle leading the hosts of Israel against its enemies in the final apocalyptic contest between God and Belial.[8] But Jesus died on the cross as a common criminal, and there was no sign of an Armageddon in sight. To most eyes, Jesus' death occasioned no miracles, no rocking of the evil world order to its foundation. Roman power remained as firmly entrenched on the day after the crucifixion as it was on the day before. To most Jews, this ended the matter. Since the priests and scribes had never "heard him gladly," this was no problem for them. For the crowds who had hoped that he "was the one to redeem Israel" (Luke 24:21), this was a disappointment, but one they had grown used to bearing. But for the disciples, who had staked everything on the truth of his message, it was an intolerable shock. Yet they, too, shared the assumption that such an end was incompatible with messianic identity, and so they scattered in dismay.

But then an extraordinary experience overtook this frightened band. The objectivity of this event can never be verified. To the outsider it must appear perhaps even as a collective "wishful thinking." To those who experienced it, it represented the dramatic influx of new understanding, the starting point for a new beginning. Could this man's hope, so vibrant and compelling, have all been for nothing? Had God played him false? Surely a miracle must have happened, unseen by other eyes, at first unrecognized even by their own. He was not dead, but still alive! Did they not feel his spirit still among them? Did they not hear his words still ringing in their ears? First one group of disciples and then another reported that they had seen him, in an unknown man that talked to them along the road to Emmaus, in a distant figure sighted along the shore as they fished. The women were the first to be sure of it. They said they had been to his tomb. His body was gone, but an angel said that he had gone ahead of them into Galilee. Finally they all believed and assembled in Jerusalem in the certainty that he was not dead, but risen, and still sojourned in their midst as a powerful, but unseen, presence that regenerated their faith. The visible miracle of the final Advent had not been disproven by his death; only postponed a little while. Now faith in its imminence must be reproclaimed in the name of the true Prophet, Jesus, whom the grave would not hold and who had been snatched up to heaven with God to appear with him at his Advent. Soon the heavens would open, just as he had expected, and God would come to overturn the evil powers and set everything to rights. Now the disciples understood the real message of his death. But they must quickly tell it to those ambivalent crowds who had first followed him, and now had turned away, supposing that it was all over. As for those priests and scribes, well, they would know soon enough who was right, for soon the clouds would burst asunder and Jesus himself would appear as the glorious Son of man beside his avenging Lord. But who in Israel had ever heard of such a Messiah?

The disciples began to search the Scriptures to affirm their faith that this redemptive event was indeed the real meaning of the ancient prophecies. In many places they found confirmation of this faith. Of particular importance were the parts of the prophet Isaiah (especially 42:52–53) which told of a rejected prophet whose suffering and death made atonement for Israel. Shortly before his death Jesus himself had linked his fate with this prophecy. This prophecy was joined to the story in the Psalms of the king, God's Anointed, who was so overwhelmed by his enemies that his soul was sinking down into Sheol, but, at the last moment, God reached down into the lower darkness and drew him up from out of many waters and established him high upon his Holy Mount and made him king over the whole earth at the time of salvation (Pss. 22; 69; 18). In Psalm 110 they found that this messianic king was to be reserved at God's right hand until God had defeated his enemies. And in the book of Daniel (7), they read of a glorious figure, like unto a Son of man, who was to appear with God at the Judgment. Clearly all these must refer to the same person. Since David died and was buried and did not ascend into heaven, and David himself, in the psalm, addresses this figure as "My Lord," this cannot refer to David himself. It must refer to his heir, the future Messiah, who is intended to be rejected by his enemies, suffer, and die, but to be resurrected from the pit and exalted into heaven at God's right hand until his enemies are defeated and he appears with God at the Judgment (Mark 12:35–37; Matt. 22:41–45; Acts 2:34–35).[9] Certain other prophetic texts pointed in the same direction. In Hosea, they read that God would revive his stricken people after two days and on the third day raise them up (6:2). In Zechariah they found many significant passages, such as the one which said that on the day of God's victory the people of Jerusalem would "look on him whom they have pierced" (12:10).

But who are the enemies of the messianic prophet? Who are those enemies who attack and almost defeat the king in the Psalms? And who are the enemies who lead the suffering prophet to the slaughter and "make his grave with the wicked"? Are they not precisely those same enemies against whom the prophets themselves are constantly railing—that stubborn taint of unbelief which has ever refused the message of repentance which God has sent through his messengers? It is the official leadership, the priests and scribes, who represent this tradition of apostasy in Israel. They are the ones who have ever resisted the Holy Spirit and killed the prophets. They are those "strong bulls of Bashan who open wide their mouths" at the threatened messianic king. They are the "power of the dog" from which he cries out to heaven for deliverance. Finally the disciples understood the real meaning of the Scriptures: that it was written that the Prophet-King-Son of man "must suffer many things, and be rejected by the elders and the chief priests and the scribes, and be killed, and after three days rise again." Jesus himself had taught this plainly during his lifetime. At that time the darkness covered their eyes, and they could understand not a word of what he said (Mark 8:27–33; Matt. 16:

21–22; Luke 9:22–27; Mark 9:30–32; Matt. 17:22–23; Luke 9:43–45; Mark 10:32–34; Matt. 20:17–19; Luke 18:31–34). But now it all became clear to them. Some of the brethren even said that Jesus himself had appeared to them on the road to Emmaus and had run through all the texts from Moses and the Prophets, teaching them that this was the true meaning of them (Luke 24:26–27). Jesus was the Prophet-King-Son of man of whom it was written that he must suffer and be rejected by the official leadership of Israel and be killed and rise on the third day to be reserved in heaven at God's right hand until God chose to reveal this secret plainly to all at the time of His Advent. Until that time, in his name and in his name alone was there salvation for Israel. Only those who believed in this midrash of the Scriptures and repented and believed in his name would be included in that remnant of Israel whom God would redeem in the last days and establish as his elect in his Kingdom. All others would be cast aside and reckoned with the Gentiles and enemies of God. Jesus was "the stone which the builders rejected," but who now "has become the head of the corner" (Ps. 118:22). He was that stone which the prophets predicted would become a "rock of stumbling to both houses of Israel" (Isa. 8:14), whom God is laying in Zion as the cornerstone and sure foundation of his people (Isa. 28:16). He is the stone that will scatter the enemies of God on the last day and become a "mighty mountain filling the whole earth" (Dan. 2:34–35). Only the community founded on this cornerstone is the true people of God and heir of the promises to Israel. Those who refused to believe in his name would be rejected from Israel and have no part in the community of salvation.

Now the Church knew that it and it alone understood the real meaning of the Scriptures. The priests of the temple and the teachers of the schools had never understood the Scriptures nor been able to recognize the mighty deeds of God (Matt. 22:29). They are the heirs of the lineage of apostasy in Israel, which has always resisted the Holy Spirit and killed the prophets, and they were destined to complete their heritage of apostasy by killing the Messiah himself. They are hypocrites and blind guides, and all who follow their lead will fall down into the pit, like the blind following the blind. Indeed, even if God sent back a man risen from the dead to tell them what was in store for them, they would not believe it, because, although they have Moses and the prophets, they do not hear them (Luke 16:27–31).

With this interpretation of the Scriptures, the disciples were ready to renew Jesus' messianic mission to Israel, now preaching that salvation is to be found only through his name. Those crowds in Jerusalem and Judea who had once heard him gladly would be told that this is the real meaning of his message. Some of the scribal class and even the priests might be expected to be impressed with the irrefutable evidence of the Scriptures —for example, that Psalm 110:1–2 cannot possibly refer to David, but must refer to his messianic heir. But the time is short. Israel might still be saved if it recognized quickly that this is the real meaning of the prophecies. They should know, too, that the official leadership could not be trusted to interpret the Scriptures correctly because they are the heirs of those who had always rejected the prophets.

Unfortunately, the times were not propitious for such a conversion of Israel's heart. As Jesus himself had said, this is an adulterous and sinful generation, unfaithful, perverse, and crooked. That spirit of apostasy in Israel, represented by the priests and scribes, possessed the hearts of the people now as never before. This is the final time of testing of Israel when it was predicted that the power of evil and unfaithfulness would be rife in the land. This is the last time of the Age of Wrath when almost all Israel is apostate. Only a faithful few will be able to hear the message and be gathered into the community of redemption. As it was in the days of Noah, so will it be in the days of the Son of man. Israel will eat, drink, marry, and give in marriage, and pay no heed to the message of repentance until the community of redemption enters into its ark and the floods come and destroy all the rest (Luke 17:26–27). To this evil and adulterous generation, no sign will be given but the sign of Jonah, that mysterious and all but unintelligible sign of the suffering Messiah who goes down into the pit. Only those who can read this sign aright and be gathered into the community assembled under it will be reckoned as members of the true Israel of God and be saved in the time of redemption (Matt. 12:39–40; Luke 11:29).

Yet the meaning of the signs of the time are plain enough for those who have eyes to see. This evil and adulterous generation can read the signs of the weather plainly enough and see that when the sky is red a storm is threatening. Yet they cannot read the signs of the times (Matt. 16:1–4; Mark 8: 11–13; Luke 12:54–56). This is that faithless Israel to whom Isaiah was sent to say: "You shall indeed hear but never understand, and you shall indeed see but never perceive." God has made their hearts dull, their ears heavy, and their eyes closed, so that they will not be able to understand the message of redemption (Matt. 13:14f. and Acts 28:27 quoting Isa. 6:9f.; cf. Mark 4:11f. and Luke 8:10), while those whom they least expect—the unrighteous ones, the unclean, the prostitutes, and the tax collectors—will go into the Kingdom of God ahead of the children of Israel (Matt. 21:31f.). Sodom itself will have it easier on the day of Judgment than the evil and unrepentant cities of Israel, for if such mighty works had been done in gentile cities, they would have been in sackcloth and ashes long ago, just as the city of Ninevah repented at the preaching of Jonah. But because Chorasin, Bethsaida, and Capernaum remain unmoved by the message, they who now exalt themselves as heirs of the Promise will be brought down to Hades (Matt. 11:20–24; Luke 10:13–15).

This is the character of the earliest Christian preaching, as we can construct it from the synoptic tradition (including the book of Acts). In its original form, Christianity appeared basically as a Jewish messianic sect with similar characteristics to other such messianic sects which arose at this period. Like the Qumran community, it claimed to represent the true Israel of the last era of world history, over against the apostate Israel of the official tradition. It demanded a conversion to its interpretation of the tradition as the means by which Jews must enter the community of salvation. Like the Qumran community, Christianity vilified the Judaism outside its converted community as apostate, sinful, worse than the Gentiles, and even of the devil. It regarded the others as fallen outside the true covenant and ranked with the enemies of God. Hypocrites, blind fools, blind guides, whitewashed tombs, serpents, off-spring of vipers, and children of hell are among the epithets heaped upon the rival interpreters of the tradition in the Gospel of Matthew. Although Matthew undoubtedly expressed a hard-ening of attitudes that came about as a result of competition between the Church and the synagogue in the Diaspora, the basic line of vilification which he represents is common to the entire synoptic tradition and did not originate with him. Indeed, Luke preserves the more ingenious and probably more primi-tive epithet that compares the Pharisees with "hidden tombs," i.e., unsuspected sources of that instant pollution such as would be caused by contact with a corpse under Mosaic Law (Luke 11:44). The Church alone is the true Plant (Israel) of God, while all the rest belong to that plant which has not been planted by God and which will be rooted up and thrown into the fire (Luke 13:3; John 15:1–6).

Like the Qumran community, the Church stood in tension with the priestly authorities of the temple. The exact character of the polemic against the temple has been obscured by the later interpretation of its destruction after 70 C.E. as punishment for rejecting Christ. But the tradition preserved by Matthew 17: 24–27, that the sons of the Kingdom are free of the temple tax, suggests an illegitimizing of the temple in principle. The tradi-tions of the cleansing of the temple and even the predictions of its fall in their original form need have been based only on the belief that its present authorities are hopelessly corrupt and that true worship must be reinstituted by God. Like the Essenes, early Christianity spiritualized temple and priestly language to refer to its own community and spiritual worship.[10]

But, even more, the Church was in tension with the rival teachers of the Law, the rabbinic schools, who formed the teaching class of the synagogues, and with the Pharisees, the superobservant rabbinic leaders. These were the authorities against whom the anti-Judaic line of the Church was to harden during the missionary experience of the first century. Moreover, it was precisely in those churches of Jewish background that we find this antipathy toward the Pharisees most strongly devel-oped, Matthew especially. Luke, as a gentile Christian, lacking this Jewish sectarian feeling of intense rivalry with the Jewish authorities, is anxious to show that all legitimate authority, Jewish and Roman, validated Christianity, while hostility to Jesus and the apostles came from persons of ill-will without authority. For this reason, Luke stresses the positive response of Pharisees to Christianity and portrays leading Pharisees as defending the apostles (Luke 13:31; Acts 5:34–9; 23:6–9; 26:5).[11]

The Church also competed with the Essenes and Pharisees in the claim to represent the true Torah, the authentic interpretation of the teachings of Moses. They, too, claimed to be the ones who had the true halakah, the "greater righteousness" (Matt. 5:20), whereas the Pharisees make void the word of God through their tradition. Pharisaic teachings were mere *human* tradition, as distinct from the *divine* commandment of Mosaic Law (Mark 7:8–9; Matt. 15:1ff.). However, the Church's halakic claims over against Pharisaic "hypocrisy" quickly dissolved, due to its early ambivalences toward the validity of the Law. Perhaps the Law itself did not represent the true will of God, but was only given because of the "hardness of heart" of apostate Israel (Mark 10:2–9; Matt. 19:1–9).

This invalidation of the temple and the Law takes the most radical form in the speech of Stephen, in the opening chapters of Acts. Here it is said that that which is called Israel had, in fact, never been the true people of God. Even from the time of Moses, apostate Israel murmured against God's prophet and rejected the Law, turning instead to the worship of the golden calf. For this reason, the covenant which God had intended to give them at Sinai was withheld until the coming of the Mosaic messianic prophet, namely Jesus. It will be the people assembled around this Mosaic prophet that will be the true people of the covenant. That which the Jews call the Mosaic Law has never represented the true will of God, nor has it been the true way of the covenant, for that Law which God had intended to give on Sinai was abrogated by Israel's apostasy at that time. The true way of the covenant is now made available again through the new Mosaic prophet who was promised by Moses (Deut. 18:15–18; Acts 7:37). The temple likewise represents no true dwelling place of God, but an idolatrous apostasy of Israel. For God does not dwell in temples "made with hands," but his true temple is the cosmos. The temple built by Solomon was contrary to God's will and an act of idolatry comparable to the making of the golden calf.

A position such as the one enunciated by Stephen was not shared by all of the Church in so radical a form. It represented a party within the Jerusalem Church called the "Hellenists" (converts from Greek-speaking synagogues in Jerusalem), whose radical position is reported to have evoked the first persecution and scattering of the Church from Jerusalem to the Diaspora. Neverthless, it represents a sectarian position that had analogies in other Jewish sects at this period. The Samaritans and the Nazaraioi (if this be really a pre-Christian sect) seem also to have repudiated the Mosaic tradition and the temple in such terms. Like them, the Church claimed to represent the true content and authority of the tradition (or perhaps better, the "idea" of the tradition), which the official representatives maintained in a false form.

However, the Church's claim to represent a "better righteousness" than the Pharisees probably had a different root than that of the Essenes. The Essenes were a superobservant halakic and priestly sect whose righteousness consisted in the claim of observing the Torah more scrupulously than anyone else.[12] The Church, however, probably even in the time of Jesus, had an iconoclastic relation to the Law that suggested a sect whose members were primarily *'am ha'aretz*, the less observant "people of the land," regarded with contempt as "unclean" by the rigorists. The polemic against the "righteous" in Christianity has a strong note of social resentment characteristic of a social group shut out of learned and observant circles and stung by the contempt meted out to the unwashed by those with the learning and means to pursue such forms of righteousness. From the beginning, theirs was a demand for a simpler and more available path of righteousness, which abrogated much of the observances of "forms" in favor of the more fundamental sentiments of justice, mercy, and faith.

The rabbinic circles, as we have seen, were not opposed to moralization of outward forms. They, too, were engaged in a spiritualizing and universalizing revolution in Judaism in their own way. To equate Christianity with an ethic of inwardness against the mere legalism and formalism, i.e., "hypocrisy," of the Pharisees is grossly unfair as a blanket indictment of the movement. And it is a falsification of the Pharisaic position and, by implication, of all rabbinic Judaism, rooted in the earliest Christian experience. Even today, much of the anti-Judaic reading of the New Testament is based on the assumption that this distinction between the "inwardness" of the Church and the "hypocrisy" of the Pharisees was literally correct. Why did the Church make this mistake about the Pharisees? Doubtless there were some among them that were "hypocrites" in precisely this sense, but they are criticized in the rabbinic tradition as well.[13] The Church's blanket indictment of this movement seems to reflect a social position in which Christians were so shut out of the observant brotherhoods that they saw them only from the "outside." So the prophetic truth of the Church's search for a more spiritual and universal ethic took on an exaggeratedly antithetical view of the "legalism" of the Pharisees. This exaggerated antithesis between Christianity's "inwardness" and Pharisaism obscured the real nature of the clash between them, as well as the actual historical role which the Pharisees were playing in contemporary Judaism as creators of a spiritualizing and universalizing revolution parallel to that of Christianity, but in conservative dress.

But the real clash between Christianity and the Pharisaic teachers was not over spiritualizing interpretations of the temple or the Law or even the belief that Jesus was the Messiah. Rather, the crux of the conflict lay in the fact that the Church erected its messianic midrash into a *new principle of salvation.* For Christianity, salvation was now found no longer in any observances—ritual or ethical—founded on the Torah of Moses, representing the covenant of the past. Rather, salvation was now found solely through faith in the messianic exegesis of the Church about the salvic role of Jesus as Prophet-King-Son of man, predicted by the prophets. Only that community gathered around this cornerstone is God's true people. All others, for whom the covenant of the past was still the foundation for the ongoing people of God, were outside the true covenant. It was not the "better righteousness," but the faith principle of the Church that was the source of the conflict between the Church, with its messianic midrash, and that Judaism which followed the midrash of the scribal schools and for whom the covenant of the past, however reinterpreted, was still normative in itself. It was this radical incompatibility between the two interpretations that caused the fierce polemic between the Church and the Pharisees. This is the real content of the continued insistence in the Gospels that the Pharisees "know nothing" of the real meaning of the Scriptures, that they are incapable of recognizing a true prophet, that they are hypocrites and blind guides. "Beware the leaven of the Pharisees" was the watchword of the Church, meaning, beware the Pharisaic midrash of the Scriptures. The Church alone has the true bread, i.e., the true interpretation. It alone has the cornerstone of the true covenant of God's people and teaches rightly about the principle for inclusion in that community. The Church's messianic midrash, therefore, had the effect of erecting a new people of God founded on a new principle of salvation, which is not available through the old covenant, but exists now as the "fulfillment" of the Scriptures, predicted by the prophets. Christianity is no mere "new patch" put on an old garment, or a new wine poured into old wine bottles. It demands a whole new "garment" and "container" of this new wine (Luke 5: 3ff.). This was the crux of the incompatibility of Christianity and the Jewish religious tradition, as interpreted by the schools. It resulted in the rapid expulsion of the Church from the womb of its mother religion with hard blows on the backsides of its ejected preachers (Matt. 10:17; Mark 13:9; Luke 21:31; John 12:42; 16:2; 2 Cor. 11:24).

This rapid expulsion of the Church from the Jewish religious community provoked a new crisis in Christian identity, since originally the Christian mission was understood exclusively as a mission to Israel (Matt. 15:24ff.; Mark 7:27). Christianity was the people of God in the sense of being the true inner meaning of the covenant, erected on the cornerstone of Israel's own messianic king, whose coming had been predicted by the prophets. Israel had no other meaning than to give birth to this foundation stone, and his coming was the entire content of the Scriptures, read "correctly." Therefore, Christianity had no religious legitimacy other than that provided by the milieu of

Jewish religious ideas. Christianity confronted Judaism with a demand for a conversionist relation to its own past that abrogated that past, in the sense that that past itself no longer provided a covenant of salvation. Christianity did not ask Judaism merely to extend itself in continuity with its past, but to abrogate itself by substituting one covenantal principle from the past for another provided by Jesus. It declared that in this cornerstone alone there is salvation, while the covenant of Moses provides no cornerstone in itself, but exists only to predict the true cornerstone.

The clash created by the preaching of Israel's salvation in this form gave the Church's evangelical progress an unexpected turn. Everywhere it preached the gospel, it found itself expelled from Jewish religious institutions. Expelled from Jerusalem by the storm over the preaching of Stephen, it went into the Diaspora. But there the Church encountered essentially the same experience, with the added vehemence of a Jewish community which had to assert its identity principle all the more clearly to prevent itself from disappearing into the surrounding gentile society. Some Jews from the Diaspora community were converted, to be sure, as some had been in Jerusalem. But these were probably those who were already somewhat Hellenized, less observant, or for various reasons ready to relax the Jewish identity principle in favor of some other key to salvation. But the representatives of the normative religious affirmation of the synagogue, as interpreted by the teaching tradition of the schools, shut their doors against Christian preachers with an unmistakable rapidity and firmness, even though they received them well at first because they came from Jerusalem. The deep hostility to the Pharisees in the synoptic tradition reflects this evangelical experience, since it was this element in the synagogues that everywhere provided the hard line of resistance in the Jewish religious community to the Christian interpretation of the Scriptures.

But this inability of Christian preaching to convert the core of the synagogue itself was complemented by an unexpected turn of events. Gentiles were attracted to Christianity and began to come in great numbers. These Gentiles came from the circle of "God-fearers," attracted to Jewish ethical and monotheistic principles, who gathered around the synagogues, but who drew back from full proselyte status. For this circle of Judaizing Gentiles, Christianity provided everything that attracted them to Judaism, without those practices which they did not want to accept. Moreover, for these Gentiles, the principle that was so offensive to the synagogue—namely the Church's insistence that one attaches oneself to the true community of the covenant, not by integrating oneself into the covenantal history of a people, but by attaching oneself to a redemptive *figure*—was no problem, since this was the customary principle of initiation into the mystery religions. The Church, then, found itself with a paradox which its first preaching had not anticipated. Rejected by Judaism, it found its fertile missionary field among the Gentiles.

Yet the Church adapted its midrash rather rapidly to accommodate this development. It is customary to regard this change from a Jewish to a gentile Church as a deep crisis that divided the early Church up through the fall of Jerusalem. The fact that the book of Acts regards this change as having come about rather early, fairly smoothly, and by the first disciples of Jesus himself is regarded with suspicion as a later apologetic.[14] Yet this writer would suggest that there are reasons for giving the account in Acts more credence. Proselytism, after all, was nothing new, but an established tradition of the synagogue. The synagogue, up to the time of Christianity, had even allowed a class of "semiproselytes" to emerge who were asked only to accept the Noachian laws.[15] Once having raised up a new covenantal principle, faith in Messiah Jesus, to substitute for that salvation that came from identifying with the covenant of the Jewish past, it was not a big step to including the Gentiles in a way that no longer demanded that they be Jews religiously. No doubt this occasioned much soul-searching on the part of the first disciples. But the compromise worked out in the book of Acts whereby Jewish converts should remain Jews in halakic observances, while Gentiles would be asked to adopt only the Noachian laws of general human decency, is by no means an inexplicable possibility for these first disciples, once we realize that they had already abrogated the intrinsic salfivic connection between such observances and entrance into the true covenant by making faith in Messiah Jesus the cornerstone (Acts 15: 19–21).

One can point to the "circumcision party" (Acts 11:2; 15:1) and to Paul's deep conflict with a Judaizing party that evidently came with the credentials of the Jerusalem Church as evidence of such a crisis (Gal. 4:17; 2 Cor. 11:5; Phil. 3:2–3). However, this circumcision party did not gather around the original disciples, represented by Peter, but around a figure who had not been a part of that original circle, namely James, Jesus' brother. The Gospels represent James as hostile to Jesus' mission during his lifetime. His entrance into the Church sometime immediately before or after the crucifixion remains unexplained in the tradition. This James was an observant Pharisee who appears to have taken over the Jerusalem church when the original disciples were driven out by the crisis created by Stephen.[16] The circumcision party, therefore, appears to represent a conservative reaction to the radical élan of the early gospel. This radical élan carried the early disciples rapidly toward the Diaspora and then toward the Gentiles, with the synagogue doors closing angrily behind them. This development then generated a conservative reaction among a Pharisaic element in the Jerusalem church, gathered around James, which was determined to hold the line against this gentilization of the Church and to insist that all converts to Christianity be fully observant proselytes to Judaism. This probably also entailed a revision of Christian covenantal theology. Christianity was interpreted more in the manner of a Torah-keeping messianic sect, such as the Essenes. Such a Jewish Christianity would regard Jesus as the Messiah designate and would await his return as redeemer of Israel, rather than see Jesus as providing an already fulfilled basis of salvation.[17]

On the other hand, the élan of the gospel toward the Gentiles was taken up by more radical figures, such as the Hellenists, and then by Paul. Paul built on the foundations laid by the Hellenists,[18] who were ready to abrogate the traditional halakic observances for Jewish as well as gentile converts. But the basis of this possibility was laid by the first disciples themselves, who had declared that Messiah Jesus alone is the cornerstone, and inclusion in the people of God is through faith in him. This viewpoint drove them into the Diaspora and then into a compromise that accepted the Gentiles on less than a full proselyte status. As the book of Acts indicates, Peter did not represent the circumcision party of Jerusalem, but stood in the position of a somewhat confused middleman between it and the radical position of Paul (Acts 10, 15; also Gal. 2). What we have here, then, is not a Jewish church, represented by Peter and James, and a gentile church, represented by Paul. Rather, we should probably think in terms of a left-wing Pauline church, a reactionary Jamesian church, and a mediating Petrine church, representing the élan created by the theology of the first disciples. This Petrine church, represented by the Gospel tradition, had from the beginning created a salvation principle that relativized the Mosaic covenant to a mere predictive status. By the second decade of the Church's mission, it had also interpreted this to mean that Gentiles could come into the people of God without accepting full proselyte status as Jews. Such Christians were probably too sentimentally attached to their own religious past to be able to regard these halakic observances as having no relevance at all *for Jews,* however. Yet this was already the implication of their position. It took a person of Paul's radical temperament to bring this out in the open and declare that Torah has no relevance for salvation for Gentiles— or Jews. If this analysis of early Christian development is correct, it would explain the rapid obsolescence of Jewish Christianity in the mainstream theology, as well as the deep hostility that Paul feels toward the Judaizing party who have taken over the mother church in Jerusalem, and yet whose position he sees as a radical backsliding on the meaning of the gospel as he has received it from the first disciples.

By the second decade of the Church's mission, this Petrine church had already reached the point where its first midrash (that Jesus is the stone the builders rejected who has become *the* cornerstone of the community of salvation) had been expanded to include the idea that God was carving out for himself a people *from among the Gentiles.* This, too, was declared to have been known and continuously predicted by the prophets. I suggest that this development took place at this early a date because the synoptic traditions, which assert the Christian covenantal principle over against that of "apostate Israel," already exists in an integral relation, in so many cases, with the idea that God, in rejecting this apostate people, is choosing the Gentiles. "The Jews"—those who adhere to the old covenantal foundation of salvation—thereby reject the gospel. So God has rejected them and is creating a new people which includes the Gentiles. All the texts about the rejection of the apostate Israel now become available for the additional idea that God finds faith among the Gentiles. In the book of Acts, this view has become formulaic. The gospel must be preached first to the Jews, for they are the people to whom this covenant was promised. But they reject it. So straightway the Church turns from the rejecting Jews to the accepting Gentiles. This pattern was based on the evangelical experience of the Church at a time not too far distant from that when Luke presents it as taking place, i.e., before and during the mission of Paul. An exegesis that added the idea of inclusion of the Gentiles to the idea of apostate Israel must then have begun to be formed in the second decade of the Church's life.

This new exegesis is expressed in the frequent correlation between the "unbelieving Jew" and the "believing Gentile." The Jewish leaders reject and kill Jesus, but the first believer is a Roman centurion at the cross (Mark 15:39). The success of the Samaritan mission added the stories about "the good Samaritan," in contrast to "the faithless Jew" (Luke 10:33; 17:16; John 4:40–42). The unbelieving Jewish cities of Chorasin, Bethsaida, and Capernaum are played against the believing gentile cities of Tyre and Sidon, who "would have repented long ago in sackcloth and ashes" if such mighty works had been done among them. The Gentiles are compared to the citizens of Ninevah, who repented at the preaching of Jonah, contrasted with the infidel Israel, who has always refused to hear God's prophets. As the final rebuke, it is said that it will be more tolerable for Sodom than for the unbelieving Jewish cities on that day (Matt. 11:20–24; Luke 10:13–15; 11:30). The saying that the men of Ninevah and the Queen of Sheba will arise to give judgment against this generation on the last day has the same *tendenz*. Both are types of believing Gentiles, in contrast to unbelieving Jews (Matt. 12:38–42; Luke 11:

29–32). Matthew sums it up by saying that the Gentiles will come from the East and the West to sit at the messianic banquet, while the sons of the Kingdom will be thrown out into outer darkness (Matt. 8:11ff.; Luke 13:25).

In the parables of the great wedding feast, those who were first invited are rejected because they refuse the king's invitation. His messengers are sent out a second time to gather in the rabble. These parables have the same implication. The rejection of the Jews implies a decision by God to include the rabble, i.e., the unrighteous (nonobservant) and the *goyim* (Matt. 22:1–14; Luke 14:16–24). Matthew makes this parable into a complete story of the Church's identity over against apostate Israel. For him, those originally invited to come are not merely too busy to come, as in Luke; they actually "seized his servants, treated them shamefully, and killed them." The king, in turn, "was angry, and he sent his troops and destroyed those murderers and burned their city." The king then sends his servants out to gather in anyone who will come. He also comes and looks over the guests during the feast and throws out the guest without the wedding garment into outer darkness. Matthew thus tells us that unrepentant Israel is rejected, but also that God will punish it by sending armies to destroy it and burn its city. The Gentiles—those originally outside the covenant—are gathered in to the people. But they are included only if their faith is true. Any Gentile who is still a pagan at heart will be damned. The community saying in Matthew that if a brother "refuses to listen even to the Church, let him be to you as a Gentile and a tax collector" (Matt. 18:17) indicates the extent to which this tradition is involved in a *reversal* of Jewish community terminology. The "righteous" (observant Jews) have become the "unrighteous" (unbelievers) who are an "abomination in the sight of God" (Luke 16:14), while the former abominations (prostitutes and tax collectors) have become "righteous" (believers). Israel is ranked with the Gentiles and the kings of the earth who are arrayed against God and his Anointed (Acts 4:25–27), whereas the Gentiles have become the "people."

All the prophetic texts saying that God will raise up salvation for Israel so that the "nations" will see it, that Israel will be a "light to the nations," and that the "nations" will be gathered into salvation on the last day—sayings which represent the universalist dimension of prophecy—now become available to the midrash of the Church to prove that God intended to gather a true people of God from among the Gentiles, even in an *antithetical relation* to an apostate Israel. This involves, at times, an extraordinary twisting of the prophetic texts themselves (which meant by this a salvation from among the Gentiles in a positive relation to the salvation of Israel, i.e., Acts 28:28, based on Ps. 67:2). In some texts, where the word *nations* in the Septuagint clearly means the "nations of Israel," this was read by the Church's midrash to mean the *gentile* nations! (Acts 15:14, based on Amos 9:11–12). The favorite passage was, of course, that drawn from Second Isaiah (i.e., 42:6), which was read to mean that Jesus, the crucified prophet, will be a "light to the Gentiles" (Acts 13:47; Matt. 12:18–21). This teaching of a destined gentile salvation to the exclusion of Israel is even read back into the beginning of Jesus' life. Simeon, at Jesus' circumcision, predicts that he will be a light to the Gentiles (Luke 2:32), while Matthew has Jesus go to live in the gentile regions of Zebulun and Naphtali before the beginning of his preaching to fulfill the saying of Isaiah that in "Galilee of the Gentiles—the people who dwell in darkness have seen a great light" (Matt. 4:12–16). Luke has Jesus undertake his first preaching in the synagogue at Nazareth by reading the great text of promised salvation for Israel from Isaiah 61:1–2, and then interpreting it to mean that this salvation will not be sent to the widows and lepers in Israel, but to those among the Gentiles. By weaving in the saying that "no prophet is acceptable in his own country" and then describing the synagogue's reaction to Jesus' midrash as one of angry ejection from the city and attempted murder, Luke makes the story of Jesus' first preaching of salvation into a paradigm of the rejection of unbelieving Israel and the election of the Gentiles (Luke 4:16–30).

The idea that apostate Israel not only is unbelieving toward the gospel, but actually tries to kill the great Messenger of God, his forerunners, the prophets, and his disciples, is of central importance to this argument. This theme provides the essential "story line" of all the Gospels, including that of John, as well as the book of Acts. What does this mean? Recent historical studies have shown that the Jewish authorities could have had, at best, a subsidiary relation to the death of Jesus.[19] Yet the Gospels elaborately play down the responsibility of the Romans, while erecting the theme that "the Son of man must suffer many things, and be rejected by the elders and the chief priests and the scribes, and be killed" into a text of key dogmatic importance. It is repeated in solemn threefold sequence in all three Gospels. The Gospel of John is built on the same story line, that "the Jews" are characterized by a desire to "kill" Jesus. The book of Acts repeats the same story line for the mission of the Church. Here, too, rejection by the synagogue constantly takes the form of "plots" by the "Jews" to "kill" the apostles.

Douglas Hare, who has examined the historical background of the theme of persecution in Matthew, concludes that execution was never any part of the disciplinary action of Jewish religious courts against Christian preachers. Flogging of dissident sectarians was a disciplinary measure used by the synagogue. This clearly was used against Christian preachers who were trying to convert the synagogue. The school at Jamnia also sent out to all the synagogues the "malediction" against sectarians which, by the time that the Gospels of Matthew and John were written, had made it impossible for a Christian actually to lead a synagogue service. But this amounted only to voluntary exclusion from the synagogue on the part of Christians who were participating in but not trying to preach to a synagogue. The synagogue was not concerned so much with excluding Christians from attending a synagogue service, as it was with excluding Christian preachers from imposing the Christian exegesis on the synagogue service itself. This discipline was exerted against Jewish Christians. The synagogue took no responsibility at all for gentile converts to Christianity.

Of the three disciples whose deaths at Jewish hands are known, Hare concludes that none reflected official decisions of the religious Sanhedrin.[20] This is probably true also in the death of Jesus, where the Sanhedrin that collaborated with the Romans was the political court of the colonial Jewish leaders and not the religious Sanhedrin condemning Jesus on religious grounds.[21] Thus Hare finds no evidence that the execution of Christians was ever any part of the disciplinary action of the Jewish religious courts acting on religious grounds. Why, then, is the condemnation and execution of Jesus by the Romans elaborately excused in the synoptics, to make the Romans appear innocent and even reluctant to "cooperate" with the Jewish authorities (an account which defies all records of the actual power relations between these two authorities), while trying to shift the blame not only to the Jews, but also on to religious grounds, i.e., blasphemy (John 19:7)?

The same biasing of history appears also in Acts. Here the "Jews" appear as constantly "plotting" against the lives of Peter and Paul, even though they don't succeed in killing either. The actual arrest of Paul in Jerusalem and his transfer to a prison in Caesarea is elaborately excused to make the Jews look responsible, while the Romans who constantly recognize Paul's innocence and want to release him, appear as innocent victims of Jewish malice. Incomprehensibly, it is said that they send him to Rome for trial only because he *demanded* a trial before Caesar, even though they themselves wanted to let him go. Finally, the account in Acts is terminated in such a way that Paul appears in Rome as an honored guest of the Romans and his actual death in Rome at Roman hands is not reported (Acts 28:17–31).

We find an extraordinary need in the Gospels to shift the blame for the deaths of Jesus and his disciples from Roman political authority to Jewish religious authority. Modern historians usually explain this as due to the exigencies of the gentile mission. Since the Christians were now preaching to the Gentiles, they wished to play down any hostility of the gentile government.[22] But it is important to note that the shift is not merely from Roman to Jewish authority, but from *political* to *religious* authority. It is important to the Gospel tradition to throw the blame for the deaths of Jesus and his disciples not merely upon Jewish (much less gentile) political authorities, but specifically upon the head of the Jewish *religious* tradition and its authority. This suggests that the purpose of this shift was not merely one of apologetics toward the Gentiles, but one, first of all, of polemic toward the Jewish religious tradition.

The idea that the religious authority of "apostate Israel" has "always" killed the prophets, and, therefore, culminates its own heritage of apostasy by killing the great messianic prophet, totally governs the entire story line of all the Gospels. Each Gospel takes the form of a mounting controversy with Jewish religious authority, expressed in the desires and/or attempts of these authorities to "kill" Jesus, culminating in his actual death. This is attributed to the elders, chief priests, and scribes. In Acts this same dogmatic thesis governs the story line, so that the rejection of the gospel by the "Jews" and their constant efforts to "kill" God's messengers result in the turn from the mission to the Jews to that of the Gentiles. The very word *Jews* in the New Testament tradition has an important resonance. The term *the Jews* is used as a constantly repeated hostile formula in Acts and John particularly. What is meant here by *the Jews?* Some recent Christian apologists have argued that this meant only the "bad authorities," not the "Jewish people" themselves.[23] This interpretation is founded on texts in the gospel tradition which reflect a time when the Church itself hoped that it would be only certain "leaders" who were "unbelievers," in contrast to the "people" (the *'am ha'aretz*), who were open to the faith.

But any significant distinction between "leaders" and "people" does not hold even for this early period, for the "crowds" are ever fickle, and this is an "evil and adulterous generation." By the time we reach the traditions which formed the usage of the word *Jews* in the New Testament tradition, this word has come to mean quite simply the "Jewish religious community," gathered in its own religious institutions and around the traditional midrash of the schools, which represented a religious consciousness that excluded the Christian midrash. The word *Jews,* in the Gospels, Acts, and Paul, means the Jewish religious community. It is in this sense that the word *Jews* becomes a hostile symbol for all that resists and rejects the gospel. In the book of Acts the term *the Jews* is used in this hostile sense about forty-five times, while the term *a Jew, Jews,* or *Jewish* is used in a descriptive sense for the religious background of Christians fewer than ten times. But the word *Jewish* is carefully avoided in talking about Christianity qua Christianity. The formula in Acts for Jewish rejection versus gentile faith is represented by a passage such as the following:

But when the Jews saw the multitudes, they were filled with jealousy, and contradicted what was spoken by Paul, and reviled him. And Paul and Barnabas spoke out boldly, saying, "It was necessary that the word of God should be spoken first to you. Since you thrust it from you and judge yourselves unworthy of eternal life, behold, we turn to the Gentiles. For so has the Lord commanded us, saying 'I have set you to be a light to the Gentiles, that you may bring salvation to the uttermost parts of the earth' " [Isa. 49:6]. And when the Gentiles heard this, they were glad and glorified the word of God; and as many as were ordained to eternal life believed. [Acts 13:45–48]

This story line in Acts culminates with Paul installed in Rome. The Jewish religious community of Rome confronts him. Their rejection of the gospel then constitutes the culminating "rejection of the Jews" and "election of the Gentiles." This is interpreted by putting together the texts of Isaiah 6:9–10 and Psalm 67:2 to show that "this people" ever hear and hear but never understand, see and see but never perceive; God is making their ears heavy and their eyes closed so that they *may not be able to believe* and that then salvation will be sent to the Gentiles, who will listen to it (Acts 28:26–28).

Why is it necessary to emphasize that the Jewish religious tradition not only rejects the gospel, but tries to kill its messengers (including its "forerunners," the prophets)? We would suggest that this theme in the Christian tradition developed from the crucial need to make religious sense out of the crucifixion itself, i.e., to provide a dogmatic necessity for the fact that the Prophet-King-Son of man is not only to be unheard by an unbelieving people, but that *it was predicted that he should be killed* by them. This is accomplished by reading back into Jewish history a pattern of an apostate Israel which has always rejected the prophets and killed them. The best text for this was Isaiah 53 where the suffering servant is actually said to have died, but the theme of suffering in the Psalms can also be read as though it referred to the actual death of the messianic king.[24] The recent innovation by Herod of erecting memorial tombs to the prophets, in imitation of the Greek practice of erecting memorial tombs to the heroes, is read in the Gospels as evidence that Jewish religious authority admits that they have always killed the prophets and are trying to expiate this crime.[25]

The basis for this interpretation of Jesus as the Prophet-Messiah who is killed by the apostate people and makes atonement for their sins lies in a popular tradition that probably arose at the time of the Maccabean struggle. In the centuries surrounding the birth of Christianity it had become common to believe that the prophets had been martyrs and, conversely, that martyrs were prophets. The Righteous Ones of the Jewish tradition were interpreted as suffering figures who died at the hands of an unrepentant and unbelieving people. The Rabbis themselves adopted this tradition and interpreted their own great teachers as such suffering prophets, as a way of calling the people to renewed faith and good works. These suffering Righteous Ones were also seen as atoning for Israel and interceding with God for Israel in their lifetime and even after their deaths.[26] Although this tradition was not clearly identified with that of the Messiah, the links between the Messiah and the final messianic Prophet made it possible for Christianity to apply this whole tradition of the suffering prophet to Jesus as the final messianic Prophet. The death of Jesus then becomes linked with the idea of a heritage of unrepentant Israel whose hardness of heart is exemplified by killing the prophets.

The Church read back into Jewish history a record of apostate Israel as rejecting and killing the prophets, in order then to read this pattern forward again to make the death of Jesus the predicted and culminating act of this history of apostasy. This dogmatic pattern can then be extended to include the messengers of the crucified Prophet: "As they have always done to the prophets, so they will do to the Son of man" becomes, "As they did to the Son of man, so they will do to you" (the Church). The pattern is, of course, extended to cover the prophetic forerunner of the Messiah, Elijah, as well. The Jews still await Elijah, but the Christians know that Elijah has already come (in the person of John the Baptist) and that they (the Jews) "did to him whatever they pleased [killed him]. So also the Son of man will suffer at their hands" (Matt. 17: 9–13; Mark 9:9–13).

This theme, that the Jews have always killed the prophets, finds its great exposition in the parable of the vineyard, found in all three synoptics (Mark 12:1–12; Matt. 21:33–46; Luke 20:9–19). Here the vineyard owner (God) leaves his vineyard (Israel) in the hands of tenants (the Jews), occasionally sending servants (the prophets) to get his share of the fruit. But these unfaithful tenants constantly beat, kill, and stone the servants. Finally, the owner sends his own son, assuming that the tenants will respect the actual son of the owner. But the tenants immediately kill the son, believing that thereby they may take perpetual squatters' rights on the vineyard. They don't have any real right to it. They are only tenants, not sons. What will the owner of the vineyard do to those wicked tenants? "He will come and destroy the tenants, and give the vineyard to others." There then follows the great "stone" text that was so central to christological midrash: "The very stone which the builders rejected has become the head of the corner" (Ps. 118:22). This tradition must have been formed quite early, prior to the letters of Paul. Paul takes for granted both this interpretation of the stone which God is laying in Zion as the stone of stumbling for Israel (Rom. 9:33, combining Isa. 28:16 and 8:14) and also the dogmatic pattern of the apostasy of Israel as one of "killing the prophets":

For you, brethren, became imitators of the churches of God in Christ Jesus which are in Judea; for you suffered the same things from your own countrymen as they did from the Jews, who killed both the Lord Jesus and the prophets, and drove us out, and displeased God and oppose all men by hindering us from speaking to the Gentiles that they may be saved—so as always to fill up the measure of their sins. But God's wrath has come upon them at last! [1 Thess. 2:14–16]

This theme, that Israel has always killed the prophets, is echoed again and again in the synoptics. It is even stated that *only* those Christian preachers who are rejected by the Jews are true prophets. Christians should beware "when all men speak well of you, for so their fathers did to the false prophets" (Luke 6:26). Stephen culminates his account of the apostasy of Israel with the judgment:

You stiff-necked people, uncircumcised in heart and ears, you always resist the Holy Spirit. As your fathers did, so do you. Which of the prophets did not your fathers persecute? And they killed those who announced beforehand the coming of the Righteous One, whom you have now betrayed and murdered. [Acts 7:51–52]

For good measure, Stephen throws in the assertion that the Jews have never kept the Law either. He had previously said that the Jewish Law is not the real Mosaic Law, since the commandments which God had intended to give on Sinai were withheld because of the worship of the golden calf. The Jews of the Mosaic tradition have never been God's people anyway (Acts 7:35–48).

The climactic text on apostate Israel as the lineage of those who murder the prophets comes from the "Q" tradition. In Matthew, this text is used to climax his great chapter of "woes" against the Pharisees:

Woe to you, scribes and Pharisees, hypocrites! for you build the tombs of the prophets and adorn the monuments of the righteous, saying, "If we had lived in the days of our fathers, we would not have taken part with them in shedding the blood of the prophets." Thus you witness against yourselves, that *you are sons of those who murdered the prophets.* Fill up, then, the measure of your fathers. You serpents, you brood of vipers, how are you to escape being sentenced to hell? Therefore I send you prophets and wise men and scribes, some of whom you will kill and crucify, and some you will scourge in your synagogues and persecute from town to town, that *upon you may come all the righteous blood shed on earth,* from the blood of the innocent Abel to the blood of Zechariah the son of Barachiah, whom you murdered between the sanctuary and the altar. [Matt. 23:29–35; author's italics]

This text is followed immediately by that of Jesus mourning over Jerusalem, "O Jerusalem, Jerusalem, killing the prophets and stoning those who are sent to you," and the judgment that "your house is forsaken and desolate," followed by the prediction that the temple will be destroyed so that "there will not be left here one stone upon another" (Matt. 24:2). But the real culmination of this whole section is Matthew 27:25, when the people of Jerusalem demand Jesus' death, crying out, "His blood be on us and on our children." This is the final doing of that which has been "foretold": the killing of the Prophet-Messiah, by apostate Israel, thereby bringing down on its head God's vengeance for the blood of all the righteous ones since the beginning of history (as well as all the Christian martyrs to come).

The Christian tradition must have reached this position rather early in its history, at a time prior to the writings of Paul. In other words, by the second decade of its mission it had come to believe that Judaism, represented by its dominant religious consciousness, was hopelessly apostate and represented a heritage of apostasy which merited its rejection as the true guardian of the vineyard of Israel and the election of the Gentiles instead. But this point of view was not created by gentile converts. It originated in an alienated and angry Jewish sectarianism which believed it had the true midrash on the Scriptures and was founded on the true cornerstone of God's people, but found itself rebuffed and rejected at every stage by the synagogue.

The anti-Judaic tradition in Christianity grew as a negative and alienated expression of a need to legitimate its revelation in Jewish terms. In the opinion of this writer, it continues on in the Church Fathers, and even to this day, as an ongoing expression of this same need by the Church to legitimate its christological midrash by insisting that this actually represents the true meaning of the Jewish Scriptures and is the divinely intended fulfillment of Moses, the Psalms, and the Prophets. It is not enough for the Christian tradition to hold this opinion. Nor is it enough to convince "a few Jews" (especially secularized Jews) that this is the case. As long as "the Jews," that is, the Jewish religious tradition itself, continues to reject this interpretation, the validity of the Christian view is in question. The "wrath upon the Jews," poured out by Christianity, represents this ever unsatisfied need of the Church to prove that it has the true content of the Jewish Scriptures by finally making "the Jews" (Jewish teaching authority) "admit" that this is the true interpretation. Until Jewish religious tradition itself accepts this as the "real meaning" of its own Scriptures, "the Jews" must be kept in the status of the "enemies of God," in order to ward off that unthinkable alternative, suppressed at the very beginning, by the decision of faith upon which Christianity was founded.

2. *The Philosophizing of Anti-Judaism in Paul, Hebrews, and the Gospel of John*

The christological midrash, and its anti-Judaic left hand, found in the synoptics, was created by the Palestinian and early Diaspora missions. This testimonies tradition forms a common base on which New Testament theology is built. Paul, Hebrews, and John all have versions of the same testimonies. However, in Paul, Hebrews, and John we find a development which builds on this foundation, but brings out its theological implications on a metaphysical level. This is done by incorporating the antithesis between the true and the apostate Israel into a world view that fuses Platonic dualism (the material and the spiritual) with messianic dualism ("this age" and the "age to come").

This Platonic dualism between the body and the soul, the material and the spiritual "worlds," had governed Philonic exegesis. However, when this spiritualizing exegesis is fused with the messianic dualism between "this age" and the "age to come," identifying the Church with the eschatological community of the Resurrection, Philo's spiritualizing exegesis, intended to vindicate the inward meaning of Jewish law, is now used to "prove" the radical supersession of Jewish law. Judaism is identified with all that is "old" and "carnal," while Christianity is spiritual and eschatological "newness." Judaism is the outward, temporal, and perishable which existed only as a shadow of the inward and eternal covenant of true Being that has now dawned through the power of the Resurrection. The Christian belongs no longer to "this age," but lives already in the eschatological "age to come." This fusion of Platonic with eschatological dualism gives the anti-Judaic argument in Paul and John a close approximation to that "demonizing" of Judaism which we found in certain forms of Gnosticism. A demonizing of Judaism was already rooted in the messianic sectarian perspective, wherein unconverted Judaism was equated with the "party of Belial." But in Paul and John, this dualism between the "sons of light" and the "sons of darkness" is incorporated into a philosophical and cosmological framework, making the "sons of light" into the spiritual, eschatological humanity, in contrast to the carnal, this-worldly humanity of unconverted Judaism.

Paul founds his mission to the Gentiles on the belief that salvation in Christ abrogates any distinction between the circumcized and the uncircumcized. Circumcision gives the Jew no elected status with God superior to the Gentile which can stand, in itself, as the basis of salvation. In respect to righteousness, Jew and Gentile are in the same situation before God. Both know God's will: the Jew through the Torah, the Gentile through the natural law of conscience. Paul thus takes up the argument found in Hellenistic Judaism, that the Torah is identical in content with the "Natural Law." But he uses it to argue that both Jew and Gentile knew God's will, and both have disobeyed. Both are equally unrighteous before God (Rom. 1). The only advantage to the Jew through the Law is really a disadvantage. Knowing the Law in explicit form, he is judged more severely. Moreover, the Law itself incites the power of sin latent in the flesh, and so makes "sin abound" in the Jew, whereas the Gentile remains "naive" about the state of his sinfulness. The Jew, who has the Law, then becomes the "lawbreaker" par excellence. He witnesses to the "nations" only the power of sin, not any superior power for righteousness. Rejecting any idea that Judaism itself can be a "light to the nations," Paul establishes the relation of Judaism to the Gentiles through the text: "The name of God is blasphemed among the Gentiles because of you" (Rom. 2:24; Isa. 52:5).

In respect to righteousness, there is no difference between circumcision or uncircumcision. Both Jew and Gentile are sold under the power of sin. Both belong equally to the sphere of the "old Adam" of finite, carnal humanity. Salvation cannot come through the works of the Law, which merely make manifest the sinfulness of the Adamic nature of fallen humanity. Salvation comes only through a new covenant founded on the risen Christ. Christ brings to an end Adamic nature and makes available for the first time a new nature that has a power for inward, spiritual authenticity. Man cannot earn his way into this spiritual humanity on the basis of his fallen, Adamic nature. He can come into it only through faith in the risen Christ. In respect to this true foundation of salvation, Jew and Gentile also are on an equal footing. The means to it is faith, and not any a priori status provided by the birth rights of an elect people. Christ brings to an end all such "boasting in the flesh," all presumption of special rights with God or priorities in salvation because of Israel's history. All such vain boasting is put to naught by the true principle of salvation that arises only when we die to all that pertains to the flesh. Paul correlates Judaism very closely with his rejection of "the flesh," "boasting" or "confidence in [circumcized] flesh," i.e., the principle that a lineage of physical descent gives special rights in the economy of salvation (Phil. 3:3–11; Gal. 6:13f.). He sees all this as belonging to the sphere of the "old Adam." By the same token, the outward observances and ordinances of Judaism—food laws, festivals, new moons, Sabbath—belong to the sphere of the "flesh." All confidence in such practices bespeaks the carnal man, puffed up in his "sensuous mind," and must be put to death before the new, spiritual man, founded on the risen Christ, is born (Col. 2:16–19).

Paul turns the prophetic distinction between inward circumcision of the heart and outward circumcision of the flesh into an antithesis (Jer. 9:25; Rom. 2:25–29). For those who are "uncircumcised of heart," their circumcision has become uncircumcision. For Paul, the call of the prophets to Israel to become "circumcised of heart" cannot take place within the sphere of Judaism qua Judaism. The Law can only give knowledge of sin, not the power to obey God from the heart. Only through the eschatological power of Christ, which abrogates the finitude of the old Adam, is there a power that can take away the "hearts of stone" and give us "hearts of flesh," i.e., inward obedience to God's will. This inward obedience is not available under the covenant of Moses, but only through the "new covenant" promised by the prophet Jeremiah (31:31; 2 Cor. 3:6). The circumcision of inward obedience is available only through baptism, through that sharing in the dying to the old Adam and the rising in the new Adam made available by the salvific action of Christ. In baptism, we "put off the body of flesh" and rise to the new circumcision of spiritual life "not made with hands" (Col. 2:11–12). True inwardness, for Paul, is eschatological. It transcends the power of finite man of the "old Creation." Only the new and eternal covenant of the Resurrection imbues us with the spiritual power to become a living Law, in whom obedience to God's commandments is written "on tablets of human hearts" (2 Cor. 3:3). Thus Paul's dualism between the old covenant and the new is a dualism between the old and new creation, between finite and eschatological man.

Paul's distinction between fleshly and spiritual circumcision is paralleled by his midrash on the "true children of Abraham." God gave Abraham the promise of salvation while he was yet uncircumcized. Abraham "believed God and it was reckoned to him as righteousness" (Gen. 15:6 [LXX]). Paul uses this text in Romans 4 and Galatians 3 to prove that Abraham is not the father of those who keep the Law in the lineage of tribal descent, but the father of those who believe apart from the works of the Law. Abraham is the father of those made righteous through faith, not the father of those who seek righteousness through the works of the Law. His fatherhood is universal, not tribal, because it is said that he was to be the father "of many nations." Reading the word *nations* (Gen. 17:5) as "Gentiles," Paul understands this to mean that Abraham is the father of a universal people redeemed by faith. He is the father of the spiritual Israel, descended not by physical lineage but through faith in the promise that was given to Abraham apart from the works of the Law. Isaac is the child of the promise. But the true spiritual Isaac is Christ, who is the child of the promise given to Abraham (Rom. 9; Gal. 3:6–9). Christians, not Jews, are the true offspring of Abraham and heirs of the promise.

Paul's argument in favor of a spiritual Abrahamic descent is coupled with proofs of the secondary and inferior character of the Law. Circumcision was not prior but secondary to the giving of the promise. But the Mosaic Law was given only four hundred and thirty years after Abraham. Therefore it cannot be the basis for redemption. The Law was "added because of transgressions." Presumably this means that God gave the Law to curb the Jews from the depths of sinfulness into which they had fallen, although this view would contradict his argument in Romans that it is the Law itself which arouses the spirit of rebelliousness. The Law, moreover, was given only through the mediation of angels (Gal. 3:16–20). By angels, Paul means those lower and inferior powers which reign over the spheres of the fallen cosmos. Thus the giving of the Law through angels means that the Law does not express the spiritual realm, but the lower realm of fallen humanity.

Yet, in another context, Paul feels the need to affirm that the Law truly came from God and is "spiritual." It does express the will of God. It is only that man is "carnal," being one body with the fallen nature of the old Adam. So the Law cannot save him, but only activate the sinful promptings of his fallen nature (Rom. 7:7–24). Yet, in the sense that the Law only "reveals sin" and gives no spiritual power for obedience, it belongs to the sphere of the old Adam. Only in the Resurrection do the spiritual contents of the Law become "written on men's hearts."

But the affinity of the Law with the sphere of sin becomes deeper in Paul's exegesis on the giving of the Law on Mount Sinai. Here the Torah is called the "dispensation of death," a mere outer shadow of that dispensation of life available through the resurrected Christ. By misreading Exodus 34:29–35 (where it is said that Moses *takes off* the veil that hides the glory of God's *Shekinah* when teaching the Law to the people), Paul argues that Moses' veiling his face when teaching the Law shows that the Law expresses that hardening of Israel's heart characteristic of the unbelief and apostasy of those under the old covenant (2 Cor. 3:7–18). The Torah lies under the power of the veil, i.e., under the power of unbelief that separates us from God's glory. This veil continues to lie upon the hearts of the people of the Mosaic covenant even to this day. Torah is to Christian revelation as a shadow is to the light. It belongs to the sphere of the perishable and the finite. Moses veiled his face while teaching the Torah, so that the Israelites should not see the end of its fading splendor, so their hearts would be hardened. "To this day whenever Moses is read a veil lies over their minds; but when a man turns to the Lord the veil is removed." As for those who claim that Paul's own Gospel is veiled and obscure, he retorts that it is veiled only to those who are perishing, i.e., to those whose unbelief marks them as belonging to the nonelect (2 Cor. 4:3).

In Galatians, Paul argues that circumcision is forbidden under the new covenant. Paul's position on this is confused because he was reluctant to demand that all those baptized from Judaism should dispense with the ordinances of Judaism in principle. In Acts 16:3, he is even said to have circumcized Timothy who was the son of a Jewish Christian mother and a gentile father. He recommends avoidance of food offered to idols in order not to scandalize the weaker brethren (1 Cor. 6:12–13; 8; 10:23–29; cf. Rom. 14). But to the man of faith such observances have become voluntary concessions to the weakness of those not fully confirmed in the freedom of Christ. They have no necessary connection with salvation. Yet in Galatians and Philippians, he argues that any imposition of circumcision is tantamount to unfaithfulness. Those who would insist that the Christian assume full proselyte status he calls "dogs" and "evil-workers" and expresses the wish that the knife may slip and finish the job of "mutilation" (Phil. 3:2; Gal. 5:12). To take on circumcision is to make oneself responsible for the whole Law. But man under the power of the old Adam must necessarily fail to fulfill the whole Law. Yet the Law says that those who do not obey all its ordinances are cursed (Deut. 27:26). All who try to add the ordinances of the Law to salvation in Christ put themselves under the power of the curse. Christ, however, has freed us from the power of the curse by taking the curse of the Law upon himself by hanging on a tree. Paul's argument is ingenious at this point. Jewish spokesmen had evidently used Deut. 21:23 (Gal. 3:13),

"Cursed be every one who hangs on a tree," to argue that Jesus could not be a righteous man, but a sinner. Paul refutes this argument by turning it upside down. It is the Law which is necessarily the sphere of the curse. All who try to live by it are under the curse (of alienation from God), while Christ, by hanging on a tree, took the curse of the Law upon himself and buried it with the death of the old Adam, rising to a new life beyond the power of the curse (Gal. 3:10–14). Such an exegesis was self-evident to Paul. But it would make little sense to any rabbinic Jew who shared neither Paul's view of the "legalism" of the Torah nor his view of its lack of spiritual power. In other words, it was an exegesis which made sense only to those who shared Paul's vision of the two aeons—the aeon of carnal, historical man and the aeon of risen, eschatological man—and who equated the Torah with the sway of the "old aeon," while believing that the spiritual power of eschatological man has already become available through Christ.

Paul's theological thinking is governed by a remarkable fusion of Gnostic and apocalyptic dualisms. In Gnosticism, there are two realms of existence: the higher, spiritual realm of true being, and a lower, carnal realm of fallen, inauthentic life, characterized by materiality and fate. This realm is separated from the power of true being. Its world rulers do not have the true power of life. Rather, they are demonic beings whose sway is that of slavery, sin, and death. These are the "archons" or "powers" who reign over the visible cosmos. This visible cosmos is not God's creation, but a realm that originates through the fall and is characterized by alienation from the true heavenly world of Light. Paul assumes a similar view of the visible cosmos when he speaks of its world rulers as "principalities and powers," "the elemental spirits of the universe," and "spiritual hosts of wickedness in the heavenly places" (Gal. 4:3; Col. 2:8; Eph. 3:10; 6:12). But Paul has fused this Gnostic world picture with the apocalyptic dualism between this "present age" of world history, dominated by the powers of wickedness, and the new "age to come," which Paul sees as eternal and spiritual in character. The two realms, the lower realm of darkness, materiality, and sin, and the higher world of eternal being, are related to each other, not on the vertical axis of inward transcendence, but on the temporal axis of historical supersession. For Paul, the critical "turn of the ages" has already taken place in the death and resurrection of Christ. The finite, historical cosmos, ruled by the "principalities and powers," has already been overthrown in principle. It has already been superseded by the new spiritual world of the resurrected body of eternal life. The finite world is fast perishing and will soon disappear altogether, while the Christian community, which already belongs to the new eternal world of the resurrection, will be caught up in the transformed, spiritual cosmos of the eschatological "new Creation" (1 Cor. 15:20–54; 1 Thess. 4:13–18).

For Paul, the reign of Torah is equivalent to the reign of these demonic powers and principalities of the finite realm. This allows Paul to equate the Torah, as the guardian spirit of the people of the old covenant, with the "elemental spirits of the universe," the false "gods" of the pagans (Col. 2:8, 20; Gal. 4:3, 8–10). While under the Torah, the people were "slaves to the elemental spirits of the universe," but now, as free sons of God in Christ, "how can you turn back again to the weak and beggarly elemental spirits, whose slaves you want to be once more," by submitting to the ordinances of the Torah? This kind of thinking allows Paul to equate the sons of the promise, while they are still under the Law, with children who have not yet come of age and who must submit to the chastisements of a slave *paidagogus*. But now that Christ has come, the sons have come into their inheritance. They have become sons of the Kingdom and are no longer under the power of the "guardians," the Torah and the elemental spirits of the universe. They have become "sons of Light" and have passed beyond the realms of enslavement to lower powers, symbolized by Greek philosophy and the Jewish Law. This is Paul's ultimate framework for rejecting the continuing validity of the Mosaic covenant.

Paul's concept of the "two aeons" lies behind his typology of the two covenants, symbolized by the two wives of Abraham, Hagar and Sarah. Hagar is the slave woman, and her offspring belong to the aeon of slavery. Sarah is the free woman, and her children belong to the aeon of freedom. Those who believe in Christ are the offspring of the free woman, while those still under the Mosaic covenant are the offspring of the slave woman. There is no common inheritance between the offspring of the slave woman and the offspring of the free woman. The slave woman and her children are cast out, so they may not inherit together with the children of the free woman. Hagar and her children stand for Mount Sinai. The children of the slave woman are the children of the Mosaic covenant, while those who believe in Christ are the sons of Sarah and belong to the spiritual Jerusalem above. Mount Sinai bears children in slavery and corresponds to the present Jewish religious community of historical Jerusalem which is "in slavery together with her children." Christians belong to the spiritual covenant. They are the spiritual children of Abraham and sons of the promise, whose mother is the spiritual, eschatological "Jerusalem above" (Gal. 4:21–31). The two covenants of Moses and Christ also correspond to the two brothers, Jacob and Esau (Gen. 25:23), where the elder is made to serve the younger. The younger abrogates the law of inheritance of the elder, heir according to the flesh, and claims the inheritance by the spiritual law of election (Rom. 9:6–13).

Paul clearly does not think of the Church as a "historical religion," which superseded Judaism in a relation of historical continuity. His "two aeons" are not two historical eras, but an antithesis between the historical and the eschatological "worlds." Judaism belongs, by nature, to the historical world of fallen, finite Adamic man. Christianity is the spiritual promise given "in history" to Israel, but which is manifest only in those final eschatological events which bring this historical realm to an end in order to found the eschatological "new Creation." The Mosaic and the Christian covenants have no common inheritance. They are like carnal man and spiritual man, intertwined within history in the same people perhaps, but now separated in the eschatological sorting of the "wheat from the tares." The Mosaic covenant is essentially carnal and this-worldly in nature. Those who belong to it will be cast out into outer darkness, like the slave woman and her child. But the spiritual sons of the promise, who have been intertwined with the people of the Mosaic covenant—but whose promise was given before it and has never been "of it"—will be caught up into the eternal cosmos, already established in Christ and soon to be fully manifest, bringing to an end the finite cosmos and its enslaved children.

Paul's world view creates several severe theological problems for contemporary exegetes. After two thousand years, his literal eschatology becomes somewhat untenable, but still more his imputed attribution of the characteristics of the eschatological to a new community of faith which itself was rapidly proving its intention of becoming "historical." These theological problems created by a "historicizing of the eschatological," in the antithesis between Judaism and Christianity, will be among the questions explored in the final conclusion of this study.

Paul's position was unquestionably that of anti-Judaism.[27] This does not, of course, mean that Jews, as a people, are excluded from becoming members of the community of salvation (Christians). The polemic against "the Jews" in Paul, as in the New Testament generally, is a rejection of *Judaism,* i.e., "the Jews" as a religious community. Judaism for Paul is not only *not* an ongoing covenant of salvation where men continue to be related in true worship of God: it *never* was such a community of faith and grace. Paul's position, therefore, is similar to that of Stephen. The Mosaic covenant is seen as belonging to a people who were apostate from the beginning. Its essential nature is that of carnality, unbelief, and hardness of heart. It belongs to the sphere of the old Adam. The covenant of the promise was given *before* the Mosaic covenant and *apart* from it, and its destiny is fulfilled with the coming of Christ. Only those who believe in Christ, whether from among the Jews or Gentiles, belong to this spiritual community of the promise. Those who imagine that the Mosaic covenant itself provides an ongoing relation to God will be cast out as sons of the aeon of enslavement.

But doesn't God have some special concern for this people as a people? Even though they presently manifest that hardness of heart characteristic of the Mosaic covenant, will God not eventually bring them into the community of the promise, that promise which was given to Abraham and which is their own intended spiritual destiny? Paul struggles with this question in chapters 9–11 of Romans. He is not quite willing to declare that historical election means nothing at all to God. So he tries out several alternative explanations for the meaning of the present apostasy of the Jewish religious community. He begins by asserting that the true Israel is the spiritual Israel. It is the Israel of the promise, not the Israel of the Mosaic covenant and the lineage of physical paternity. Only the sons of the promise, believers in Christ, the spiritual offspring of Abraham, are the true children of Abraham and heirs of his promise. Then Paul asserts God's sovereign right to have his way with his own creatures. If he made the people of the Mosaic covenant as vessels of wrath made for destruction, in order to reveal the sons of the promise as vessels of his glory, that is God's business. No creature can question the "why" of such divine doings. That God intended to gather this community of the promise from among the Gentiles, Paul proves with a quotation from Hosea (2:23; Rom. 9:25): "Those who were not my people I will call 'my people' "; and from Isaiah (65:1; Rom. 10:20): "I have been found by those who did not seek me." On the other hand, the people of the Mosaic covenant are that apostate people of whom the prophets say: "All day long I have held out my hands to a disobedient and contrary people" (Isa. 65:2; Rom. 10:21). Only a remnant from among this apostate people were intended by God for repentance and salvation. This remnant is already represented by the Jewish Christians who have believed. Therefore, God has not rejected his people, for this remnant has been saved.

But Paul is not quite satisfied with this solution. He wants some soteriological significance for the "unbelief of the Jews." He demands a religious meaning to this refusal of the Jewish religious community to accept Christian faith as their intended spiritual destiny. Paul finally finds his way to affirm such a religious meaning for the unbelief of the Jews, as well as God's continued concern for his people's final salvation, by proclaiming the discovery of a "mystery" (Rom. 11:25). According to this "mystery," the Jewish religious community has been hardened, so that the Gentiles might be gathered in. This is preeminently the work of God's grace, for they are grafted onto the stem of Israel that remains rooted in the history of God's elect people. As soon as this ingathering of the Gentiles is complete (and Paul evidently expected this to take place quickly, perhaps with the completion of his missionary circuit around the Mediterranean world as far as Spain),[28] God would mysteriously unharden the hearts of the Jews. Then they, too, would be gathered into the one community of salvation. At this time, Christ will return to complete the work of salvation by abolishing the world of the old Adam and establishing the eschatological new Creation. The "conversion of the Jews," then, becomes in Paul the last event in the historical economy of salvation. It shows that God has not cast off his people ultimately, but has reserved them in their present state of apostasy until the final ingathering of the elect.

This "mystery" in Paul does not suggest in any way an ongoing validity of the Mosaic covenant as a community of salvation in its own right. Contemporary ecumenists who use Romans 11 to argue that Paul does not believe that God has rejected the people of the Mosaic covenant speak out of good intentions, but inaccurate exegesis.[29] For Paul, there is, and has always been, only one true covenant of salvation. This is the covenant of the promise, given *apart from the Law*, to Abraham and now manifest in those who believe in Abraham's spiritual son, Christ. The people of the Mosaic covenant do not now and never have had any way of salvation through the Torah itself. God never intended to save his people through the Law. The veil under which the Mosaic Law was given manifests its essential nature as a religion of unbelief. God intended his people to transcend the Mosaic covenant by becoming children of faith in that promise given to Abraham apart from the Torah and manifest in Christ in the last days. The Jews now refuse to enter this community or recognize it as the spiritual lineage of the Abrahamic promise. But this is only a temporary hardening of their hearts, which will be removed in the culmination of God's Plan for the salvation of all the elect. God has not "cast off his people" only in the sense that he intends to bring them to this conversion to the Church at the end. Paul's proclamation of the "mystery" of Israel, therefore, contains no hint of any intention of allowing a place for the ongoing validity of the Mosaic covenant as such or any spiritual relation to God that can be found through Judaism. In this sense, he enunciates a doctrine of the rejection of the Jews (rejection of Judaism as the proper religious community of God's people) in the most radical form, seeing it as rejected not only now, through the rejection of Christ, but from the beginning. The purpose of Paul's "mystery" is not to concede any ongoing validity to Judaism, but rather to assure the *ultimate vindication of the Church*. If the Church is the eschatological destiny of Israel, then this truth must finally win out by having the "Jews" themselves testify to it. They must admit finally that it is not through Torah, but through faith in Jesus as the Christ, that they are intended to be saved.

THE EPISTLE TO THE HEBREWS.   The Epistle to the Hebrews parallels Paul in its fusion of spiritualizing and eschatological interpretations of the Jewish Scriptures. The revelation in Christ supersedes the "old covenant" in time. It is the "new covenant" against an "old" one which has grown obsolete and is perishing. But the new covenant also transcends the old, spiritually. It is the true, inner, spiritual meaning of that of which the old is a mere anticipation, shadow, and outward figure. Spiritualizing exegesis has been fused with messianic midrash in such a way that Philo's "inner and spiritual" meaning of the text now becomes antithetical to the outward forms of Jewish religion, superseding them in time. But the ultimate framework for the contrast between the two covenants in Hebrews, as in Paul, is one of an absolute contrast between the historical and the eschatological. Judaism is not merely superseded historically, but absolutely. It is the mere finite, mutable and carnal, in contrast to the eternal, immutable and spiritual. However, unlike Paul, Hebrews is more concerned with the temple cultus than with the Torah. The author wants to show that Christianity has the true eternal meaning of the priesthood, while leaving behind those "former priests many in number" (7:23), whose outward and repeated sacrifices have no spiritual efficacy.

The author of Hebrews possessed an extensive tradition of christological testimonies and probably worked from a written handbook of testimonies which had been gathered out of their scriptural contexts.[30] He takes for granted a number of correlations and misreadings of the Greek text as christological readings of the Psalms and Prophets. For example, he reads Psalm 8:4–6, "What is . . . the son of man, that thou carest for him? Thou didst make him for a little while lower than the angels," as a testimony to the *kenosis* of the divine Logos (Heb. 2: 6–7). Hebrews takes over the Philonic doctrine of the cosmological Logos as the theological identity of Christ, a development which also appears in Paul's letter to the Colossians (1: 15ff.) and in the prologue to the Gospel of John. By making the Logos christological, however, it ceases to be a spiritual reality that grounds the present creation and human history, as in Philo. Instead, it becomes the form of the divine world which is revealed only at the end of time, superseding history. Hebrews takes over Philo's use of the Logos as the spiritual meaning of temple, sacrificial, and sacerdotal language. But the priestly mediatorship to the true heavenly sanctuary, which Philo saw as the inner meaning of the Jewish cultus, is used in Hebrews to relegate the Jewish cultus to the temporal, carnal plane, superseded by the spiritual, eternal priesthood of Christ. The eschatological Logos does not provide an inner meaning for historical realities, but abrogates history to enter the eschatological sanctuary of the heavenly "new Creation."

The Epistle opens with an argument for the superiority of the Son of God to the angels. As in Paul, the angels are probably thought of as the guardian spirits of the temporal creation, in contrast to the Son of God who is the form of the eschatological, spiritual creation to come. The revelation of the old covenant was given by angels, testifying to its temporal, inferior character, whereas Christian revelation was spoken directly by the Son in the last days (1:2; 2:1–3). Moses was only a servant in God's house, while Christ is the son and builder of it (3:2–6). The Torah is only a shadow of the good things to come, not the true form of these things (10:1). All the "Old Testament" worthies—Abel, Enoch, Noah, Abraham, Sarah, Isaac, Jacob, Joseph, Moses, Joshua, Rahab, the judges, and prophets—were witnesses to the coming of Christ. They did not possess this revelation in its fulfilled spiritual power. They lived by faith in a future spiritual coming. They did not live in the presence of what was promised, but only in anticipation of its coming at the end of time, acknowleding that they were strangers and exiles on earth. Their status was merely predictive in relation to the real revelation which has come in Christ. They themselves are "made perfect" only by being taken up into the christological faith of the Church (chap. 11). Moreover, the Exodus community of old was rebellious against its leadership in Moses. Because of their unbelief, Moses swore that they would never enter his rest. But the promised rest was not to be found in the land of Canaan, but only in the eschatological peace of the Kingdom of God. It is into this eschatological rest that the true people of God shall enter, while the disobedient people of the old covenant have been disbarred (3: 18–19; 4:3–10).

But the real concerns of the christological exegesis of Hebrews center on the temple cultus. The author finds in Melchizedek the type of the eternal priesthood of Christ, in contrast to the Levirite priesthood, which never had any spiritual power. Its priests were mortal, and so had to succeed each other in temporal succession, while the priesthood of the Logos-Christ is eternal. Their sacrifices must be constantly repeated, for they gave no permanent forgiveness, while the forgiveness of sins found through the sacrifice of the body of Christ is once-for-all. Quoting Psalm 40:6–8 in the Septuagint text, he argues that God never took any pleasure in Old Testament sacrifices:

Sacrifices and offerings thou hast not desired, but *a body thou hast prepared for me.* [Heb. 10:5]

The Hebrew text reads "Thou has given me an open ear." By reading the text in the Greek mistranslation, Hebrews establishes the psalm as a favorite text for the supersession of the sacrifices of the "Old Testament" by the final, once-for-all sacrifice of the "body" of Christ.

Like Paul, Hebrews constructs a spiritual line of faith from the Jewish past which is the true line of descent of the Church. Melchizedek stands for the type of the eschatological priesthood. The faith of the Old Testament worthies awaits Christ. But even for them, there was no present spiritual power, but only anticipation of "things hoped for, the conviction of things not seen. By it the men of old received divine approval" (11: 1). But the religion of Torah and temple sacrifice belonged irrevocably to the temporal, finite sphere which is now perishing. The people who cling to this religion, and imagine thereby to win God's approval, belong to the heritage of apostasy of those who worshipped the golden calf. Its Law did not give them inward obedience. Its covenant was temporal and doomed to vanish. Its sanctuary was a mere outward "copy," "made with hands," of the heavenly sanctuary. Its sacrifices had no power of forgiveness.

Christ is the eternal High Priest, seated on the right hand of the Father, who makes ultimate reconciliation with God in the sanctuary of heaven itself. The Levirite priests were allowed to enter only the outer tent of the sanctuary for those daily sacrifices. But they entered the inner tent only once a year. This is a type of the two aeons. The outer tent is the temporal creation which is growing old and ready to vanish away, while the inner tent is the type of the eternal, eschatological creation. This Day is drawing very near (10:25). The daily sacrifices of the Levirite priests belonged to the temporal creation and remained always external, mortal, and spiritually impotent. The new covenant writes the commandments of God on the innermost heart (8:8–10, quoting Jer. 31:31–33). Soon this present mutable creation will be shaken to its very foundations and swept away, while the immutable world of heaven will remain. This is the inner tent into which the great High Priest, the Logos-Christ, is leading his true people. We have no abiding city here on earth. Like Christ, who was sacrificed "outside the gate," we must go outside the city gates (outside of "this world") to seek the eternal Jerusalem to come. Ours is not the temporal and perishable covenant of Mount Sinai, but the eternal covenant of the heavenly Zion (12:18–22; 13:14).

The Epistle ends with a strong polemic against apostasy to Judaism. Now it becomes apparent what the purpose of this entire midrash has been in this letter. The author is a pastor addressing a Jewish Christian community, probably in Alexandria, which is in danger of backsliding into Judaism and interpreting their faith as an allegory of Jewish religious observances, in the manner of Philo's interpretation.[31] He is intent to warn his people that an absolute line separates the Jewish forms from Christian faith. The two cannot be interpreted as the outward form and inward meaning of the same covenant. The inward, spiritual, and eschatological meaning is related antithetically to the old covenant, rendering it obsolete. "We have an altar from which those who serve the tent [i.e., "Jewish" fleshliness and finitude] have no right to eat" (13:10). Those who slip back into the old forms and make their Christianity a mere inward gnosis of Judaism commit an apostasy from which there can be no forgiveness. Like Esau of old, they sell their birthright to the promises of God and fall irrevocably on the side of the apostate community of Israel which has been forbidden to enter God's rest (12:16–17).

THE GOSPEL OF JOHN. In the Gospel of John, the philosophical incorporation of anti-Judaic midrash reaches its highest development in the New Testament. Here the antitheses between the old and the new, the temporal and the eschatological, the outward and the inward, the carnal and the spiritual have been so completely sublimated into an antithesis between a fulfilled spiritual universe poised over against a fallen universe of darkness, symbolized by "the Jews," that the language of the "two aeons," drawn from apocalyptic futurism, has been almost entirely absorbed into the language of vertical and inward transcendence. Instead of "two aeons," we have "two worlds": the spiritual world of light "above" and the dark world of alienation from the divine "below." "The Jews" are programmatically identified with this false principle of existence of the world of darkness below. John's midrash works constantly between the eternal, spiritual meaning of every symbol and its carnal, inauthentic mode of appropriation in Judaism. Jesus is the "good wine" of true spirituality who comes at the end, taking over and transforming the water pots of the Jewish rites of purification, when the earlier "inferior wine" had run out (2:3–11).[32] Jesus is the true spiritual temple in his resurrected body, in contrast to that Jewish temple which will be destroyed. Jesus is the spiritual waters of eternal life, not the water of Jewish and Samaritan rites, from which one will "thirst again" (4:6–15). He is the spiritual bread of truth which fills the hunger of the soul, in contrast to that perishable bread, even that manna which the Jews ate in the wilderness, which did not last (6:4–58).

Jesus is the true spiritual principle of Israel. He is the good shepherd who knows who are the elect of God, as they know him. He also gathers the elect from among all the nations. He is more than just a shepherd. He is the Way of life of the true people of God. He is *Torah*. He is the "door" by which the sheep enter the sheepfold. The Jewish teachers are not true teachers. They are mere hirelings and robbers. They try to climb into the sheepfold by the wrong door (i.e., by the wrong exegesis). They desert the sheep in time of crisis. Jesus alone is the good shepherd. All who came before him were thieves and robbers, who sought only to kill, steal, and destroy (10:1–18). Likewise, Jesus is the true vine of God. (The "vine" symbolized the true form of Israel.) Only those who abide in the true vine bear fruit unto eternal life. The rest, who do not abide in the true vine, wither and die and are gathered together and thrown into the fire of eternal judgment (15:1–18).

For John, the crucial issue between the Christian community and its Jewish opponents is the christological exegesis of the Scriptures. This is based on his theological principle that only through Christ is there access to the Father. Through Christ alone the Father is revealed. Only those who know Christ know the Father, and apart from knowledge of Christ, there is no knowledge of God. Therefore, the Jews, by rejecting christological exegesis of the Scriptures, are completely incapable of knowing their true meaning or of finding in them true knowledge of God. It is this principle that lies behind John's repeated insistence that the Jews have never known God (5: 19–47; 7:28; 8:19, 24–27, 47; 15:21; 16:3). It is impossible for the Jews to know God, for God is known only through the Son. Only those who read the Scriptures christologically come to a knowledge of God through the Scriptures.

And the Father who sent me has himself borne witness to me. His voice you have never heard, his form you have never seen; and you do not have his word abiding in you, for you do not believe him whom he has sent. You search the scriptures, because you think that in them you have eternal life, and it is they that bear witness to me; yet you refuse to come to me that you may have life. [John 5:37–40]

"The Jews" are the type of the "unbelievers," who see and see but never perceive. Even a man blind from birth "sees," i.e., recognizes Christ. But the Pharisees, although physically sighted, are blind. If they were really blind, they would have no guilt. But because they say "we see," i.e., think they are the disciples of Moses, their guilt remains. Jesus gives sight to the blind and reveals the blindness of those who think they are sighted (9:28–41).

But "the Jews" are not merely dull-witted in their unbelief. For John, the "unbelief of the Jews" points to a much deeper theological mystery. "The Jews," for John, are the very incarnation of the false, apostate principle of the fallen world, alienated from its true being in God. They are the type of the carnal man, who knows nothing spiritually. They are the type of the perishing man who belongs to the "time" of the world, but, unlike the spiritual brethren of Jesus, can never recognize the *kairos* of the eternal event (7:6). Because they belong essentially to the world and its hostile, alienated principle of existence, their instinctive reaction to the revelation of the spiritual Son of God is murderousness. What they do recognize is that in Christ their false principle of existence has been unmasked and comes to an end. So whenever the light breaks through in their presence, they immediately seek to "kill him." In this murderousness they manifest their true principle of existence. They show that they are "not of God," but "of the Devil," who was a liar and a murderer from the beginning:

Why do you not understand what I say? It is because you cannot bear to hear my word. You are of your father, the devil, and your will is to do your father's desires. He was a murderer from the beginning, and has nothing to do with the truth, because there is no truth in him. When he lies, he speaks according to his own nature, for he is a liar and the father of lies. . . . The reason why you do not hear them [the words of God revealed in Jesus] is because you are not of God. [John 8:43–47]

The ultimate contest between Christ and "the Jews" in John, therefore, is over Jesus' identity as the incarnate manifestation of God through whom alone there is access to the Father. Jesus poises his I AM, identifying himself as the one revelation of, and way to, the Father, over against the rage and murderousness evoked in "the Jews" by this declaration. Either this revelation is true, or else it is the highest possible blasphemy. John goes out of his way to make it appear that blasphemy is the central reason why "the Jews" want to kill Jesus. When they finally hand him over to Pilate and insist that he be crucified, they are explicit in their insistence that it is by the Jewish law against blasphemy that he must die "because he has made himself the Son of God" (19:6–7). John goes the farthest of all the Gospels in depicting Jesus as actually being crucified *by the Jews*.[33] He makes Pilate refuse to crucify Jesus under Roman law, while the Jews insist that he die by the Jewish law of blasphemy. Intimidated by the Jews, Pilate hands Jesus "over to them to be crucified." Pilate himself stands by as an aggrieved bystander and even quasi believer, who insists on affixing the title "King of the Jews" to the cross of Jesus, as a witness to his true identity, over against the protests of the Jews (19:6–22). For John, it is crucial that Jesus be crucified, not by the Romans as a political dissident, but by the Jewish religious authorities for the religious crime of blasphemy. This means that the One who is the unique revelation of God in the world, God's very self-manifestation, who can use the divine I AM to identify himself, is killed by the Jews as an explicit rejection by them of this divine identity. Thus John moves the "crime of the Jews" very close to what will become the charge of "deicide," i.e., that the "Jews," in killing Jesus, commit the religious crime of rejection and murder, not merely of God's prophet, but of God's revealed self-expression.

This murderousness of "the Jews" toward Christ naturally extends itself to his Church. As Jesus is in the Father and the Father is in him, so his disciples abide in Jesus and Jesus in them. Through him, they abide in God, just as he abides in God. They are the extension of his incarnate revelation of God in the world (chap. 15). "The Jews," on the other hand, represent the ever hostile principle of "the world" toward this manifestation of God. As they did to Jesus, so they will also seek to do to his disciples, who manifest his ongoing life in the world. The reverse side of the christological principle is that "he who hates you, hates me, and he who hates me hates the Father." Since Christ has come into the world and the Jews have hated him, they have manifested their true nature as haters of God. This was "to fulfill the word that is written in their law, 'They hated me without a cause'" (15:25; Ps. 35: 19). Because "the world" hates you (the Church), as it has hated Christ before you:

They [the Jews] will put you out of the synagogues; indeed the hour is coming when whoever kills you will think he is offering service to God. And they will do this because they have not known the Father or me. [John 16:2–3]

John apparently represents a time in the Church's mission when the malediction of Jamnia against sectaries was in effect.[34] Like Matthew, he makes the ejection of Christian preachers from the synagogues a central symbol of this principle of hostility of "the Jews" against the prophets of Christ. This is the ongoing expression of their "hatred" of Christ and, through Christ, their hatred of God. The Jews are represented in the Gospel as constantly attempting to throw those who believe in Christ "out of the synagogues" (7:13; 9:22; 12:42). At the conclusion of the Book of Signs and preparatory for the culminating drama of the crucifixion, where all that has previously been revealed in symbols will now be accomplished, John sums up the nature of apostate Israel:

Though he had done so many signs before them, yet they did not believe in him; it was that the word spoken by the prophet Isaiah might be fulfilled. . . . "He has blinded their eyes and hardened their hearts, lest they should see with their eyes and perceive with their heart, and turn for me to heal them." [John 12:37–40]

Studies of the anti-Judaic aspect of the New Testament frequently object to any characterization of this line in John as being truly anti-Semitic, even though he, more than any other New Testament writer, uses the term *the Jews,* in preference for words for Jewish authority figures, in this consistently hostile manner (some sixty times throughout the Gospel).[35] It is argued by such apologists that this antithesis between the "sons of light" and the "sons of darkness" is an allegory which John has demythologized. It is not intended to refer to a division between Christian believers and "the Jews" in any literal sense, but rather to the two modes of existence of man, to the division between faith through grace and the fallen, apostate man. These are not two modes of existence which divide Christian from Jew, but which divide man from himself. This schism searches each man's heart to see where his treasure really lies. This indeed is the authentic theological meaning of the division between "believers" and the "apostate." It is the only authentic way to read the antithesis between the "believer" and "the world" (qua "the Jews") in John. Modern exegetes read this antithesis in the Gospel "correctly" (in a theological sense) when they automatically demythologize it in this way.

Unfortunately, for almost all of Christian history, this antithesis has not been read in this demythologized way, but literally. This is because John himself, as well as the other New Testament writers, did not demythologize this antithesis. On the contrary, they mythologized it! They projected a theological division within man into a division of identity between two interpretations of faithfulness to God. The Christian community, reading the Scriptures christologically, are the *only ones* who abide in the Father. The Jewish community, which reads the Scriptures as a testimony to an ongoing covenant of the past, are "the children of the Devil who have never known me or the Father." By mythologizing the theological division between "man-in-God" and "man-alienated-from-God" into a division between two postures of faith, John gives the ultimate theological form to that diabolizing of "the Jews" which is the root of anti-Semitism in the Christian tradition. There is no way to rid Christianity of its anti-Judaism, which constantly takes social expression in anti-Semitism, without grappling finally with its christological hermeneutic itself.

Chapter 3

The Negation of the Jews
In the Church Fathers

1. *The Character of the Patristic*
Adversus Judaeos *Tradition* *

The primary materials for studying the attitudes toward the Jews in the Church Fathers are the *adversus Judaeos* writings. These writings are remarkable for their preservation of the archaic testimonies tradition. As such, they represent a continuous tradition of christological and anti-Judaic midrashim on the Old Testament, which was the earliest form of Christian theologizing. As we have seen, this method preexisted and is the hermeneutical basis of the New Testament. This tradition continues in the Church Fathers as an expanding collection of themes and proof texts designed to prove, on the one hand, Christology, and, on the other hand, the reprobation and "blindness" of the Jews. In the patristic period, the Old Testament continues to be the Bible of the Christian Church for this midrashic work. New Testament references come to be added to those of the Old Testament, and the New Testament layer of interpretation is gathered up into the patristic rendering of

* Abbreviations of Patristic texts that appear in this chapter are to be found on p. 181f.

this tradition. But the *adversus Judaeos* tradition, down into the medieval period, continues to be one of christological and anti-Judaic midrash on that Scripture which was the sole Bible of the Christian Church before there was a written New Testament.

These writings appear in various forms. The underlying form is simply that of a collection of Old Testament texts, with one or two New Testament texts appended, arranged under a series of headings. The *Three Books of Testimonies Against the Jews,* by the third-century African Father Cyprian is such a collection.[1] The first book of testimonies expounds such anti-Judaic themes as these: (1) that the Jews have fallen under divine wrath because they departed from God and have followed after idols; (2) that they disbelieved in and killed the prophets; (3) that it was foretold that they would reject the Lord; (4) that the Jews would not understand the Scriptures, but that they would become intelligible (to the Church) after Christ came; (5) that the Jews would not understand Scripture unless they believed in Christ; (6) that they would lose Jerusalem and the promised land; (7–18) that all the tokens of the old dispensation would cease and that a new law, election, leadership, and prophecy would take its place; (19–24) that the younger people, the Gentiles, would replace the Jews as God's people. Collections of proof texts are arranged under each of these headings. The second book of testimonies contains christological proofs, similarly arranged under a series of headings, and the third book contains testimonia about Christian moral regulations. A similar book of testimonies, primarily christological in character, was composed about 400 C.E. and included in the writings of Gregory Nyssa.[2] *Questions to Antiochus Dux*[3] and *Contra Judaeos* by the sixth-century Spanish Father Isidore of Seville[4] are smaller collections of testimonia, similarly arranged according to christological and anti-Judaic topics.

This testimonies tradition underlies other writings devoted to the anti-Judaic theme. The basic themes, method of interpretation, and concatenation of texts can be built up into sermons, treatises, imaginary dialogues, and even stories and dramas. A treatise may choose to expound on a single anti-Judaic theme, as does Novatian's *On Jewish Meats*.[5] Or it may cover the whole scope of anti-Judaic themes and bring to bear numerous proof texts for each theme, as these were known in the tradition of a particular writer and as he himself chose to develop them. Tertullian's *Adversus Judaeos* is the best example of such a comprehensive tract.[6] *Demonstrations against the Jews*, by the Syrian Father Aphrahat, expounds a series of standard themes.[7] Other shorter, general tracts we might mention here are the *Expository Treatise against the Jews,* attributed to Hippolytus,[8] the *Demonstration to Jews and Greeks that Christ Is God* by John Chrysostom,[9] the *Contra Judaeos* by the Arian bishop Maximinus,[10] and the simple but powerful *Tractatus Adversus Judaeos* by Augustine.[11] The most famous case of sermonic use of this material are the eight sermons against the Jews which John Chrysostom preached in Antioch in 386–8 C.E.[12] The Syrian Fathers Ephrem,[13] Isaac of Antioch,[14] and Jacob of Serug[15] also preserve anti-Judaic writings in sermonic form. The early second-century treatise ascribed to the apostle Barnabas as an "epistle" probably had, as its core, a baptismal sermon.[16]

At a period contemporaneous with the latest books of the New Testament, the imaginary dialogue became a favorite Christian method for presenting this material. The lost dialogue of Jason and Papiscus (mid-second century) represents this genre.[17] It is the beginning of a long line of such dialogues that continue to the end of the Byzantine period, such as the *Dialogue of Timothy and Aquila;*[18] the *Dialogue of Athanasius and Zacchaeus;*[19] the *Discussion of the Archbishop Gregentius with the Jew Herban;*[20] the *Discussion of Zacchaeus the Christian and Apollonius the Philosopher;*[21] the *Discussion between Simon the Jew and Theophilus, a Christian,* attributed to Evagrius;[22] the *Dialogue of Papiscus and Philo;*[23] the *Discussion of St. Silvester with the Jews at Rome;*[24] and the *Dialogue on the Blessed Trinity* by Jerome of Jerusalem;[25] and the *Trophies of Damacus,* by a Syrian monk[26]—to mention only the best-known dialogues up to the seventh century C.E. Some of these dialogues seem to be based on actual, formal disputations between Jews and Christians. But they are so dominated by the Christian presuppositions, and even by magical details, that it becomes difficult to separate elements of fact from fiction. These dialogues are almost useless as sources for what Jews might actually have said about Christianity.[27] The Christians' opponents are the Jews of Christian imagination. The most elaborate of such dialogues is Justin Martyr's *Dialogue with Trypho*,[28] which purports to be an informal conversation with a learned Jew.

The testimonies material could also be elaborated into a liturgical drama, as in the pseudo-Augustinian *Altercation between the Church and the Synagogue* (itself originally a sermon) which had an extensive life in the medieval period.[29] The dialogue form could spin off into imaginary stories, in which Jewish unbelief is overcome by a combination of argument and miracle. Such is the sixth-century Ethiopic *Teachings of Jacob*.[30] This is the story of a Jew who suffered forced baptism under the Emperor Heraclitus. He was taught the inner meaning of his unwelcome faith by Christ in a vision. He is then portrayed as teaching this same teaching to a reluctant and then believing Jewish community, similarly baptized by imperial decree. It is typical of the dialogue literature to portray heavenly power as the supplement to Christian argument in overcoming what is seen as the semidemonic "unbelief of the Jews," not to mention its role in salving Christian bad conscience in episodes of forced baptism. The tradition of christological and anti-Judaic midrash on the Jewish Bible here appears in the mouth of a miraculously converted Jew, who is portrayed as convincing his fellow Jews of the truth of the Christian hermeneutic.

The anti-Judaic arguments can also be found embedded in a three-cornered debate between pagan philosophy, Judaism and Christianity, as in Origen's *Contra Celsum*.[31] Origen refutes the attack on Christianity of the philosopher, who, in turn, claims to be quoting a Jewish polemic against Christianity. Celsus has no high opinion of Judaism either, but he prefers it to Christianity on the grounds that it is, at least, the ancestral faith of an ancient people, while Christianity is an upstart heresy that has departed from its own ancestral customs. In Eusebius[32] and Augustine[33] the anti-Judaic theses appear a an intrinsic part of their presentation of salvation history. John Damascene includes a short polemic against the Sabbath in his summa on the *Orthodox Faith*.[34] Prudentius' long poem on the Incarnation devotes a section to the blindness and reprobation of the Jews.[35] Lactantius devotes a portion of the *Divine Insti-tutes* to the topic, and Athanasius, in his treatise *On the Incar-nation of the Word,* devotes a section to refuting Jews and pagans.[36] The tradition is virtually absent from Clement of Alexandria, who is close in spirit to Philo in his reconciliation of the biblical and the philosophical traditions. Irenaeus, in his treatise against the Gnostics, devotes considerable time to clarifying the continuity and discontinuity between Judaism and Christianity.[37] Generally, the anti-Judaic and the anti-pagan apologetics remain separate and distinct agendas. The *adversus Judaeos* writings use midrashic methods, and the *adversus nationes* philosophical and rationalist methods.

However, simply to list treatises, sermons, dialogues, and major sections of writings devoted to this theme is to give a misleading impression of its importance. In actuality, the *adversus Judaeos* tradition represents the overall method of Christian exegesis of the Old Testament. Any sermons, com-mentaries, or teachings based on scriptural exegesis of the Old Testament, and even of the New Testament texts where Jews are mentioned, will reflect this tradition of anti-Judaic midrash. It was virtually impossible for the Christian preacher or exegete to teach scripturally at all without alluding to the anti-Judaic theses. Christian scriptural teaching and preaching per se is based on a method in which anti-Judaic polemic exists as the left hand of its christological hermeneutic.[38]

Since this subject is so broad and basic to patristic thought, it is discussed within modest limits in this chapter. An attempt is made to present a general profile of the major themes found in the *adversus Judaeos* tradition, as well as the method of proof-texting these themes from the Old Testament. Hopefully this will provide a summary of the anti-Judaic theses which were generally accepted as a part of the content of classical Christian theology. This tradition informed the prevailing way in which the Christian community was taught, through its preachers and teachers, to look at, not only the Jews of Old Testament and New Testament times, but at the Jewish community of their own times.

Other important tasks are beyond the scope of this study. The christological side of the Christian hermeneutic cannot be covered in detail. Since this tradition is one of Old Testament exegesis, it is a potential gold mine for the study of variant textual readings and for the lineage of various textual interpretations from author to author. A number of the texts used to prove the Christian position were based on disputed translations of the Septuagint, not to mention dubious splicing of texts from different sources, and readings that are nowhere else found. Many of these readings were canceled from the Jewish side by the new Greek translation made by Aquila in the early second century. This gave rise on the Christian side to the charge that the Jews had "altered the Scriptures" to circumvent the Christian interpretation.[39] Very few Christian writers, even among the New Testament authors, could read Hebrew, so this left Christianity in a self-enclosed position in its defense of the Septuagint as the "inspired text" after the Jewish community had repudiated it. A comparison of Christian with rabbinic exegesis, to discover to what extent there was interdependence or even interchange between the two traditions or specific texts, would be another area worth further study.[40]

In this chapter, however, I will attempt only to provide a profile of the nature of the anti-Judaic argument in Christian theology in the period from the second century to about the sixth century. This exposition will, in turn, provide the basic framework for understanding the way in which the doctrines on the Jews were translated into a theological-juridical principle for defining the status of Jews in Christendom. It is here that we find the connection between theological anti-Judaism and anti-Judaism as a legal, sociopolitical modus vivendi in Christian society. This only became possible when and where the Church was established as the official religion of the state. However, the ultimate purpose in this study is theological. Having shown the way anti-Judaism was incorporated as a legal principle to lay the basis for the persecution of the Jewish people in Christendom, we will turn to a criticism of the essential underpinnings of these doctrines theologically. Then it will be necessary to ask, "Is it possible to eliminate anti-Judaism from Christianity and still affirm Jesus as the Christ?"

The *adversus Judaeos* tradition was a literary tradition, the themes of which remain quite constant from the second to the sixth centuries. Much the same themes appear in writings before and after the Constantinian establishment and in the Syriac as well as the Greek and Latin Fathers. This should not lead us to imagine that it was only a literary tradition, however. The same repertoire of themes was constantly adapted by each author to the specific occasion and context in which he wrote. The tradition was a tool of active polemic between the two faiths. It expresses Christian self-affirmation in the face of a live and proselytizing Judaism that continued to challenge Christianity. Unfortunately, a study of the context of each writing must be largely passed over in the present chapter. It is hard to do justice to the exegetical side of the tradition, the use of particular texts and their interpretation from author to author. This could be a subject of many monographs. Rather, this chapter will concentrate on what is most important from the point of view of doctrinal history: namely, the themes of the anti-Judaic tradition. These are what is most constant in the tradition. Each author makes his own selection and organization of themes and texts. But these are secondary to a broad continuity of basic tenets. This chapter provides a composite *adversus Judaeos* presentation, indicating the elaborations of ideas in different authors and giving an overview of the hermeneutical method and types of texts used to establish these themes. These themes are arranged under the two major headings in which they typically appear: (*a*) the rejection of the Jews and the election of the Gentiles, and (*b*) the inferiority and spiritual fulfillment of the Jewish law, cult, and scriptural interpretation. In a final section, we will discuss the social context in which the Christian polemic took place and how the Jewish teachers and religious structure interacted with it.

2. *The Rejection of the Jews and the Election of the Gentiles*

JEWISH HISTORY AS A TRAIL OF CRIMES. The reprobation of the Jews is based, finally, on the assertion that they rejected Jesus as the Christ. But, as in the New Testament, the Church Fathers projected this final act of apostasy backward and constructed a view of Jewish history as a trail of crimes. They wanted to show that this was not a recent and forgivable misstep on the part of the Jews: they have ever been apostate from God. So the rejection and murder of Christ is the foreordained conclusion of the evil history of a perfidious people. As in the New Testament, with the death of Christ, the Jewish people are said to "fill up the measure of their sins."[41] The core of this theme is still that of killing the prophets.

The Son of God came in the flesh for this purpose, that he might bring to summation the total of sins of those who persecuted his prophets to death. [*Ep.* Barn. 5, 11]

That the Jews never heard the prophets, always rejected the prophets, ever refused to repent at the prophets' call, and, finally, regularly killed the prophets is repeated throughout the anti-Judaic writings. Texts such as the following could be cited as proofs that Jewish apostasy from God and murderousness toward the prophets have always characterized their history.[42]

Nevertheless they were disobedient and rebelled against thee and cast thy law behind their back and killed thy prophets. [Neh. 9:26]

The prophet Elijah calls out:

The people of Israel have foresaken thy covenant, thrown down thy altars, and slain thy prophets with the sword; and I, even I only, am left; and they seek my life, to take it away. [1 Kings 19:10; cf. Rom. 11:3]

Lactantius adds that they killed the prophets with "exquisite tortures."[43]

But this list of the crimes of the Jews has been considerably expanded in the Church Fathers. The Jews are not only prophet killers, but idolaters, law breakers, and sinners of every description. This proclivity for vice and idolatry is usually presumed to have begun with their stay in Egypt. The Fathers claim the Patriarchs as ancestors of the Church and assume a patriarchal history of unspotted virtue. The evil nature and history of the Jews begin with the Egyptian sojourn. There they are said to have picked up an incorrigible proclivity for idolatry and vice. The Mosaic Law with its cultic and dietary commandments is then seen as a curb upon this Egyptian depravity. God restrained their appetites with dietary laws and gave them a regulated cult to "innoculate" them against even worse idolatry. Eusebius states this myth of Jewish degeneration in Egypt by saying that "everything that Moses forbade they had previously done without restraint."[44] Idolatry, polytheism, lying, incest, and murder—indeed, all the crimes forbidden in the Law previously had characterized their "wild and savage life" in Egypt. Aphrahat adds the ingenious idea that all the animals they are forbidden to eat were the food they ate with the Egyptians, while the animals they are allowed to eat (sheep, calves) were those they previously had worshipped in Egypt.[45] Chrysostom typifies the life of the Jews in Egypt by saying that they "built a brothel in Egypt, made love madly with the barbarians, and worshipped foreign gods," a statement which he incorrectly ascribes to Ezekiel.[46]

Once out in the desert, the Jews were unable to shake off the evil habits they had picked up in Egypt and fell straightway into idolatry. As in the Stephen tradition in Acts, the golden calf is regularly cited as the type of the Jewish mania for idols. It is the paradigm of their rejection of God which will end in God's rejection of them. For Barnabas, indeed, God already rejected the Jews as a result of their making of the golden calf. Moses broke the tablets to signify that God had withdrawn their election, preserving it instead for the Christian Church.[47] Prudentius allusively links up the golden calf with the "deafness" of the Jews to the Word of God, suggesting that they impaired their "hearing" when they gave over their earrings to make the idol:

Have these truths soaked into the ears of the Jews? . . . But all the trappings have vanished from their ears and gone to fashion a cast head of Baal, robbing the ears of their honor. [Prud. *Apo.* 321–25]

Some of the patristic writers also speak of the Jews as resisting and disbelieving Moses, and even trying to kill him. Chrysostom declares that they continually tried to kill Moses.[48] But this theme is not prominent, perhaps because its possibilities are outweighed by the desire to deprecate the Mosaic tradition as well.

When in the Promised Land, the Jews did not repent, but continued to run after idols. Here, every prophetic text which rebukes the people for rebelliousness, unfaithfulness, and "whoring after the foreign gods of Canaan" can be ransacked to provide a description of what "the Jews" were like in Old Testament times. Since the gentile Church has recently come from paganism, this would seem to be a dubious charge. But the Fathers surmount this by a remarkable piece of historical compression wherein the proclivity of the Jews for idols in Old Testament times is contrasted with the "faithful Gentiles" who have turned from idols to the worship of the true God. For example, Tertullian says:

According to the divine Scriptures the people of the Jews quite forsook God and did degrading service to idols and, abandoning the Divinity, surrendered to images. . . . And, in later times, in which the kings were governing them . . . they did again worship golden kine and groves and enslave themselves to Baal. Whence it is proven that they have ever been guilty of the crime of Idolatry, whereas our lesser or posterior people [the gentile Church], quit the idols . . . [and] converted to the same God from whom Israel, as we have shown above, departed. [Ter. *Adv. Jud.* 1][49]

In a series of startling antitheses, Ephrem, the fourth-century Syrian Father, plays the tale of Jewish idolatry against the final rejection of Christ:

What is thine iniquity, O Daughter of Jacob, that thy chastisement is so severe? Thou hast dishonored the King and the King's Son; thou shameless one and harlot! The King was dishonored in the wilderness and the King's Son in Jerusalem. The Father was exchanged for the calf and for sundry similitudes, and the Son was exchanged for a thief and a blood-shedder. And the Spirit of the Lord they did vex among strange nations. The Trinity that was of old she despised and behaved herself madly, and loved vain gods and devils and fortunes and images. For Saturn had honor paid to him and the Word of God was dishonored. Chemosh was beloved, and the gracious Son insulted. Tammuz was near and dear, and the Lord on High rejected and despised. Astaroth was paraded in every place, and the Heavenly One was put aside. Baal was honored by sacrifices, and the Messiah was persecuted by the impure. Bats and ghosts were worshipped in her chamber, and He, on whose nod the earth hangs, was smitten with palms in the streets. [Eph. *Rhy. C. Jud.* 15]

Other crimes are also brought in to extend this picture of Jewish sinfulness. The Jews are said to have ever been blasphemers against the Name of God (Isa. 52:6: "On your account My Name is continually reviled among the Gentiles").[50] They have always been rebellious and resisted the Spirit (Isa. 64:2: "All day long I stretch my hands to a disobedient and gainsaying people").[51] They were gluttons (Ex. 32:6: "This people sat down to eat and drink and rose up to play"),[52] sensualists (Deut. 32:15: "Jacob waxed fat and began to kick"),[53] and adulterers (Jer. 5:8: "They became furious, wanton steeds. They neighed each one for his neighbor's wife").[54] Chrysostom especially embroiders on this theme of Jewish "sensuality" which he links with rebelliousness against God:

As an animal, when it has been fattened by getting all it wants to eat, gets stubborn and hard to manage, so it was with the Jewish people. Reduced by gluttony and drunkenness to a state of utter depravity, they frisked about and would not accept Christ's yoke. [Chry. *Or. C. Jud.* I, 2.]

The theme of Jewish sensuality can be fused with the general ontological dualism of Christian theology which describes the Jews as the people of the outward "letter," against the Christian people of the "spirit." The Fathers feel full license to describe Jewish "outwardness" not merely in terms of literalism over against the Christian allegorical interpretation of Scripture, but as though the Jews were actually addicted to the vices of the flesh, in contrast to Christian asceticism. Ephrem the Syrian speaks of the synagogue typically as a "harlot." This language is drawn from Hosea, but is presumed to apply to contemporary Jews. The synagogue is said to have been cast off by God "because she was wanton between the legs."[55] Aphrahat equates Jerusalem with Sodom and Gomorrah, using a text that is frequently cited by other patristic writers against Judaism.[56] Like those legendary cities of vice, Jerusalem, declares Aphrahat, will never be rebuilt. John Damascene says that God gave the Jews the Sabbath because of their "grossness and sensuality" and "absolute propensity for material things" ("On the Sabbath" IV, 23).

Perhaps the most extraordinary theme in this repertoire of sins is the charge that the Jews were infanticides and sacrificed their children to demons. Psalm 106:37 (a standard source for the patristic "catalogue of crimes") was the basis for this idea. Chrysostom, in his sixth sermon, draws particularly on this and other sources to portray Old Testament people as inveterate debauchers and idolators who "sacrificed their sons and daughters to demons." Chrysostom repeatedly speaks of the Jews as "godless, idolators, pedicides, stoning the prophets and committing ten thousand horrors" (*Or. C. Jud.* 6, 2). In his fifth sermon, he also declares that they were cannibals, eating their own children (*Or. C. Jud.* 5, 6: Deut. 28:56 and Lam. 4:10). By the third century, this myth of Jewish history as a trail of crimes was sufficiently fixed so that Hippolytus could sum up the matter in this fashion:

Why was the temple made desolate? Was it on account of the ancient fabrication of the calf? Or was it on account of the idolatry of the people? Was it for the blood of the prophets? Was it for the adultery and fornication of Israel? By no means, for in all these transgressions they always found pardon open to them. But it was because they killed the Son of their Benefactor, for He is coeternal with the Father. [Hipp. *C. Jud.* 7]

The purpose of this "catalogue of crimes" is to provide the heritage for the final apostasy of the Jews in the killing of the

Messiah. The "nature" of the Jews becomes fixed through this history as one of rejection of God and monstrous evil, and the logical culmination is the murder of God's Son, justifying then God's final rejection of them. God is portrayed as ever wrathful against them, receiving nothing but unresponsiveness and crimes in return for his efforts to reform them. Most of the Fathers do not go as far as Barnabas in regarding the Jews as already rejected on Sinai, for this takes the point out of that drama of crimes which leads to the final act of apostasy. Most stress the idea that they always found forgiveness up to that point. Nevertheless, the catalogue of crimes has the effect of making the Jews appear de facto an apostate people throughout their history, who, in fact, never accepted God. God's efforts on their behalf were futile. In his forbearance, he kept trying again, sending prophets to turn them from their evil ways and again receiving perfidity and murder in return. With the killing of Christ, the final evidence is in that the Jews are not suitable to be God's people. They are then rejected irrevocably for another people, the gentile Church, who will respond to God.

The crime with which the Jews are charged in the death of Jesus is seldom directly described as deicide in the pre-Nicene Fathers, although this idea is implicit as soon as Jesus is identified as the incarnate Son of God. Most pre-Nicene Fathers follow the New Testament tradition which links Jesus with the martyred prophets. They describe the crime as the culmination of the killing of the prophets in the killing of that ultimate messianic envoy from God predicted by the prophets. To reject the Messiah is to reject the promised salvation and to put oneself beyond the pale of God's designated means of salvation. With the more developed Nicene theology, the nature of the crime could be escalated and the Jews described as enemies of God who committed a crime of cosmic treason and *lèse majesté* against the Sovereign of the universe. Killing Christ becomes a crime of cosmic regicide. This became particularly true after Christianity had been integrated into the empire and began to identify the emperor as the legitimate "vicar of Christ on earth." Chrysostom particularly is fond of this imperial language:

If someone had killed your son, could you stand the sight of him or the sound of his greeting? Wouldn't you try to get away from him as if he were an evil demon; as if he were the Devil himself? The Jews killed the Son of your Master. . . . Will you so dishonor Him as to respect and cultivate His Murderers, the men who crucified Him? [Chry. *Or. C. Jud.* I, 7]

A few lines later, Chrysostom specifically calls the crime that of "deicide" (*theoktonian*) and identifies the worship of the synagogue with service to demons.

The evil nature supposedly characteristic of the Jews of the past, climaxing in the crucifixion, is typically applied to contemporary Jews in the patristic writings. Origen speaks of Jews of his day as "the sons of those who rejected Moses in the desert."[57] Isidore declares that the evil nature of the Jew never changes, citing Jeremiah 13:23: "Can the Ethiopian change his color or the leopard his spots?"[58] Augustine, in his tract *Against the Jews,* speaks of the Jews as filled with bitterness and gall like that which they gave Jesus to drink on the cross (5). He regards Jewish responsibility for the crucifixion as a kind of inherited trait:

"For the wickedness of my people he was led to death" (Isa. 53:8). This is said about Christ, whom you, in your parents, led to death. [Aug. *Adv. Jud.* 7 (10)]

Chrysostom also assumes that all the crimes and vices which he ascribes to Jews of old can also be attributed to contemporary Jews. However, with his penchant for rhetorical antitheses, he turns the idea of Jewish inheritance of their parents' crimes into a startling chiasmus almost incomprehensible except to those schooled in patristic figurative exegesis. The Jews are said to have been prone to every vice, idolatry, and lawlessness in olden times. Yet God did not cast them off. Now that they have committed the ultimate crime, they are beyond divine forgiveness. So now, although they strictly observe prayers and fasting, keep the Mosaic Law, and do not worship idols, stone prophets, or eat their children, they nevertheless are much more hated by God than before. Formerly, they are said to have broken every commandment, when God wanted them to keep them. Now that Christ has come, they perversely insist on keeping every detail of the Law, just when God wants to abrogate it. In either case, they always do just whatever it is that God doesn't want them to do. Thus, according to Chrysostom, their present virtues are much worse in the eyes of God than their former vices, for they stand under the mark of guilt for Christ's murder and their fidelity to the Law now expresses their ongoing refusal to turn to Christ. Chrysostom can, therefore, feel justified in applying all the language of idolatry, harlotry, and demonism to the present law keeping and worship of the synagogue, to describe the synagogue as a brothel and a house of demon worship.[59]

THE "TWO PEOPLES" IN THE OLD TESTAMENT. The hermeneutical method for proof-texting this tale of crimes supposedly characteristic of the Jews in Old Testament times consists of splitting the right hand from the left hand of the prophetic message. The prophetic dialectic of judgment and promise is presumed to apply, not to one people, the Jews, but to two peoples, the Jews and the future Church. This means that all the statements of divine wrath and judgment, which the prophets used as a language of ethical exhortation to that one people whom they also expected God would redeem, are read schizophrenically. Every negative judgment, threat, or description can then be taken out of context and read monolithically as descriptive of "the Jews." The positive side of the prophetic message—the traits of faith, repentance, and future promise— are said to apply not to the Jews, but to the future Church. By this method, one gains an unrelieved tale of evildoing and apostasy said to be characteristic of "the Jews," divorced from the message of forgiveness and future hope, which is applied to the Church. This turns the Jewish Scriptures, which actually contain the record of Jewish self-criticism, into a remorseless denunciation of the Jews, while the Church, in turn, is presented as totally perfect and loses the prophetic tradition of self-criticism! This also means that the heroes of the Old Testament become the lineage of the Church, while the Jews are read as a people who never accepted or responded to their prophetic leaders and teachers. Since the Christian exegete is a biblical literalist in seeing the Scriptures as written "by God," through the prophets and heroes, it was not necessary to ask, sociologically, how this document could have been preserved as the Scriptures of a people who "never heard the prophets." The Old Testament itself is made to yield the tale of Jewish apostasy and the election of the gentile Church. By dividing prophetic wrath from prophetic promise, one makes the Old Testament a text for anti-Judaism, on the one hand, and for ecclesial triumphalism, on the other.

Augustine delineates this hermeneutical method explicitly in his *Tract Against the Jews*. The Jews are said to be incurably carnal-minded and unable to understand the spiritual meaning of the Scriptures. Vainly do they imagine the promises made to Israel to refer to themselves. But the people who are called "from the rising of the sun to the setting thereof" (Mal. 1:11) cannot be a local tribe, but only a universal spiritual people, the Church. The Jews, however, belong to those "enemies" of God referred to by the psalmist, speaking in the person of the Davidic king:[60]

My God shall let me see over my enemies; slay them not, lest at any time they forget thy law. Scatter them by thy power. [Ps. 58:12; Aug. *Adv. Jud.* 7 (9)]

The Jews unknowingly mediate the Law to the Gentiles, the people called from the rising to the setting of the sun, while testifying in their own Scriptures to their own reprobation. When the Jews hear the prophet say such things as "for he has cast off his people, the House of Israel" (Isa. 2:6), they should acknowledge that "this is us." But when the prophet says such things as "O House of Jacob, come, walk in the light of the Lord" (Isa. 2:5), they should know that this refers to the universal, spiritual people, who come into being through faith in that Messiah whom the Jews themselves killed (Aug. *Adv. Jud.* 8 [11]).

The two peoples, then, the reprobate Jews and the gentile Church, are believed to be already known and predicted and even anticipated in the Hebrew Scriptures. All the Righteous Ones of the Old Testament belong to the lineage of the Church, while "the Jews" are the "enemies" of the Davidic king of the Psalms and the Suffering Servant of Isaiah. They are the subject of the wrath of the prophets.

Old Testament polygamy provided the Church with the central images of this idea. The practice of concubinage often resulted in rival wives and rival brothers who contended for the heritage of the patriarch, e.g., Sarah and Hagar and their respective sons, and the two wives of Jacob. The Church especially used the story of the rival sons of Isaac, Jacob and Esau, as an image of the "two peoples." The biblical and talmudic tradition in Judaism also used these images to contrast the legitimate people of God with the alien people. For the talmudic tradition indeed it is the Church which is Edom and Esau, while the Church claims that it is Jacob and the Jews are Esau![61] The Church especially seized on the line in Genesis 25:23 where it is said that "two nations" are in the womb of Rebekah and "the one shall be stronger than the other, the elder shall serve the younger." Unquestionably, this refers to the Church, the gentile people, who came after the Jews but overcame them, while the elder people, the Jews, are made to "serve" the younger people, the Church.

Maximinus, in his treatise *Contra Judaeos,* lists a whole series of such patriarchal sibling rivalries which prefigure the supersession of the elder people, the Jews, by the younger people, the Church. There are Ishmael and Isaac; Esau and Jacob; Jacob's elder brother and Joseph; Manasseh and Ephraim. The two tablets of Moses—the first of which was broken and the second of which prefigures the New Law of the "new Moses," i.e., Christ—also have the same meaning, according to Maximinus (*C. Jud.* 1). Maximinus begins his list of prototypes of the sibling rivalry of the Church and the Jews with Cain and Abel. Cain symbolizes the Jews, while Abel, killed by the elder brother and replaced by the mysterious Seth, symbolizes the murdered and resurrected Christ. Other Fathers also make Cain a symbol of the Jews. According to Tertullian, God rejected the bloody sacrifices of Cain, i.e., the Jewish sacrificial system, while accepting the unbloody spiritual worship of Christians (Ter. *Adv. Jud.* 5). Chrysostom makes a similar exegesis of the sacrifices of the two brothers (Chry. *Or. C. Jud.* I, 7).[62]

Aphrahat identifies the passage in John 8:44, "Your father was a murderer from the beginning," with Cain. He declares that the father of the Jews is not Abraham, but Cain (*Dem.* 16, 8). Ephrem explicitly identifies the reprobate status of the Jews in the exile with that of the wandering Cain:

Today the glory has passed from the people of Israel and they stand among the nations ashamed, as Cain was, at their unnatural deed. [Eph. *Rhy. C. Jud.* 8]

Augustine is also fond of the Cain-Jews analogy.[63]

The two brothers motif provided the Church not only with the notion of a younger people who supersedes an elder, but also suggested that the elder was now in a servile status in relation to the younger. When the image of Cain is added to this idea, the Jew becomes the murderous elder brother now forced to wander the earth as a reprobate among the nations, i.e., the gentile Church! This theological motif is a typological ancestor of the medieval myth of the Wandering Jew. In the words of the fourth-century poet Prudentius:

From place to place the homeless Jew wanders in ever-shifting exile, since the time when he was torn from the abode of his fathers and has been suffering the penalty for murder and having stained his hands with the blood of Christ, whom he denied, paying the price of sin. . . . This noble race [is] . . . scattered and enslaved. . . . It is in captivity under the younger faith . . . a race that was formerly unfaithful confesses Christ and triumphs. But that which denied Christ is conquered and subdued and has fallen into the hands of Masters who keep the Faith. [Prud. *Apo.* 541–50]

The antithesis between the two peoples also drew on the image of the two wives of Abraham, Sarah and Hagar, and the two wives of Jacob, Rachel and Leah. Paul provided the basis for the interpretation of the two wives of Abraham (Gal. 4: 21–31), as he did also for that of Jacob and Esau (Rom. 9:13). In Paul, the Christians are the children of Sarah, offspring of Isaac-Christ, while the Jews are the children of the slave woman, Hagar. Augustine especially used this Pauline exegesis, and it was to become the stock image in the medieval Church for the doctrine for the "servitude of the Jews."[64] For Augustine and other Fathers, the Jews are the "carnal men," against the Christians, who are the "spiritual men," children of the eschatological Jerusalem. Hagar is the fallen, earthly Jerusalem, who is in bondage together with her children (both political servitude under "the nations" and moral servitude to "earthly things"). Sarah's children are those who have been freed by Christ and belong to the Heavenly City above.[65]

A parallel analogy of the Church and the Synagogue was drawn from the story of the two wives of Jacob:

Also Jacob received two wives; the elder Leah, with weak eyes, a type of the Synagogue; the younger, the beautiful Rachel, the type of the Church, who also remained long barren and afterwards brought forth Joseph, who also was himself a type of Christ. [Cyp. *Test.* 20][66]

This image of the "weak-eyed Leah" could be mingled with the Pauline image of the "veil" that lies over the eyes of the Jews, blinding them to the truth, to provide an image of the "blindness" of the Synagogue. Medieval cathedrals were commonly to use this image of the two wives, the Church and the Synagogue, one beautiful and triumphant, and the other dejected, with a blind over her eyes.[67]

The image of the "two wives" also suggested the scriptural image of Israel as "bride" of Yahweh who, in her apostasy, is excoriated as a harlot. The Church was the legitimate bride of God, while Israel is the harlot who has been given a bill of divorce and sent away by God for her many sins. The Syrian Fathers Ephrem and Aphrahat particularly play on this image of the bridal Church (drawing on Revelation 19:7–8 and the ecclesiological interpretation of the Song of Songs) and the harlot synagogue. Using the language of Oriental divorce practices, Ephrem paints this picture of Israel's "divorce" by God:

She despised the voice of the Prophets and the preaching of the Apostles. . . . He wrote and delivered to her the divorcement as being rejected and polluted. He took the veil from her head and from her eyes also chastity. He stripped her of her ornaments and doubled back and lifted up her covering. He took her necklace from her neck and took away her bracelets and her armlets and as an adulteress and a harlot He drove her out and sent her forth from His chamber. And she sat without a veil and with her head uncovered and disgraced. [Eph. *Rhy. C. Jud.* 13]

This language is less central in Aphrahat, but it also appears in his *Demonstrations Against the Jews:*

Concerning them Hosea preached when he called them a licentious and adulterous woman. He said concerning the congregation of Israel, "remove her licentiousness from her face," and concerning the congregation of Judah, "remove her adultery from between her breasts" (Hos. 2:2). The Prophet spoke concerning both their congregations and called them licentious and adulterous when he said at the end of the verse, "If she does not remove her licentiousness from before her face and her adultery from between her breasts, then I shall throw her out naked and shall abandon her as on the day she was born.". . . Israel has played the whore, and Judah has committed adultery. And the people which is of the peoples [the Church] is the holy and faithful people, which has gone down and adhered to the Lord. [Aph. *Dem.* 16, 3][68]

A blending of the whore image with that of the rejected bondswoman of the patriarchal stories occurs in the pseudo-Augustinian *Altercation Between the Church and the Synagogue.* The synagogue is a mere handmaiden who has tried to usurp the place of the true Bride of the Lord. The prophets testify to her true status as a servant who was only intended to prepare the place for the true Bride. They also testify to her "adulterous ways," her crimes and idolatry. The synagogue is described as a wicked, conniving woman who has been "caught in adultery more than once," and still has not given up all her stolen ornaments and false claims. Her sign of election, circumcision, is itself disgraceful, for it signs an organ which must be covered and is used only for shameful deeds, while the Christian is chastely signed on the forehead. The Church is the true Bride of the Lord foretold by the prophets (quoting the Song of Songs). The treatise cites not only the biblical texts of reprobation, but also the political status of the Jews, as a people who are forbidden the holding of any office in the (Christ tian) Roman Empire, to prove that God is against them.[69] The altercation is arranged in the form of a court hearing of disputed claims of possession. It was performed as a liturgical drama in medieval times.

THE ELECTION OF THE GENTILES. The heart of the *adversus Judaeos* tradition is the proof of the election of the gentile Church and its inheritance of the election of the rejected Jews. This idea in the Church Fathers most often is presented as an antithesis between "the Jews" and "the nations," i.e., the Gentiles. The Jews are that people that has never heard the prophets and is finally cast off for rejecting the Messiah. A new people, the believers from "among the nations," has taken their place as the elect people of God. There is little attempt in the patristic tradition to maintain the idea of a Jewish remnant in the Church as the stem into which the Gentiles are "ingrafted." The relationship becomes primarily one of substitution. The reprobate, unbelieving Jews are cast off, and the believing gentile people take their place.

But the patristic tradition does not see this simply as an event that divides the "new people" from the "old" at the time of Jesus. The gentile Church is seen as implicit in the Old Testament too. It is prefigured and foretold in the ancient heroes and prophets. The gentile Church has ever been the ultimate meaning of Israel. The prophets foretold that Jewish election was temporary and provisional only, and that the Jews were finally to be rejected. The relation of the election of the Jews to that of the Church remains blurred in the patristic account. But the dominant tendency follows the line we saw in the Hellenist Stephen, in Acts, and in Paul. Essentially, there is one covenant, *promised* to Abraham, *foretold* by the prophets, and *fulfilled* in the gentile Church, who accepted the Messiah promised to Israel. The Jews assume the status of a people on probation who fail all the tests and finally are flunked out. The message of election refers to a believing people. The Jews proved through their history that they are not this people. So the believing people becomes a historical reality only with the gentile Church. The Old Testament heroes and prophets are leaders without a people, standing as the lineage of the Church, preparing the way for the Messiah and the people who will respond to God. The Jews are that people who "ever resisted the Holy Spirit" from the time of Moses to Jesus. So, in a sense, they were never really elected, because their status remained provisional. Since they never accepted God, the covenant with them was abortive and was dropped finally in favor of that people who did accept God, the prophets, and the Messiah. The Church assumes the status of the "true Israel" (cf. Just. *Dial.* 123). The prophets already knew and foretold that the believing people would be a gentile people "called out from among the nations." The Old Testament references to election refer to this believing people, while the passages about apostasy, wrath, and rejection refer to the Jews. The period of God's unsuccessful efforts with the Jews runs only from Moses to Jesus, for the patriarchal period is detached from Jewish history and becomes the prehistory of the gentile Church. The prophets are a line of witnesses leading to the Messiah and the Church.

The Pauline doctrine that the true sons of Abraham are those who, like Abraham, are justified by faith apart from circumcision is repeated to show that it is the Christians who are the true heirs of the promise to Abraham (Gen. 15:6; Rom. 4:3; and Gal. 3:6–9). God's promise to Abraham that he would make him the "father of many nations" (Gen. 17:5) is cited to prove that the descendants promised to Abraham are not the Jews, but "the nations," i.e., the Gentiles. Abraham's promised fatherhood is realized only with the creation of a believing people from among the "nations."[70] Isaac of Antioch creates a vivid image to describe this relationship between the circumcized Jews and the true Israel, the uncircumcized gentile Church:

Abraham was stamped like a vessel because of the treasure that was in him. And the seal continued in your generations because of the treasure that was in you until now. Now . . . the treasure has come forth. . . . In you it was in custody and was safeguarded, and it was preserved under the stamp. To me it was given for use. Therefore I do not circumcize myself like you. . . . O nation [Jews], you were the guardians of the riches that were preserved for the nations [gentile Church]. . . . Its rightful owners have taken the trust, and you are concerned with the regulations. Unseemly are the seals . . . when the garment on which they were are worn out. They were trampled and fell and were cut off. . . . Behold they are ruined, destroyed, and despoiled, and yet they are proud of the seal upon them. [Is. Ant. *Hom. C. Jud.*][71]

Jewish circumcision is not a mark of true election. It is merely the seal on a treasure bag kept by guardians for the true heir, who has now claimed the inheritance and discarded the outward seal and container. The Jews are left holding an empty bag; they are clinging to the outward vessel and seal whose inward contents has been taken by the "rightful owner."

  The basic method of proving the election of the Gentiles in the patristic writings, as in the New Testament, is to read all the texts about Israel as a "light to the nations," the future sway of the Davidic king over "the nations," and praise for non-Hebrew peoples, as prophecies of the gentile Church. These texts are read antithetically to the texts condemning Israel, to prove the rejection of the Jews and the election of the people from among the nations. Texts used for this purpose are myriad, and here are only a sampling of the method. Key texts were found in the Psalms, which promise to Israel's king great sway among the nations, and in the Suffering Servant passages of Isaiah. Since Christ was identified with the Davidic king of the Psalms and with the Servant of Isaiah, the subject of these texts was presumed to be Christ. If the subject is Christ, then his enemies must be the Jews! The nations to be conquered and the nations to be converted are the gentile believers. Since the enemies of the psalmic king were his rivals, often rival kings of other nations, this means the Church must read the references to "nations" and "enemies" in the Psalms very selectively to make antithetical what is often identical! The strong bulls of Bashan who open wide their mouths (Ps. 22:13) are the Jews who crucify Christ, while the nations whom the Davidic king will conquer in Psalm 2 or Psalm 110 are understood as that gentile people that will be converted to Christ. The Church reads texts such as "Thou art my Son; this day I have begotten thee. Ask of me and I will give the nations as thy inheritance" (Ps. 2:7–8) as a statement addressed by God to Christ promising him the gentile Church as his inheritance (cf. Ter. *Adv. Jud.* 12). By juxtaposing such texts with others, such as "On your account the name of God is blasphemed among the Gentiles" (Isa. 52:5), read as referring to the unbelieving Jews (Ter. *Adv. Jud.* 13), one reads the Psalms and Prophets as texts for the election of the Gentiles and the reprobation of the Jews. The gentile Church is the faithful people, who are referred to by such texts as: "I will change the speech of the peoples to pure speech, so that all of them shall call on the Name of the Lord" (Zeph. 3:9); "Many and strong peoples shall adhere to the Lord" (Zech. 2:11); "The peoples shall abandon their idols" (Jer. 6:19); "I have found a people who did not seek me" (Isa. 65:1; cf. Rom. 10:20); and "Those who are not my people I shall call my people" (Hos. 2:23; cf. Rom. 9:25). The reprobate Jews appear in such texts as "I have abandoned My House; I have abandoned my heritage. I have given my beloved into the hands of his enemies" (Jer. 12:7–9), and "Let me blot out this people and I shall make you into a people which is greater and more worthy than they" (Ex. 32:10).[72]

This gathering of the faithful people from among the Gentiles is understood in the Fathers, as in the New Testament, as the fulfillment of the messianic expectation of the ingathering of the nations to Zion at the time of redemption. By the same token the Church hotly denies the rival claim of the synagogue that this ingathering is taking place in the gentile proselytes to Judaism (cf. Just. *Dial.* 122). The gentile Church is itself seen as a sign of messianic fulfillment. The nations all believe in Christ and flow into Zion from whence goes forth the good news of the gospel, while the Jews disbelieve and are abandoned:

I shall open my gates with joy and the hosts of the Gentiles shall enter into thee and become in thee an elect people and the Lord shall reign over Zion and many peoples shall come and worship me in Jerusalem. . . . Then Zion spake, weeping distractedly: The Lord hath left me because I have provoked Him and God hath forgotten me; yes, He hath rejected me. [Eph. *Rhy. C. Jud.* 20]

Needless to say, this exegesis calls for extraordinary distortion of the actual meaning of the biblical texts. There the Israel which is chastised and the Israel whose messianic fulfillment is predicted are the same. The messianic fulfillment of Israel includes the ingathering of believers from among the nations. In the Church's reading of these texts, however, the messianic Israel is identified with the believing Gentiles, in antithetical relationship to the chastized Israel, the reprobate Jews.

In the period after the establishment of the Church as the religion of the Roman Empire, this argument, that the gentile Church is a messianic fulfillment, takes on a new political tone. The universalism of the nations, gathered in the Church, is equated with the universal sway of the Christian Roman Pax. The ecumenical empire comes to be identified with the millennial reign of the Messiah over the earth. In fulfillment of the promises to the Davidic king, in Christendom Christ reigns "from sea to sea and from the river to the ends of the earth" (Ps. 72:8).[73] All nations gather into the Kingdom of Christ. The Jews alone are in exile "among their enemies." But since their enemies, the nations, now equal the elect gentile Church, the reversal of Jewish messianic hope is total. All nations are redeemed at the coming of the Messiah except the Jews!

Chrysostom particularly is notable for this triumphalistic language which identifies the Church of Christendom with the millennial reign of Christ over the "whole world."[74] This required a highly ideological reading of the success of the Church. The overthrow of paganism by the Church is regarded as the vanquishing of all idolatry. Everywhere ancient error and superstition are replaced by the true faith. Since the pagan gods are demons, this also means that Christ has vanquished the demons. Belial has been bound and his sway over mankind has been conquered. Christ has established his reign over the earth. Christendom is God's Kingdom Come! With all men united in the one catholic faith and universal empire, strife ceases and the reign of peace and brotherhood prevails. The success of the Church is viewed as though it were already completely universal. The ideology of the empire, which regarded itself as universal and disregarded those outside its bounds, is fused with the messianic universalism of the Church. Christendom is the realization of the messianic prophecy that "all . . . the nations shall worship before him" (Ps. 22:27). Christ has established his reign over the earth and made "his enemies his footstool" (Ps.

110:1). The house of God has been established on the mountain of Zion and all nations flow to it. As for the Jews, it is of them that the messianic king speaks when he says: "As for these enemies of mine who did not want me to reign over them, bring them here and slay them before me" (Chry. *Dem. Jud.-Gen.* 4, quoting Luke 19:27). This same blending of messianic and Roman imperial universalism appears typically in Eusebius:

As the knowledge of the one God and the one way of religion and salvation, even the doctrine of Christ, was made known to all mankind; so at the self-same period, the entire dominion of the Roman empire was being vested in a single sovereign, profound peace reigned throughout the world. And thus by the express appointment of the same God, two roots of blessing, the Roman empire and the doctrine of Christian piety, sprang up together for the benefit of men. . . . The falsehood of demonic superstition was convicted and the mutual hatred of the nations removed. At one same time one God and the knowledge of that God were proclaimed to all. One universal empire prevailed and the whole human race, subdued by the controlling power of peace and concord, received one another as brethern. Hence as children of one God and Father, owing true religion as their common mother, they saluted one and welcomed one another with words of peace. Thus the whole world appeared like one well-ordered and united family. [Euseb. *Or. Con.* 16, 4–7]

This triumphalistic interpretation of the victory of the Church is less prominent in writings before the political establishment of Christianity. Yet, even in pre-Nicene writings, the successful mission of the Church is used as proof that "God is on our side."[75] Earlier writers appear more aware of the gap between the actual state of the world and those messianic promises of peace and glory which were, in the Jewish tradition, the meaning of the messianic coming. Pre-Nicene writers cover this discrepancy by claiming that the Scriptures teach *two advents* of the Messiah, one in humility and suffering and the second in glory. It is because the Jews fail to understand this prophetic teaching of the two advents that they falsely regard the crucifixion as a refutation of Jesus' messiahship. The persecution of the Church continues this mission of the suffering Christ, while the glorified Christ will come at the Second Advent.[76]

In Eusebius and Chrysostom, this sense of a gap between the suffering state of present reality and the messianic promises seems to have vanished. The establishment of the Church is taken as a realization of messianic glory and the universal sovereignty of God's Kingdom over the whole world. Christian conversion among many groups is taken as that ingathering of all nations in worship at Zion of messianic expectation (reading the ingathering at Zion spiritually, as the gathering into one faith). A similar dispersion of Jewish believers throughout the whole world, however, is taken as exile and reprobation (Zion, for them, being interpreted as purely local). Unconsciously, a double standard for interpretation of historical facts is employed. The persecution of the Church is construed as holy martyrdom, while the persecution of the Jews is read as divine wrath. The success of the Church in the empire is seen as proof that God is "on our side." At this time in Persia, the Jews are temporarily secure, while the Church is persecuted. When they point to this fact as an indication that God is against the Christians, saying "Where is your God?" this is regarded as false caviling on their part.

The Syrian Father Aphrahat answers these Jewish charges by calling on the Jews to remember their own tradition of martyrdom and to recognize that those who suffer in God's name suffer righteously. The Christians persecuted under the Persian regime are martyrs to the faith. Yet Aphrahat does not hesitate to equate Jewish misfortune with divine wrath. He declares that Jerusalem, like Sodom, will never be rebuilt and will remain desolate until the end of time. In vain do the Jews look for an end to their captivity, for the city is to be "in desolation until the completion of all things has been decided" (Dan. 9:27). Persecuted Christians are God's beloved witnesses. Persecuted Jews are unrepentant sinners to whom the prophets said "in vain have I smitten your sons, but they did not take correction" (Jer. 2:30; cf. Aph. *Dem.* 21). In Chrysostom's sermons, it is said that no commonality exists between the sufferings of martyrs and the sufferings of thieves, grave robbers, and sorcerers —Jewish suffering falling in the latter category. Christians love the martyrs (including the Maccabean martyrs!) who suffered for Christ's sake. But they loathe the Jews who suffer the just punishment of thieves.[77] Even the martyrs take great delight in Chrysostom's polemic against the Jews:

The martyrs especially hate the Jews, for the reason that they love so deeply the One who, by them, was crucified. The Jews said, "His blood be on us and on our children," while the martyrs shed their own blood for Him whom they destroyed. Thus they will listen to these words with pleasure. [Chry. *Or. C. Jud.* VI, 2]

THE REPROBATAON OF THE JEWS. It is axiomatic in the *adversus Judaeos* tradition that Jewish reprobation is permanent and irrevocable. The left hand of Christian victory and messianic ingathering is Jewish rejection and exile. God's discipline of the Jews held out the possibility of forgiveness until the death of the Messiah. Thereafter their reprobation is permanent.

You can hear the wailing and lamentations of each of the prophets, wailing and lamenting characteristically over the calamities which will overtake the Jewish people because of their impiety to Him who had been foretold. How their Kingdom . . . would be utterly destroyed after their sin against Christ; how their Father's law would be abrogated, they themselves deprived of their ancient worship, robbed of the independence of their forefathers, and made slaves of their enemies instead of free men. How their royal metropolis would be burned with fire, their . . . holy altar undergo flames and extreme desolation, their city be inhabited no longer by its old possessors, but by races of other stock, while they would be dispersed among the Gentiles throughout the whole world with never a hope of any cessation of evil or breathing space from troubles. [Euseb. *D. E.* I, 1][78]

As signs of their rejection, Jewish Law has been revoked by God, and they are perverse for continuing to observe it. Their cultic center is destroyed. The temple, the priesthood, the sacrificial system have all been terminated. The Jews celebrate the festivals illegitimately in the Diaspora, for God decreed in the Law that these festivals were to be observed only in the temple in Jerusalem. Judaism, as a vehicle of valid worship of God, has been terminated with the destruction of the priesthood and the temple. Jews are renegades from God in continuing to maintain the festivals outside this assigned context.

This interpretation of the destruction of the temple also presumed a double standard for judging similar developments in the Church and the synagogue. The noncultic worship of the Christian Church is regarded as the fulfillment of that universal spiritual worship among the nations predicted by the prophet Malachi (1:10–11).[79] But the Church strictly rejects the notion that this same noncultic development is legitimate for the Jews. This means that Christianity either ignores or illegitimizes the synagogue as an institution and rabbinic noncultic development of Judaism. With a kind of Sadducean literalism, Christianity identifies valid Judaism with the temple cultus and the Aaronite priesthood. The fall of the temple and the priesthood is then claimed as a divine obliteration of legitimate Jewish worship. Jews have now lost all their tokens of divine favor, all vehicles of divinely ordained communication with God. They are exiles from the one God-given center of worship in Jerusalem, and so bereft of valid prayer and sacrifice. In continuing to observe the ancient festivals in their rabbinic adaptation to the synagogue and the home, they break the Law. Chrysostom especially heaps endless vilification on the synagogue as a diabolical place where Jews, lawlessly, continue to observe Passover and other feasts and fasts. He proves in detail from the Scriptures that Passover could only be observed in Jerusalem. And so the synagogue celebrates it in the Diaspora contrary to divine ordinance.[80] Both the prophets and Christ, and even historians, such as Josephus, are brought forward to prove that the destruction of the temple is intended to be permanent. Three times the Jews attempted to rebuild it (under Hadrian, under Constantine, and under Julian), and each time their impious efforts were beaten back by God.[81] Christ himself decreed that "Jerusalem will be trodden down by many Gentiles until the times of the many Gentiles are fulfilled," that is, until the end of history, in Chrysostom's free rendering of Luke 21:24 (*Or. C. Jud.* 5, 1).

All the various prophetic texts which envision desolation and exile as a result of sin are employed by the Church as predictions of this final state of desolation and exile of the Jews.

Your country is desolate. Your cities are burned with fire: your land strangers shall devour in your sight, and the daughter of Zion shall be left deserted. [Isa. 1:7–8; Cyp. *Test.* I, 6]

The book of Daniel is searched to show that three captivities were predicted for the Jews. The first two (Egyptian and Babylonian) were given precise time limits. The restoration promised to the Jews has already been fulfilled in their restoration after these two captivities. But from the third captivity there will be no restoration. It was given no limit and was intended to last to the end of history.[82] In vain do the Jews look for a Messiah to deliver them from captivity. The Messiah has already come and they have rejected him. As a result, they are to stand under divine reprobation forever:

"Let their eyes be darkened that they see not." And surely ye have been darkened in the eyes of your soul with a darkness utter and everlasting. For now that the true light has arisen, ye wander as in the night and stumble on places with no roads and fall headlong, as having forsaken the way that says, "I am the Way." Furthermore hear this yet more serious word: "And their back do thou bend down always." That means, in order that they may be slaves to the nations, not four hundred thirty years, as in Egypt, nor seventy years, as in Babylonia, but bend them to servitude, He says, "always." How do you indulge vain hopes, expecting to be delivered from the misery which holds you? [Hipp. *C. Jud.* 6]

Hippolytus continues with the exposition to suggest that the Jew's back is to be beaten down always in retribution for beating Christ. Augustine also dwells on this mistranslated text from Psalm 69, which Christianity interpreted as a prediction of the details of the crucifixion by the Jews. Twice, in his short treatise against the Jews and again in the *City of God*, he reiterates the fateful phrase "their back bend thou down always."[83]

Chrysostom, as always, waxes purple on the subject:

It is because you killed Christ. It is because you stretched out your hand against the Lord. It is because you shed the precious blood, that there is now no restoration, no mercy anymore and no defense. Long ago your audacity was directed against servants, against Moses, Isaiah and Jeremiah. If there was wickedness then, as yet the worst of all crimes had not been dared. But now you have eclipsed everything in the past and through your madness against Christ, you have committed the ultimate transgression. This is why you are being punished worse now than in the past. . . . If this were not the case God would not have turned his back on you so completely. . . . But if it appears that He has utterly abandoned you, it is evident from this anger and abandonment that He is showing even to the most shameless that the One who was murdered was not a common law-breaker, but was the very Lawgiver Himself, and the Cause, present among us, of innumerable blessings. Thus you who sinned against Him are in a state of dishonor and disgrace, while we who worship Him, though we once were less honored than any of you [i.e., as gentile pagans], are now established through the grace of God in a more respected position than any of you and in greater honor. [Chry. *Or. C. Jud.* VI, 2–3]

For Chrysostom, God is always in there punching, on the side of the Christians and against their enemies!

Eusebius connects this curse upon the Jews with the Pauline notion of the "curse of the Law," which is to fall on those who cannot keep the commandments in full (Deut. 27:26; cf. Gal. 3:10–11).

Therefore the Jews, because they rejected the Prophet and did not harken to His holy words, have suffered extreme ruin, according to His prediction. For they neither received the Law of Christ of the New Covenant, nor were they able to keep the commands of Moses without some breach of his Law, and so they fell under the curse of Moses, in not being able to carry out what was ordained by him; being exiled from their mother city, which was destroyed, where alone it was allowed to celebrate Mosaic worship. [Euseb. *D. E.* I, 7, 28c]

Several writers connect the giving of circumcision with the Hadrianic law forbidding the Jews to enter Jerusalem after the Jewish Wars. They conclude that circumcision was given by God to the Jews, not as a sign of divine favor, but as a mark of their future reprobation, so they might be recognized by those presently occupying the city and prevented from reentering it. Circumcision becomes a mark of Cain, ensuring the permanent exile and wandering of the Jews over the earth. (The fact that many other Near Eastern people also practice circumcision was momentarily ignored.)

Justin Martyr says:

> For the circumcision according to the flesh, which is from Abraham, was given for a sign, that you may be separated from other nations and from us, and that you alone may suffer that which you now justly suffer, and that your land may be desolate and your cities burned with fire, and that strangers may eat your fruit in your presence and not one of you may go up to Jerusalem.[54]

The *adversus Judaeos* tracts and sermons are remarkable for their relative lack of an appeal to the Jews for conversion. This note is more prominent in the dialogue writings which aim at giving proofs of the truth of the Church's christological exegesis and end in miraculous conversions of the Jewish disputants. The treatises do not deny that the Jews will be saved, if they repent and accept Jesus as the Christ. But the emphasis is on the proofs of the righteousness of the Church and the eternal reprobation of the Jews qua Jews. This indicates that the writings aim primarily at shoring up Christian self-understanding, rather than at dialogue with real Jews. Chrysostom's sermons are notable for their complete lack of any note of appeal to the Jews to be converted. His concern for the "fallen brethern" is solely for the Judaizers, i.e., Christians who participated in Jewish feasts and fasts. The Jews themselves appear as quasi-demonic figures, completely beyond either divine mercy or Chrysostom's evangelical concern. Augustine's treatise, on the other hand, follows closely Paul's position in Romans 9–11. Augustine appeals to the Jews to recognize that the Christians are the true spiritual Israel, the fruit of the scriptural promise. He concludes by calling them to repent and come into the Christian Church. But neither does Augustine, any more than Chrysostom, hold out any hope that the Jews have an ongoing vehicle of salvation *as Jews,* i.e., within Judaism. Only by becoming Christians, now or at the end of time, will they be saved. As Jews, they are reprobate throughout history until the final coming of Christ convicts them of their blindness. Here and now, Jewish misery is the testimony to the victory of Christ's Church and the wrath of God upon those who fail to believe in Christ. Augustine also includes the idea that Jewish dispersion functions as a witness to the Church, preparing pagans for Christianity through the Law and witnessing to that Christ whom their Scriptures predict. This more positive idea of Jewish witness is especially Augustinian and was to be the double-sided view of Jewish exile typical of the medieval Latin Church.[85]

As for the continued Jewish hope for a Messiah to deliver them from the exile, this was vain and perverse on their part. The Church Fathers often seem to assume that the Jews really know that Christ has already come. How could they fail to know, since their own Scriptures predict the events fulfilled by Jesus in precise detail? Thus Jewish claims to be unable to recognize Jesus as the Messiah expected by the Jewish people testify to their unwillingness to repent from their evil ways.[86] The book of Daniel is used to compute the exact time when the Messiah is to appear, and it is shown that this has already past.[87] Besides, there is no longer any chrism to anoint him, the priesthood having fallen; no longer any homeland in which he can be born, the Jews being in exile.[88] Clearly, the time predicted for the appearance of the Messiah must have been prior to the exile and the fall of the temple, while these disasters must be the result of the failure of the Jews to accept him. As for that Messiah for whom the Jews continue to hope, that is madness and perversity on their part. Several writers even suggest that the Messiah for whom the Jews hope is actually the Anti-Christ. This notion was also to be incorporated into the baptismal ritual for converted Jews in early medieval times.[89] The Jews, having killed Christ, are on the side of the demons whom Christ comes to defeat. The Messiah in whom they hope must be that Anti-Christ who Christ said would be falsely expected in the last days (Mark 13:22).[90] But the grapevine of Israel has already produced the messianic blessing. With his coming, "the grapecluster of blessing was taken from the branch, and the entire branch was given over to destruction" (Aph. *Dem.* 23, 20).

3. *The Inferiority and Spiritual Fulfillment of Jewish Law, Cult, and Scriptural Interpretation*

The Christian way of dealing with the Jewish Law and cult is to prove that the Jewish understanding of these things is unworthy and "carnal," while the Christian possesses the "spiritual" realization of that which the Jew clings to in a merely outward way. But, beyond this, there is also the characteristic assertion that the Law and the cult were intrinsically unworthy. They were given in a punitive way, rather than out of a redemptive purpose by God. They have now been relegated, both in form and content, to historical and moral obsolescence. Both of these arguments rest on the assertion that the Jews cannot interpret Scripture. The Jew sees only the letter, while the Christian discerns its true spiritual meaning. For those who ask why Christians do not keep the Jewish rites, the apologist Diognetus replies indignantly:

As for those who think they can offer Him sacrifices with blood and fat and holocausts . . . they differ in nothing, so it seems to me, from those who show the same devotion to deaf idols. . . . But now, as to certain ridiculous matters that call for no discussion—such as their scruples in regard to meat, their observance of the Sabbath days, their vain boasting about circumcision, and the hypocrisy connected with fasting and the feasts of the new moon—I don't suppose you need any instruction from me. For how can it be other than irreligious to accept some of the things God has created for men's use and to reject others, as though some were created for a good purpose and others were useless and superfluous? And how can it be other than profane to lie against God, pretending that He has forbidden us to do a good deed on the Sabbath day? And is it not ridiculous to boast of a mutilation of the flesh as a sign of a chosen people, as though on account of this they were particularly loved by God? Take again their constant watching of the stars and moon in order to make sure of the observance of months and days and to commemorate the dispensations of God and the changes of the seasons according to their own whims, making this season a time of feasting and that one a time of fasting. Who would look on all this as evidence of religion, and not, rather, as a sign of folly? And so, I hope I have said enough to show you how right the Christians are in keeping away from the plain silliness and error, the fussiness and vaunting of the Jews. [Diog. *Ep.* 3–4]

THE INFERIORITY OF THE LAW.   In the ·Fathers there is developed the notion of a pre-Mosaic religion which is the prehistory of Christianity, relegating Judaism to a Mosaic intermediate period. This idea has no counterpart in the New Testament, although an incorrect reading of Romans 2:14–15 might suggest such an early period when the Gentiles obeyed the Law "from the heart."[91] It appears to have been derived from a combination of Jewish haggadah on the virtues of the patriarchs and the Greek concept of a primordial era of virtue before the iron age of evil manners.

Eusebius especially develops this myth of the pre-Mosaic era when all men were virtuous naturally. The patriarchs were not Jews, but, like the Christians, a universal race, "neither Jew nor Greek." No idolatry or crime existed in this period. Virtue reigned, but without law, through the universal law of conscience inscribed on the heart. This is the "natural law" which coincides with universal morality. This religion alone is universal and spiritual, knowing no boundaries. Abraham, as the "father of many nations," could have intended to spread only this universal natural religion, which is suitable for everyone, and not Judaism, suitable only for the Jews. Needless to say, it is this universal, spiritual religion, written not on stones but on hearts (Jer. 31:31; cf. Heb. 8:8–12 and 2 Cor. 3:2–3), which has now been restored in its final fulfilled form by Christ. The universal spiritual Law of Christ, then, is not only a "new covenant," but a restoration of the original covenant and universal spiritual religion of patriarchal mankind before the Mosaic period.[92] This original, universal, spiritual religion is often identified with the Decalogue. The Ten Commandments represent the basic Law of God which persists through all changes, while the Law of Moses is a temporary law given only to the Jews.[93] This idea drew on the Jewish concept of the Noachian laws,[94] but in a way that makes this universal law superior and the Mosaic Law inferior. The temporality of the Mosaic Law is established by proving that circumcision and Sabbaths were not observed until the time of Moses and so could not have been necessary for righteousness. The Pauline idea that Abraham was justified by faith prior to circumcision shows that faith, not circumcision, redeems.[95] The Christians are the seed of the pre-circumcised, believing Abraham.

The Mosaic Law then assumes the status of an intermediate era, existing on a lower moral level than the spiritual, patriarchal faith restored by Christ. The Mosaic Law is not only morally inferior, but intended by God to be strictly limited in time (from Moses to Christ), in place (to be observed only in Palestine), and in use (to be observed only by the Jews). Moreover, its purpose was not redemptive but punitive. It was not given to lift the Jews up to a higher moral level than the Gentiles, but rather to restore them to that level of minimal humanity from the bestiality into which they had fallen in Egypt. It was given to restrain vice, not to inculcate virtue. It was a preparatory training for the Jews, who are morally worse than all other people, to prepare them for the "natural law" restored by Christ! (Here we see the complete reversal of the talmudic concept of the relationship between Torah and the Noachian laws.) It is not applicable to anyone else; it cannot redeem, and it has now been revoked by God, so the Jews are contumacious in continuing to observe it.

The laws given by Moses were intended to restrain all the vices into which the Jews had fallen in Egypt. God gave them food laws to restrain the inordinate gluttony which was their wont.[96] He gave them the cultic law to restrain their avidity for idolatry.[97] God actually hates cultic worship, but he allowed the Jews to have a legalized form of it to prevent them from running wild after the idols. In Chrysostom's colorful language:

And this is what God did. He saw the Jews raving mad, choking themselves in their lust for sacrifices, and ready if they didn't get them to desert to idolatry . . . or rather, not ready to do so, but already doing so. Then it was that he permitted the sacrifices. [Chry. *Or. C. Jud.* IV, 6]

The Fathers are a little confused about why God gave the Sabbath and circumcision. They quote prophetic texts, e.g., Isaiah 1:13, to show that God certainly doesn't like the Sabbath observance. Some authors hit on the idea that it was merely to give "natural rest,"[98] and anything "natural" can't be redemptive. Others suggest that it was to restrain the Jews' love for material gain.[99] Without the Sabbath, they would have been piling up wealth all the time. Others make a complete circle and declare that, since the Jews "pollute" the Sabbath, God gave it to them to reveal how they are polluting it.[100] Circumcision is purely national, given to the Jews to separate them from the surrounding peoples who practice idolatry.[101] But since all the world is now Christian, this is now unnecessary. Only a few of the Fathers repeat the novel idea that circumcision was also given punitively, as a mark of the future reprobation of the Jews.[102] But others suggest that it is certainly an indecent sort of mark, restraining sexual proclivities, in contrast to the chaste Christian sealing "on the forehead."[103] Besides, women can't be circumcized, which shows its inferiority to Christian baptism, which signs men and women alike.[104] All such laws apply only to people of inordinate appetite for vice, who need extra restraints, i.e., Jews. They are unnecessary for the righteous, i.e. patriarchs and Old Testament heroes . . . and Christians. The text from Ezekiel 20:25, "I gave them statutes that were not good and ordinances by which they could not have life," is cited to prove that the Mosaic Law is an evil law, given punitively and not expressive of the true will of God.[105]

THE SPIRITUAL FULFILLMENT OF THE LAW. The Christian argument against the Law included not only the idea that the Mosaic Law was abrogated, and so Christians do not have to observe it, but also that it was spiritually fulfilled. The Christians do not observe its outward form, but its true inward meaning. Christians, not Jews, are the true "Law keepers." They are the ones from whom God has removed the "hearts of stone" (outward observance) and given "hearts of flesh" (inward spiritual obedience). They possess that new Law of inward obedience of the prophetic promise of the "new covenant" (Jer. 31:31).[106] Christ is the "new Lawgiver like Moses," who gives a universal spiritual law "written on hearts."[107] Moses' upraised arms were a sign that God intended the Jews to be saved, not through the Law, but through the cross.[108] The true Law of God for all mankind goes forth, not from Sinai, but from Zion, as the prophets foretold.[109] The Jews, when the Law was given, never observed it anyway, because God ever rebuked them for their "lawlessness." Now that it is abrogated, they wrongheadedly continue to observe it, showing their lawlessness in a new way. Since it is impossible to fulfill the Law perfectly and to be saved under it, the Jews fall under the "curse" of the Law, which God pronounced against those who break it.[110] By observing it "out of season," they are also going against God's will.[111] So either in observing it or breaking it, they are lawless. The Christians, however, are those who have been redeemed from the curse of the Law. They have been relieved of its outward observances. But, having been given the inward obedience of the new covenant, they observe the real meaning of the Law inwardly. They are the spiritually lawful, while the Jews are lawless.

In this interpretation of the inward observance of what the Law merely "symbolized" outwardly, the Christians are dependent on the spiritualizing exegesis of Hellenistic Judaism. But the Christians interpret the relationship of outward form and inward meaning antithetically, while Philo interpreted it sacramentally. Thus Christian exegesis of the Law falls into the camp of those Allegorists whom Philo condemned for claiming to fulfill the spiritual meaning, while discarding the outward commandment. Christian exegesis, however, joined spiritualizing exegesis with messianic sectarian exegesis to make the relationship of outward letter and spiritual meaning supersessionary. The right to claim inward fulfillment, while discarding outward form, belongs to the messianic dispensation realized by the messianic Lawgiver, Christ.

The notion of spiritual fulfillment of the Law focused on a limited number of items. The prophetic commandment to "circumcize your hearts, not your flesh" is taken to mean that the real meaning of circumcision is repentance. The Christians, who are the repentant ones, are the truly circumcized—the "circumcized of heart," while the Jews, who are "puffed up" in their vain, fleshly claims about "carnal" circumcision, are "uncircumcized of heart."[112] For Augustine, circumcision means putting off the "old man" of unfaithfulness and carnality.[113] For John Damascene, circumcision is "cutting away all fleshly desires."[114] Lactantius adds the bright idea that the tip of the penis resembles a heart, and so the rite itself was intended by God to symbolize its inward meaning.[115] The ancients before Moses were righteous apart from circumcision, and it is unnecessary now. Indeed, those who continue to observe it, now that Christ's law of spiritual fulfillment is come, war against salvation. Isaac of Antioch repeats Paul's declaration that it would be better if such people went all the way and castrated themselves.[116] The stone knives of Joshua, by which God commanded him to circumcize the people of Israel a "second time," signify this second circumcision of Jesus (Joshua), which circumcizes the heart, not the flesh; "the Stone" being, of course, a name for Christ.[117]

Dietary laws are dealt with in a similar spiritualizing manner. These laws were given to the Jews to restrain their gluttonous ways. But, in keeping with their "carnal minds," they understand them only outwardly, as a taboo upon "unclean animals." But no animals can be "unclean," because all animals are a part of God's creation, and so are "very good." The very idea that some animals are unclean is an insult to the goodness of God's creation.[118] The real meaning of the laws is inward, not outward. The various animals forbidden symbolize various brutish and swinish ways. God intended us to avoid, not the animals, but the bestial ways, symbolized by the animals. Novatian contains the most detailed allegorization of the food laws, but the same idea appears in other writers.[119]

The Sabbath, likewise, has its real meaning spiritually. The Sabbath was not observed by the patriarchs and was not binding on the righteous even in Mosaic times. Joshua marching around Jericho for seven days, the priests who officiated in the temple on the Sabbath, and the Maccabees who fought on the Sabbath are cited to show the relativity of Sabbath observance.[120] The notion that one day should be set apart as a day "outside" the work of creation insults Creation. The seventh day is just as much a part of the world as any other day.[121] The real spiritual meaning of the Sabbath is the eschatological day beyond Creation. Sabbath signifies God's rest, that heavenly Kingdom into which Christ is leading us, as a new Joshua.[122] The Christian Sunday, which is the "eighth day," symbolizes this eschatological day beyond Creation, and not the Jewish Sabbath, which belongs within time.[123] God, in the Old Testament, stated that he cannot endure the Sabbath (Isa. 1:13), showing that God did not mean for us to observe the Sabbath, but rather its spiritual meaning. John Damascene, as an ascetic, can turn the argument around and declare that the Jews are niggardly in setting aside only one day a week to think about God. That God had to command such an observance shows how unwilling they were to lift their eyes up to spiritual things. The Christian (monk), however, sets aside not merely one day but all his time to contemplation of heavenly things. He lives his whole life "out of this world" in the eschatological day of the "new Creation." The Christian, not the Jew, possessed the real inward meaning of the Sabbath, while discarding its outward observance.[124]

This Christian spiritualization of the Law is notable for the meagerness of its actual knowledge of the Law. The Torah itself has shrunk to a few observances of the sort that any Gentile might be expected to know as distinguishing outward marks of the Jew. There is no evidence of any contact with the more developed halakic exegesis of the Rabbis. The Christian rejection of the Law assumed a simplified stereotypic form with the Pauline church of New Testament times. Thereafter there seems to have been little or no contact with the actual thinking of Jewish halakah or knowledge of the more developed halakah of the Rabbis.

THE INFERIORITY AND SPIRITUAL FULFILLMENT OF THE CULT. The arguments about the inferiority and spiritual supersession of the cultic law is similar in method. But here the argument gained an added edge because of the interpretation of the fall of the temple cultus as a sign of punishment for the crucifixion. Here, too, the prophetic passages, which rebuke cultic practices without obedience, are cited in such a way as to make it appear that God "always" rejected the cult: "I hate, I despise your feasts, and I take no delight in your solemn assemblies" (Amos 5:21); "What to me is the multitude of your sacrifices? says the Lord; I have enough of burnt offerings. . . . Incense is an abomination to me. I cannot endure your new moons and Sabbaths and assemblies" (Isa. 1:11–13); "Collect your flesh and your sacrifices and eat, for on the day that I brought them out of Egypt I did not command your fathers concerning burnt offerings and sacrifices" (Jer. 7:21f). God hates the sacrificial cult and allowed it only as a temporary antidote to worse idolatry. But it never expressed his true will. Moreover, all the cultic law was made strictly local, to show that it was intended to restrain the excessive proclivity to idolatry of the Jews and could not be spread by them to other peoples. This limitation in location shows that it was never suitable for a universal faith.

Moreover, now that the temple has fallen and the cult can no longer be observed, this localization is the definitive proof that God has abolished the legitimacy of Judaism. The legitimate cult of Judaism was limited strictly to the temple cult under the Aaronite priesthood. In continuing to observe the fasts and festivals outside Jerusalem (in their rabbinic adaptation to the synagogue), the Jews break God's Law. While claiming for itself spiritual supersession of the Law and cult, Christianity seeks to confine Judaism to Sadducean cultic literalism to illegitimize its ongoing existence.[125]

Chrysostom expresses this view of the cult, using his favorite image of God as a doctor who gives the Jews temporary medicine to cure their "fever" for idolatry:

God did the same [i.e., acted as a doctor]. After permitting them to offer sacrifices, He allowed them to do so nowhere else in the world except in Jerusalem. Then after they had offered sacrifices for a short time, He destroyed the city. Like a doctor who broke the dish, God intended by demolishing the city to lead the Jews away from the practice in spite of themselves. For if He has said plainly, "Keep off," they wouldn't have consented willingly to giving up their mania for sacrifices ... after God made the city a sort of keystone holding the whole Jewish worship together, when He overthrew the city, He destroyed the entire structure of their way of life. [Chry. *Or. C. Jud.* IV, 7 (881)]

True sacrifice to God is not the temple cult of bulls and rams, but the sacrifice of the contrite heart. True worship of God is the spiritual service of prayer predicted in Malachi 1:11:

From the rising of the sun to its setting my name is great among the nations, and in every place incense is offered to my name, and a pure offering.

As we have seen, rabbinic Judaism used a similar spiritualization to argue that the temple cultus could be legitimately replaced by the worship of the contrite heart, prayer, and deeds of loving-kindness.[126] But Christianity either ignored or tried to illegitimize this parallel universalism and spiritualization of worship in the synagogue. "Among the nations" was read as though it meant "by the nations," i.e., by the Gentiles, to argue that such universal spiritual worship could not be realized by Judaism, but must refer to a new cult promised by Christ, superseding the cult of the temple.[127] By interpreting Judaism as confined to the Aaronite cultic form of worship, Christian universal, spiritual worship was made antithetical and supersessionary to Jewish local, cultic worship. By destroying the cult, God brought legitimate Judaism to an end and made the Jews a wandering people without a legitimate vehicle of divine service. Universal, spiritual divine service can only be realized in the Church.

Other cultic symbols are also presented as spiritually fulfilled in Christianity. The true temple is not the temple "made with hands," but the spiritual temple of the Holy Spirit in the body of each believer. This concept is found in Paul and repeated in the Fathers.[128] Barnabas follows Hebrews' messianic interpretation of the Philonic tradition, making the cosmic sanctuary into the eschatological sanctuary of heaven.[129] The true temple was also identified with the risen Body of Christ, again a New Testament idea (John 2:19–21). Thence the true temple comes to be identified with the Church, the body of believers who represent the extension of the risen Body of Christ throughout the world.[130] Eusebius goes so far as to identify the New Jerusalem and restored temple of the messianic age with the Church of the Holy Sepulcher, built in Jerusalem in the fourth century by Constantine's mother, Helena. This idea is also found in the seventh-century *Dialogue of Gregentius and Herban,* showing that the Eusebian idea continued to be current.[131] Generally, however, the "true temple" is identified with what are seen as pneumatic realities and not with any new building in Christendom.

The idea that Christianity also has a new priesthood only emerges gradually in the Church, with the development of the Eucharist as a cultic rite. A few early writers follow Hebrews in seeing Christ as the priestly Logos mediating in the heavenly sanctuary, replacing the Aaronite priests who were "many in number." Melchizedek represents this priesthood of Christ, which is superior to Abraham's descendent Aaron, just as Abraham showed by asking for Melchizedek's blessing.[132] By the middle of the fourth century, it becomes common to talk of a

Christian priesthood, which represents this Melchizedekian priesthood of Christ. The Eucharist is identified with the spiritual worship of bread and wine offered by Melchizedek. The Eucharist also comes to be seen as the specific meaning of that spiritual worship promised by Malachi (1:11). Chrysostom especially dwells on this idea of the Christian priesthood replacing that of Aaron:

"If perfection had been attainable through the Levitical priesthood . . . what further need would there have been for another priest to arise after the order of Melchizedek?" (Heb. 7:11), rather than the one after Aaron. It is clear from this that the former priesthood had come to an end and a different one, very much better and more sublime, had been introduced in its place. [Chry. *Or. C. Jud.* 7, 5]

Various writers follow the mistranslation of Psalm 40:6: "Sacrifices and offerings thou hast not desired, but a body hast thou prepared for me; in burnt offerings and sin offerings thou hast taken no pleasure" (Heb. 10:5f.), to prove that God has abolished the Jewish temple cult in favor of a new cult of the Body of Christ.[133]

Similarly it is said that the Jewish Passover is only a sign pointing to the true Paschal Lamb, Christ. Now that the true meaning of Passover has been established in the Church, the Jews have no further right to celebrate Passover. According to their own cultic Law, the Passover lamb could only be sacrificed in Jerusalem. Now that they are exiled from the city, this is a sure indication that God has abolished the outward sign of the Jewish Passover for its inward meaning, the Christian Pasch. The Jews celebrate Passover in the Diaspora illegitimately. Some patristic writers allegorize the Passover in other ways, speaking of the unleavened bread as a symbol of sincerity, etc.[134] But these allegorical midrashim are crowded out by the much more impressive understanding of the Passover as fulfilled in the central Christian mystery of the death and resurrection of Christ.[135]

The Christian use of Philonic allegorical interpretation of the Torah and the cult, then, contained in itself a growing contradiction. Originally, Philo understood the allegorical meaning, not as antithetical to the outward commandment, but as the inward meaning of the commandment. When Christianity fused the Philonic dualism of letter and spirit with the messianic dualism of the historical age and the messianic age, this made the relationship of letter and spirit antithetical and supersessionary. This was originally done in a mood of expectation of imminent eschatological crisis. But when the contrast between the "two eras" is no longer that between the historical age and the eschatological age, but becomes a contrast between two historical eras, the Mosaic era and the Christian era, then Christian spiritualizing interpretation is identified with what is, actually, simply a new set of disciplinary and cultic practices. Fasting and abstinence from meat becomes a new Christian dietary law. Sunday becomes the new Christian Sabbath. Baptism becomes the new Christian sign of election. Eucharist becomes the new Christian cult. The Church begins to develop a new priesthood to serve this cult. The Church is the new temple, and Easter the new Passover. But one interprets these things as though they were purely pneumatic realities, to be contrasted with Jewish "outwardness." This means that Christianity is blind to its own outwardness and "bodiliness." The critical principle, represented by Philonic allegory and prophetic denunciations of hypocritical ritual, is alienated and projected as a "Jewish sin." Judaism becomes all that is merely outward, forgetting that the standards for this view of authenticity were originally that of Jewish self-criticism. This self-criticism only made sense when taken together with the outward commandments. Christian practices are seen as purely spiritual, as eschatological realizations. Alienating the critical principle as "Jewish sin," one loses this critical principle for criticizing the gap between outwardness and inwardness in the Church. Christian spiritualization becomes false consciousness about its own reality, fantasizing its own perfection and unable to cope with its own hypocrisy.

CHRISTOLOGICAL FULFILLMENT OF THE SCRIPTURES. The christological interpretation of the Old Testament is basic to the *adversus Judaeos* tradition and Christian theology generally. Much of the anti-Judaic writings concern themselves with the demonstration of the christological meaning of the Old Testament against the Jews. The manifestations of God are said to be actually revelations of the Father through the Son, or the Logos. The plural in the Genesis creation story ("Let us make man in our image," Gen. 1:26), the three men who appear to Abraham (Gen. 18:2), and other passages are said to be revelations of the Trinity.[136] Not only the general promise of Jesus as the Messiah, but every detail of his life, passion, death, resurrection are said to be revealed explicitly in the Old Testament.[137] There has been no attempt to treat this christological side of the anti-Judaic tradition in this study. However, the christological method of interpretation also implied a polemic against the ability of the Jews to interpret their own Scriptures, and this element is pertinent to the present study.

The Jews are said to be incapable of understanding or interpreting their own Scriptures or even finding God in them. The Jews are "blind," "hard of heart," and a "veil lies over their eyes." All this prevents them from seeing the inner meaning of the text, i.e., its christological meaning. But Jewish blindness is also a function of Jewish "literalism." Jews are "carnal men," as distinct from the Christian "spiritual men." The christological meaning is presumed to be the spiritual, or inward, meaning. The Jews see things only from the outside and are incapable of discerning the spiritual meaning. Lacking such spirituality in themselves, naturally they are unable to see the spiritual meaning of Scripture, i.e., its christological meaning.[138] The general line of thinking here follows the Pauline doctrine of Jewish blindness, the Johannine doctrine of Jewish carnality and even demonism, and the Matthean view of Jewish hypocrisy. Irenaeus follows John in saying:

Therefore the Jews departed from God, in not receiving his Word, but imagining that they could know the Father apart by Himself, without the Word, that is, without the Son; they being ignorant of that God who spake in human shape to Abraham and again to Moses. . . . For the Son who is the Word of God arranged these things beforehand from the beginning. [Iren. *Haer.* IV, vii, 4]

Christ is the incarnation of God's Word. It is through the Word that the world was created, all the Scriptures revealed, and God's creation providentially directed. It follows, then, that the Jews, in not receiving Christ, do not and never have received God's Word, and have never known God through their Scriptures, since these Scriptures are revealed through God's Word. In John's imagery, "Only through Christ do we come to the Father."

It is presumed that with the coming of Christ the prophetical gifts were transferred to the Christians.[139] The Holy Spirit now resides with the Church and is lost to the Jewish people. This somewhat contradicts the theological dictum that the Jews could never read the Scripture spiritually, not receiving it through the Word. But total consistency is not expected in such polemics. Several of the Church Fathers also preserve the theme, found in the Gospels, that the Jews can't read Scripture because they believe their "teachers." They depart from Moses in favor of "their traditions."[140] This fundamentalist argument assumes that Moses' teachings are good, and the Jews have erred by preferring "human tradition," i.e., the exegesis of the scribes and teachers, to the direct word of Scripture. This thesis cannot be brought into harmony with the anti-Mosaic and anti-Torah aspect of the Christian position. It is preserved in the Church Fathers primarily as a remnant of a buried stage of controversy between Jesus and the early Church and the Jewish teachers. It does not suggest any fresh contact with rabbinical teachings on the part of the Fathers. The Christian hermeneutic, however, remains implicitly anti-talmudic and was to make this explicit in its historical dealings with Judaism. Just as the Jews have no right to adapt the cult to the synagogue, so the ongoing hermeneutic that allowed the Jews to leap the disaster of the Jewish Wars and survive in the Diaspora is regarded as illegitimate by Christianity. Talmudic teaching is regarded as that "veil" over the Scripture that induces blindness and leads the Jews down the wrong path. If the teachings could be stripped off of the plain word of Scripture, Christian exegetes assume that its christological meaning would become evident and indisputable.

In Paul and Hebrews, the clash between the two eras is still primarily a clash between the historical era of finite man and the eschatological era of redeemed man, in a framework of expectation of the imminent end of the world. When the eschatological era is historicized as the Christian era, one then comes to draw a line across history at the time of the birth of Jesus that is treated as though it coincided with the transition from "sin" to "grace," from the old man of finitude to the new man of redemption, from outwardness, carnality, and unfaith to inwardness, spirituality, and the age of faith. The Jews receive the negative side of all these dualisms. The Jews are the men of the letter, against the Christian understanding of the spiritual meaning. The Jews are the carnal men, confined to a bodily level of existence, against Christians, who live on a higher plane, morally and ontologically. The Jews are the blind, against Christians, who see and believe. But this negative side is also treated as a temporal sequence from one to another, so everything Jewish also becomes obsolete and has no further right to exist now that the spiritual meaning has come. The outward form predicts and anticipates the inward meaning and becomes obsolete when the spiritual meaning has arrived. Augustine is most rigorous in his treatment of the Jews as the carnal men, who belong on a lower plane of moral existence and have become obsolete, now that spiritual fulfillment in Christ has come. Augustine is careful to avoid any purely racial interpretation of these dualisms. This judgment does not apply to Jews who believe in Christ. It applies to Judaism and to Jews, in the sense of those who cling to the way of Moses and do not accept the Christian interpretation. Those who accept the Christian exegesis belong to the spiritual Zion; while those who do not, belong to that earthly Jerusalem that is in bondage to "material things":

When the Jews hear these words, they take them in their natural meaning and imagine an earthly Jerusalem which is in slavery with her children, and not our eternal mother who is in heaven. [Aug. *Adv. Jud.* 5 (6)]

The Jews and their rites are said to "have remained stationary in useless antiquity" (Aug. *Adv. Jud.* 6 (8)). They belong to the Israel "after the flesh," in contrast to the Christian spiritual Israel. When the Jews refuse to acknowledge the Christian exegesis, they prove themselves to be the fleshly Israel which can only know things after the flesh:

The Israel, however, about which the Apostle says: Behold Israel according to the flesh (1 Cor. 10:18), we know to be the natural Israel; but the Jews do not grasp this meaning and as a result they prove themselves indisputably natural. [Aug. *Adv. Jud.* 7 (9)]

Everything in Judaism becomes "Old Testament" in relation to the Christian "New Testament." The relationship between the two testaments becomes a triple supersession: a supersession ontologically, morally, and historically. Everything Jewish is, at best, an outward "shadow," which symbolizes on a bodily level the spiritual meaning realized in the Christian dispensation.

However, this spiritualizing direction of the Christian antithesis between the old and the new is implicitly contradicted by its incarnational direction. If the Jewish dispensation is the "carnal" as contrasted with its spiritual meaning, it is also the "shadow" which is fulfilled by the coming of the spiritual realization "in the flesh." The Jews are carnal, but somehow they are also *insubstantial*—merely outward shadows of the good things to come. Here is Chrysostom's rendering of this idea in Hebrews (10:1):

"For since the Law has but a shadow of the good things to come instead of the true form of these realities, it can never, by the same sacrifices offered year after year, make perfect those who draw near. Consequently when Christ came into the world, He said, sacrifices and offerings Thou hast not desired, but a *body* hast Thou prepared for me," calling the Incarnation the entrance of the Only Begotten into the world, since it was through the Incarnation that Christ came to be with us, not exchanging one location for another (for how could He who is everywhere and fills everything?), but by being manifested to us through flesh. [Chry. *Or. C. Jud.* VII, 3; *PG* 48 919–20]

This unresolved fusion of spiritualizing and incarnational fulfillment means that what becomes bodily and historical in Christianity is treated as though it were pneumatic and eschatological. The Christian alienation of the critical principle, and the projection of its negative side as the identity of the Jews, also has the effect of losing that critical principle in the Church. The Church deals with its own "body" as though it were the eschatological Body of Christ and becomes unable to criticize the gap between outwardness and inwardness, finitude and spirituality in its own identity. In this one-sided appropriation of the redeemed side of all the basic dialectics of human existence, the theological basis is laid for ecclesial infallibilism.

4. *Theological Polemics and Judaeo-Christian Relations in Patristic Times*

THE INTERACTION OF JUDAISM WITH THE CHRISTIAN POLEMIC. The rabbinic response to the Christian polemic is a subject of which no thorough exploration exists. The Rabbis wrote no *adversus Christianos* tracts that have been preserved, although pagan controversalists were aware of popular Jewish works refuting Christianity.[141] It is difficult to ferret out material intended to refute Christianity in the Talmud, because the Rabbis refer to it allusively and indirectly, using the word *min* (heretic). It is only by study of the context of each statement that an informed guess can be made about what material is directed against Christianity and what against other heresies. The Rabbis saw all Christianity as forms of heresy, so where the Christian scholar would distinguish attacks on Christianity from attacks on Christian Gnosticism, Jewish-Christianity, etc., the Rabbis would attack all of these as *minim*. Hence the rabbinic attack on the *minim* probably include many kinds of Christianity today unknown to us. A detailed discussion of this topic is beyond the scope of this study or the competence of this author. However, a few general remarks will be given here to set the Christian polemic in its context in Jewish-Christian relations in patristic times.

Neither Judaism nor Christianity ever confronted the substance of the other's arguments. Each operated within presuppositions which were mutually exclusive. So no real dialogue was possible. The Rabbis did not discuss the Christian exegesis of particular texts in any detail, because the assumptions of this exegesis were, for them, impossible. The Christian polemicists did little to familiarize themselves with the authentic mind of rabbinic Judaism. With few exceptions, most had not really studied rabbinic exegesis.[142] The Jew in the dialogue represents what the Christians thought Jews would say rather than representing an authentic dialogue where the Jew is allowed to give his own argument in his own terms.[143] Nevertheless, this should not lead us to suppose that the disputes were not real and that Christians were not in fact replying to a real polemic that was taking place between the two faiths.

Yet despite the fact that the Rabbis responded to Christianity only in hints in the material that has been preserved, there is evidence that the Rabbis were very aware of the threat of Christianity and concerned to refute it and to teach their people to refute it, especially in the period surrounding the Jewish Wars (70–150 C.E.), when Christianity still appeared as an internal Jewish movement attempting to proselytize the synagogue directly. It was at this time that the "curse" against the *minim* was handed down to prevent any Christian from taking over the synagogue and making Christian exegesis normative in it.[144] This was a period of perhaps the most catastrophic events in Jewish history until the Nazi era, a time when the very survival of Judaism appeared to be at stake. In addition to the terrible losses suffered in the rebellion, Jews in Diaspora experienced massacres and persecution. The spread of a sect at this moment announcing that God had rejected the Jewish people appeared to the Rabbis to be as profound a threat internally as their social reverses were externally. The Rabbis mobilized all their energies to exclude the Christian exegesis from the synagogues and to center Jewish life around the Torah. It was in this period that the basic estrangement of Judaism and Christianity took place and when it is possible to speak of Judaism as "persecuting" Christians. Christian preachers were flogged for attempting to proselytize the synagogues. Jewish authorities were also anxious to demonstrate to the Roman authorities that Christianity was not a legitimate form of Judaism that should enjoy the status of a *religio licita* with Judaism. In this way, they were seen by Christians as aiding in the persecution of the martyrs by Roman authorities. There is no evidence that the death sentence against Christians was ever actually passed by Jewish courts, however.[145]

On the Jewish side, this period of active struggle changed when Christianity became gentile. Jewish authorities could only exercise discipline against Jewish Christians who continued to attend and to try to proselytize the synagogue. But there is reason to think that Jewish spokesmen continued to actively dispute with Christians into the fifth century and that the term *minim* came to be used not just for Jewish Christians, but for Christianity as a whole.[146] Judaism responded to Christianity by strongly consolidating itself around its rabbinic leadership and reaffirming its basic self-understanding. The idea that the Gentiles were elected, while Israel was rejected, was not even discussable as far as the Rabbis were concerned. But the Rabbis were sensitive to the argument that the fall of the temple was a sign of God's wrath, for they also interpreted this as a punishment for sin. But for them it was not a punishment for not accepting Jesus, but for not being obedient to God's commandments. The remedy for this was Torah-obedience. The Rabbis strongly reaffirmed the continued election of Israel and spoke in moving terms about the love relationship linking God and Israel. This election of Israel does not exclude the salvation of the Gentiles, for the two are coordinate, not mutually exclusive, ideas in rabbinic thought.[147] The prophecy of Malachi 1:11 is fulfilled in the fact that in all parts of the world the Torah is studied in the dispersed Jewish community.[148] The ingathering of Gentiles is found in proselytes to Judaism, not in Christians.[149] God's Holy Presence goes with Israel into the Exile.[150] God's wrath is a healing wrath that carries its own remedy, not a rejection. The covenant between God and Israel is permanent and irrevocable, for God is like a passionate lover who must ever seek his beloved Israel. God's election of Israel is based, moreover, on Israel's response to God. God chose Israel because she, of all the nations, accepted the Torah, while the other nations rejected it.[151] If Israel has not yet attained full fidelity, the way to that fidelity is marked out by God's gift to Israel in the Torah. God's promise, once given, can never be revoked. God and Israel are like father and son or like lovers who must ever seek each other out and can never be finally separated.[152]

As for Christians, they are, in the rabbinic view, apostates and idolators.[153] They are apostates in deserting God's appointed way of salvation in Torah. They are idolators in adding to the name of God the name of a man. They are worse than the *goyim,* who are ignorant of God. For they have known God, but have false ideas about him (*Shabbat* 13:5). The Rabbis answer Christian exegesis particularly on the question of divine sonship. God has no son, and the Messiah will be a human being, not a divinity. Psalm 110 refers to Abraham, and not to a divine person. Melchizedek, indeed, lost his priesthood to Abraham precisely because he committed the sin of putting the name of a man before that of God.[154] There can be no concept of a "second god" associated with the one God of Israel. Any disruption of the unity of God, any placing of a man beside the Name of God is that idolatry which automatically cuts the one holding such views out of the Book of Life. The various passages which Christians used to prove the Trinity in the Old Testament refer either to angels, with whom God associated himself in creation and revelation, or to the great angel Metatron.[155] The Messiah will indeed come and restore Israel to the land. Then the temple will be rebuilt, the priesthood and temple cultus restored, the Gentiles flow in to worship God at Zion. But there is no possibility of claiming that he has already come when this redemption has not occurred.

As for Jesus, the Rabbis' ignorance of him is complete. They assume him to have been an evil man, a law breaker. Like Balaam, he was a magician who led many Israelites astray. The fact that he was crucified proves him to have been a criminal and no savior. The Christian claim that he was born of a virgin was received scoffingly by the Jewish community, who punned on the similarity between the words *virgin* and *prostitute* in Greek (*ek parthenou, ek porneias*) and referred to him as the son of a prostitute and a Roman centurion, Pantera. In rabbinic opinion it was better for a Jew to die than to be cured in the name of "Joshua ben Pantera."[156] This jibe seems to have circulated internally in the Jewish community, but was unknown to the patristic polemicists, however. The success of Christianity, far from being a proof of God's favor, is an expression of that messianic woe whereby the whole world is to be delivered over into heresy in that time of troubles before the coming of the Messiah. Jewish exile under the pagan state, Edom, is itself seen as an expression of this premessianic time of troubles. This judgment on the empire was to be transferred to the Christian state after Constantine.[157]

The Rabbis also affirmed the Torah, together with all the *halakoth, midrashim,* and *haggadoth,* as essential for salvation. They made haste to close the gaps which Christianity sought to open between the patriarchs and Moses, between Moses and the oral Law, and finally between Jews and the gentile convert. The gentile convert must show his goodwill by being able to accept the whole Law. If so, he is as dear to God, perhaps dearer to God, than the born Jew.[158] This allows the synagogue to distinguish between the gentile convert and the Christian. The oral Law is no recent addition, but was all revealed on Sinai together with the written Torah. The worship of the golden calf was a sin, but no unforgivable apostasy. Indeed, when Moses broke the first tablets of laws, God comforted him by giving him a second and far better Law, to which the whole oral Law had been added. The giving of the ritual Law, following this fall, was no punishment, but indeed the proof that God had forgiven his people.[159] The patriarchs, too, are not to be distinguished from the Mosaic obedience, for they too obeyed the Law before it was given. Some Rabbis even claimed that Abraham observed the most minute regulations. It is suggested that the patriarchs were born circumcized.[160] When a *min* inquires as to why God didn't create all men circumcized if it was necessary for salvation, the Rabbis replied that creation is imperfect and can do with some improving.[161] Thus, although the Rabbis seldom directly reply to Christian tenets or specific exegesis, the Talmud contains a wide-ranging refutation of the structure of the *adversus Judaeos* tradition, which takes the form, less of direct argument with Christians, than of defensive affirmation of the Jewish point of view. In a sense, the whole Talmud is a refutation of the anti-Judaic exegesis and a rigorous response of Judaism to the catastrophies that threatened to overwhelm the religious community-identity of the Jewish people.

After the second century, this period of active attack on Christianity in rabbinic Haggadah seems to disappear.[162] Christianity comes to be seen as a separately organized community outside of Judaism. The situation remained different in Iran, where both Christianity and Judaism remained minority faiths under the Zoroastrian empire, and alternatively suffered persecution. Here, the Christian community continued to be drawn from Jewish converts. Persian Christianity remained much more Jewish in spirit, and the Church and the Rabbis were rivals for the allegiance of the untutored Jewish population.[163] When Christianity became the religion of the Greco-Roman Empire, moreover, Christians in Persia were viewed as partisans and potential traitors to the West, while Jews in the Christian empire were viewed as potential traitors to Persia. Many of the arguments over the Law, which were settled in the Western churches by the second century, were still live issues in the Persian church in the fourth century.

JUDAIZING AND ANTI-JUDAISM: THE SERMONS OF JOHN CHRYSOSTOM. In the Christian Roman Empire of the fourth century, a new development in the relationship of Christians to the synagogue took place. The Christian "Judaizer" was of a different character than the militant Jewish Christian convert who sought to proselytize the synagogue in the earlier period. The Judaizing Christian was a Christian, not necessarily of Jewish background, who was attracted to Jewish rites and traditions, while remaining within the mainstream Church, which now had become the official imperial religion. The Judaizing Christians came to the synagogue, not to convert it, but because they saw it as the roots of their own Christian practices. This Judaizing Christianity is to be distinguished from "Jewish Christians," such as the Ebionites, who existed as a separately organized sect. The Judaizing Christians arose as a popular movement within the Catholic Church, especially in those areas where there was a visible Jewish population alongside the Christian one, such as in Antioch, and among Oriental Christians close in language and culture to the Jews. Such Judaizing Christians practiced circumcision as well as baptism, followed dietary laws and rites of purification, observed the Sabbath as well as Sunday, and participated in Jewish fasts and feasts, such as New Year, the feast of Tabernacles, and the fast of Yom Kippur. They continued to date Easter by the Jewish calculations of Passover and celebrated the Pasch on 15 Nisan, regardless of the day of the week on which it fell. They also associated with the synagogue in other ways. They appealed to the Rabbis as charismatics who were regarded as gifted exorcists and healers. Since many Christians attended only the liturgy of the Word in the Church, it was easy to substitute the similar service of the synagogue on occasion for regular worship. The clapping and good fellowship of the synagogue appears to have contrasted favorably with growing pomp and long rhetorical sermons of the Church. Some of this Judaizing movement had a superstitious element to it, such as the amulets worn especially by the women.[164] But it is evident that the movement as a whole was not superstitious, but rather a sincere, if eclectic, emotional attraction which continued the identification of Christian traditions with their Jewish foundations. Officially, the Rabbis disapproved of such assimilation without full commitment. But, in practice, the synagogue tolerated the Judaizing Christians as "semiproselytes," much as they had previously tolerated the "God-fearing pagan," as a "stranger within the gates."[165]

The history of the Church's response to Judaizing is one of continued effort to separate Christian from Jewish practices, but with a tradition that stubbornly continued to remind the Christian of his Jewish roots. Paul himself was of two minds on this, tolerating Jewish practices for Christians recruited from the Jews, but fanatical in his insistence that any effort to impose this as normative for Gentiles is a legalism that cancels salvation in Christ. By the second century, this latter position, for all Christians regardless of background, became the standard position of the Western Church Fathers. In a famous correspondence between Jerome and Augustine in the late fourth century, the question of the validity of Jewish Christianity in apostolic times and their own times is discussed. Augustine takes the position that, because of their cultural background, this was legitimate in Paul's time for those of Jewish background crossing over to the "Israel after the spirit." Jerome believes such practices always were apostasy and denies that Paul was really ever a "Jew to the Jews." But both agree that the continued observance of the Law by Christians now is inadmissible. To combine

Jewish practices, such as the Sabbath, dietary laws, or circumcision, with Christianity now is to deny that salvation comes through Christ *alone*.[166]

The problem of separating Christian from Jewish practices proved difficult, however, especially among Oriental Christians. The cultural ties to circumcision, the Sabbath, and Passover were deep and not easily rooted out. The Church early transferred its holy day to Sunday and correspondingly tried to "secularize" the Sabbath in its hermeneutics. The interpretation of Easter as Passover itself represents a Judaizing accommodation to the continued observance of this Great Feast, but it attempted to reinterpret it completely. The first day of Passover, 15 Nisan, a day of joyous celebration for the Jews, became a Christian day of mourning for the crucifixion of Jesus by the Jews. Jews and Christians changed their fast days so they would not coincide. The Jews fasted on Monday and Thursday, the Church on Wednesday and Friday. This meant that the joyous Jewish Sabbath evening service became a weekly Christian day of fasting and mourning, again commemorating the crucifixion by the Jews. Thus, the Christian fasts and feasts themselves were constructed as anti-Judaic commemorations. The greatest days of Jewish joy became the darkest days of Christian anti-Jewish memories. But even these changes did not sufficiently sever the Christian from the Jewish rites on the popular level, and some Christians continued to observe both in tandem. With the Council of Nicaea, the Church officially declared that Easter is never to be observed in the same week as Passover. The Church is to calculate the season differently from the Jews, accusing the Jews of departing from the ancient customs. But large sections of the Oriental Church refused to go along with these rulings. Easter continued to be observed as the Sunday within the octave of 15 Nisan or, by the rigorous, on the day of 15 Nisan. Others simply observed both the Orthodox Easter and also Passover. The controversy continued through the end of the fourth century and full unity around the new Orthodox dating was not secured in the Greek Church until the eighth century.[167]

The city of Antioch had long had a large and prosperous Jewish community, and it was here that the followers of the Nazarene were first called "Christians." Even in apostolic times, the Church at Antioch seems to have been divided into a Judaizing group, that was gathered from Jewish and Jewish proselyte background and who continued Jewish practices and rabbinic exegesis, and a Gnosticizing group that declared a radical separation between the God of Israel and the Christian Savior (such as the disciples of Saterninus and Cerdo the Syrian). The Jewish community itself was Hellenized and continued to attract its own proselytes and semiproselytes. It was in this atmosphere that Judaizing Christians in Antioch of the later fourth century found an open door in the synagogue to support their continued attachment to those practices which had now been declared heresy by the Great Church.[168] This group continued to be members of the Catholic Church (it being illegal to be a Christian sectarian by this time!), but eclectically combined this with the practices, fasts, and feasts of the synagogue. It was against this group that John Chrysostom railed in his eight sermons preached in Antioch in 386–87 C.E. (Chry. *Or. C. Jud.*). Three of these sermons were preached in the fall of 386, two before the great New Year's Day of the Trumpets, the Day of Atonement, Yom Kippur, and the Feast of Tabernacles (Ors. I and II); and a third after the Jewish rites were over (Or. VIII). One sermon was preached in the spring of 387 at the time of the Jewish Passover (March 31) against Judaizers who were observing Easter and Passover together (Or. III). Three more were preached before New Year's Day, Yom Kippur, and Tabernacles the following fall (Ors. IV–VI), and one after these observances were over (Or. VII).

The sermons of John Chrysostom are easily the most violent and tasteless of the anti-Judaic literature of the period we have studied. But they differ from the *adversus Judaeos* writings generally only in the frenzied quality of the rhetorical tone and the immediacy of the Jewish community which is attacked. In basic doctrines, John Chrysostom is at one with the dominant trends of the Church's anti-Judaic hermeneutic. The hermeneutical method, the basic concepts that have been traced in these other writings, are the same as that used by Chrysostom, whose sermons are a veritable pastiche of Old Testament quotations used anti-Judaically. The difference between the treatise of Augustine and the sermons of John Chrysostom does not lie in any difference of basic doctrines about the status of the Jews, but in the fact that Augustine writes in the detachment of his study with no Jewish threat in sight, while Chrysostom speaks in the heat of battle. What Chrysostom's sermons bring into unmistakable clarity is the contemporary reference of the anti-Judaic doctrines. The doctrine of the reprobation of the Jews here appears, not as the condemnation of Jews of past times, but as the way of viewing contemporary Jews. Again, this is true of the other anti-Judaic writings as well. In Chrysostom, however, its direct use as the way the Christian is actually to view the Jew across the street is uppermost.

Chrysostom's basic theme is the complete illegitimacy of the synagogue as an ongoing vehicle of relationship to God. With the abrogation of the Law and the fall of the temple, Judaism as a divinely founded pipeline of divine grace is over. For the Jews to continue to observe the Law, now that it has been abrogated, is "lawless," paralleling the lawlessness of the ancient Jews who broke the Law when God wanted them to observe it:

I say "lawlessness" because these things are practiced when they are no longer appropriate. There was a time when it was necessary to observe them, but that time is now passed. Hence what was lawful once is unlawful now. . . . I wish to assail the Jews directly, so let me give them a big lesson and show how the Jews, by continuing to fast at the present day, are dishonoring the Law and trampling on God's ordinances, always doing everything opposite to what God approves. When He wanted them to fast, they anointed themselves and grew fat. Now when He wants them not to fast, just to be different, they fast! When He wanted them to offer sacrifices, they ran off to idols. And now when He doesn't want them to celebrate Festivals anymore, they are eager to hold them. This is why Stephen told them, "You always resist the Holy Spirit." For this one thing alone, said he, have you shown any enthusiasm, for doing the opposite of anything God requires—exactly as they are doing now. [Chry. *Or. C. Jud.* IV, 4; *PG* 48, 876]

It is illegal to sacrifice the Paschal lamb anyplace but in Jerusalem. Now that the temple is destroyed, the old festival of Passover has been terminated and replaced by the Christian Pasch. Illegally do the Jews continue to celebrate it in their synagogues. Still more insane are the Christians who imitate their lawless practices:

Unleavened Bread does not pertain to the Jews anymore. And neither does the paschal festival. But to see that Unleavened Bread does not pertain to the Jews anymore, listen to the Lawgiver: "You shall not be at liberty to keep the Passover in any ordinary city which the Lord your God gives to you, but only in the place in which His name shall be invoked" (Deut. 16:5–6), meaning, of course, Jerusalem. Do you see how God first restricted the feast to one certain city, and then later destroyed that very city in order to lead them. even against their will, away from that way of life? [Chry. *Or. C. Jud.* III, 3; *PG* 48, 865–66]

The Jewish priesthood has been brought to an end with the temple. The Jews now have no lawful ministry. The present leaders of the Jews are no better than hucksters, with no valid ordination:

Where are your sacred things now? Where is your High Priest? Where are his robe, and the oracular breastplate, and the Urim? Don't talk to me about those "Patriarchs" of yours, those hucksters and traders, men full of wickedness. What sort of priest can there be, pray tell, when that ancient unction is no more, nor any other ritual? What sort of priest can there be. I ask, where there is no sacrifice, or altar, or service of worship? . . . These men called patriarchs among the Jews nowadays are not priests but only pretend to be such and play as if they were in the tabernacle. . . . When Scripture says Aaron was ordained with these things, sanctified, and with them made atonement to God, and yet none of them occur anymore among you, neither sacrifice, or burnt offering, or sprinkling of blood, or anointing with oil, or tent of testimony, or designated number of days to stay inside, it is quite clear that the Jewish priest today is unordained and impure and polluted and profane and that he is a provocation to God. For if he cannot be ordained otherwise than by these means, it follows inevitably, when they are absent, that no priesthood exists among the Jews. [Chry. *Or. C. Jud.* VI, 5–6; *PG* 48, 911, 912]

The Jewish temple has fallen, never to be rebuilt, despite three impious efforts by the Jews to defy God's clearly stated will on this matter.[169] The synagogue is no substitute for the temple, and, indeed, to go there to celebrate the ancient festivals is no better than to visit a brothel, a robber's den, or any other indecent place. Christ himself will judge those who fraternize with his murderers:

This is what you ought to fear lest on that Day you hear the One who is to judge you say, "Get away. I do not know you. For you fellowshipped with those who crucified Me, and contending with Me, you revived festivals which I had terminated. You ran to the synagogues of the Jews, who sinned against Me. And whereas I destroyed the temple and turned that sacred edifice and its awesome contents into a ruin, you reverenced buildings which are no better than taverns or robber's dens". . . . For if their place of worship was a den of robbers in those days, when what pertains to their way of life still prevailed, if a person should call it a brothel today, or a criminals' hangout, or a resort of demons, or a citadel of the Devil, or the ruin of souls, or a cliff and a pit of complete destruction, or any other name whatever, he would speak more kindly than the place deserves. [Chry. *Or. C. Jud.* VI, 7; *PG* 48, 915]

Wrongly do the Judaizers protest that the place is hallowed because it contains the Word of God, for the Word of God hallows only that place where its true meaning is understood and taught. The Jews, who are blind to the true meaning of Scripture, no more hallow their illegal synagogues by keeping the Scriptures there than places of pagan demon worship were hallowed when the Ark of the Covenant was captured by the Philistines or when the Septuagint was deposited in the Serapeum by Ptolemy Philadelphus:

Tell me, if you saw some famous man, respected and distinguished, being taken off to a tavern or a criminals' hangout and insulted there, beaten, and made to undergo fierce drunken behavior, would you honor that place because a great and illustrious man had stood there and been abused? I doubt it. Wouldn't you rather hate and shun it all the more for this very reason? Apply this to the synagogue. The Jews took both Moses and the prophets in there, not to honor them, but to outrage and dishonor them. When they say that these holy men neither knew Christ nor anything about His Advent, how much worse could they insult them? For when they accuse them of not recognizing their Lord, they make them partners in their own iniquity. The Jews act so offensively against these holy men that we must hate them and their synagogue all the more. [Chry. *Or. C. Jud.* I, 5; *PG* 48, 850][170]

As for the present feasts and fasts of the Jews, they are completely illegitimate and impious:

Nowadays everything among the Jews is a game, and a sport and a disgrace and a piece of huckstering, replete with inordinate wickedness. [Chry. *Or. C. Jud.* VI, 6; *PG* 48, 913]

In vain do the Judaizers appeal to the holiness of fast days, for God regards not the deed, but the intention. Murder is good, if God commands it. But fasting is evil and no better than a drunken orgy, if God has commanded that its observance be terminated:

If you see [a man] fasting against God's will, then despise and hate him more than if he were a drunken and carousing sot. . . . Oh, theirs is no fast, but a crime and a sin and a fault. . . . What do you go to see in the synagogue of those God-fighting Jews anyway, tell me? Men blowing trumpets! What you ought to do is stay home and weep and sigh for them, because they are fighting against the commands of God and dancing with the Devil. For just as I said before, whatever is done contrary to God's will becomes the basis for incalculable punishments, even if at some time in the past God has permitted it. [Chry. *Or. C. Jud.* IV, 3, 7; *PG* 48, 874–75, 881]

The Christians listening to Chrysostom should do everything in their power to hunt down the misguided Judaizers, just like hunters tracking wild animals, and persuade them by any method to abandon their evil fraternizing with Christ's murderers. Even if one must drag them into one's house by force and eat in front of them to make them break their godless fast, this is better than to allow them to fast with the Jews on Yom Kippur (Chry. *Or. C. Jud.* VI, 7; *PG* 48, 916). But the Christians should not let it be known how many of their members have Judaized during the fast, lest their enemies exult, but go secretly and confront their fallen brethren with opening questions such as:

"Tell me, do you praise the Jews for crucifying Christ and for, even to this day, blaspheming Him and calling Him a lawbreaker?" Beyond a doubt if he is a Christian, he will refuse to say so. . . . After you have gained his goodwill, start in again and say, "How is it then that you are able to fellowship with them? How can you share in their festivals and fasts?" Accuse the Jews of arrogance. Recount every one of their violations of the Law, which in recent days I have recounted to you; every proof of lawlessness which I have derived from the place, the time, the temple, and the predictions of the prophets. Show that there is no rhyme or reason for what the Jews are doing, and that they will never restore their former way of life and that it is not lawful for them to observe this sort of celebration outside of Jerusalem. Remind them too of Gehenna and of the trial held there and of the fearful judgment seat of Christ and of how we shall give an account of all these things and of that certain punishment (not slight) which awaits those who dare to do such things. [Chry. *Or. C. Jud.* VIII, 5; *PG* 48, 935]

As for the Jews themselves, they are demonic in every way. No reproach can come close to describing the infamy of these people and the disgracefulness of their place of worship:

I know that many people hold a high regard for the Jews and consider their way of life worthy of respect at the present time. This is why I am hurrying to pull up this fatal notion by the roots. . . . A place where a whore stands on display is a whorehouse. What is more, the synagogue is not only a whorehouse and a theater; it is also a den of thieves and a haunt of wild animals . . . not the cave of a wild animal merely, but of an unclean wild animal. . . . The Jews have no conception of [spiritual] things at all, but living for the lower nature, all agog for the here and now, no better disposed than pigs or goats, they live by the rule of debauchery and inordinate gluttony. Only one thing they understand: to gorge themselves and to get drunk. [Chry. *Or. C. Jud.* I, 3, 4; *PG* 48, 847, 848]

The synagogue is not only a place of vice and impiety. It is a haunt of the demons. The very souls of Jews are haunts of demons. Wrongly do Christians look for healing from the Jews, for demons cannot heal. Or even if they do heal, they heal by the power of the Devil and not that of God. Better to die, than to be healed by demons and lose one's soul (Chry. *Or. C. Jud.* I, 6–7; *PG* 48, 852–55).

When the time for meeting calls you to Church, if your wives are indifferent . . . but if they respond with alacrity when the devil calls to the trumpets, you fail to hold them back, but let them get caught in crimes of godlessness and drawn away into immorality. For harlots and effeminates and the whole company of the dancing floor habitually gather there. But why am I talking about the immorality that goes on there? Are you not afraid that your wife will come away from that place possessed with a demon? Didn't you hear the argument in my earlier sermon which proved clearly that the demons inhabit the very souls of the Jews, as well as the places where they gather? Tell me, how do you dare to return to the congregation of the apostles after you have cavorted with demons? After you have gone off and joined those who shed Christ's blood, how can you keep from trembling when you return and eat from this holy Table and drink this precious blood? Does it make you shudder? Doesn't such lawlessness appal you with terror? . . . Rescue them with every earnestness. Snatch them out of the devil's teeth and bring them to me on the Day of the Fast so that . . . we may with one voice praise God, the Father of our Lord Jesus Christ, to whom is glory into the ages. Amen. [Chry. *Or. C. Jud.* II, 3; *PG* 48, 861–62]

In these sermons, Chrysostom never actually tells his people to do any violence to the Jews themselves or their synagogues, although he is very free to declare that he "hates them," that "God hates them," all the prophets "hate them," and the holy martyrs "hate them." He even talks metaphorically about the Jews as "fit for slaughter":

When animals have been fattened by having all they want to eat, they get stubborn and hard to manage. . . . Another prophet intimates the same thing when he says "Israel ran about madly like a heifer stung by a gadfly" and still another calls her "an untrained calf." When animals are unfit for work, they are marked for slaughter, and this is the very thing which the Jews have experienced. By making themselves unfit for work, they have become ready for slaughter. This is why Christ said, "Ask for my enemies, who did not want me to reign over them, bring them here and slay them before me." [Chry. *Or. C. Jud.* I, 2; *PG* 48, 846][171]

What is evident is that the Jews, for Chrysostom, never appear as "brothers," potential brothers, or even as human beings. His evangelical concern is only for the Judaizers. They are the "fallen brothers" who must be rescued from the devils, the Jews. Chrysostom does not even favor the Jews with any expressions of hope that they might be converted. He seeks to convert only the Judaizers. But the Jews themselves, in Chrysostom's sermons, have passed beyond the pale of humanity altogether into the realm of the demonic.

These sermons were preached in an excitable, faction-ridden Hellenistic city, where the Jews had been the subject of communal violence before, especially during the Jewish Wars. Such sermons as these gave the blessings of the Church's greatest preacher, "the Golden-mouthed," to what was now a government-sanctioned destruction of Jewish civic status and an increasing tendency for religion to become the vehicle for popular violence against the Jews. On the other side of the Jewish and Judaizing population, there was a pagan and gentile-Christian population, happy to attack this minority group who had lived in their own communally-governed section of the city since Hellenistic times. In the early fifth century, waves of violence broke out against the Jews in Antioch, with the first recorded Christian charge of Jewish "ritual murder." The great synagogues of the city were destroyed. Simon Stylites, the famous saint, intervened to prevent the governor from making reparations to the Jews. Eruptions of communal violence against the Jews continued to characterize Christian Antioch in the fifth and sixth centuries, until, in a final effort at mass conversion and an outbreak of massacre, the Jews were expelled from the city altogether.[172]

Theologically, Christians and Jews in patristic times had positions that were mutually exclusive, each claiming to be the sole legitimate heir of the biblical faith. Jews were no more tolerant of Christians than Christians were of Jews, although the Jewish view of "the nations" allowed Jews to coexist with Christians and with peoples of other faith, provided they let the Jews be themselves, whereas Christian universalism could allow for no such place for the non-Christian. By the same token, the Jew could tolerate a Judaizing Christian in the synagogue, although not a proselytizing Christian in the synagogue, while the Christian could not tolerate a Judaizing Christian in the Church. Nevertheless, the Christian view did allow for a place for the Jews to continue to exist. The Jew was allowed to exist, indeed commanded to exist in the Christian era, not as one with a legitimate vehicle of religion in his own right, but in the negative space of divine reprobation and as an eventual or ultimate witness to the "truth" of the Church. Anti-Christianity was an extrinsic and defensive need for the synagogue, which was over as soon as the Church was organized outside the walls of the Jewish community. For Christianity, anti-Judaism was not merely a defense against attack, but an intrinsic need of Christian self-affirmation. Anti-Judaism is a part of Christian exegesis. Anti-Christianity is not properly a part of Jewish exegesis. The *adversus Judaeos* literature was not created to convert Jews or even primarily to attack Jews, but to affirm the identity of the Church, which could only be done by invalidating the identity of the Jews. All of this might have remained theoretical, however, if Christianity and Judaism had both remained minority religions in a pagan (Zoroastrian or Moslem) state, as they were to continue to be in Persia. In the fourth century, however, Christianity became the religion of the Greco-Roman Empire. What had previously been theology and biblical hermeneutics now was to become law and social policy.

Abbreviations of texts used in chapter three

Diog. *Ep.*	*Epistle of Diognetus*
Did.	*Didache* or Teachings of the Apostles
Ep. Barn.	*Epistle of Barnabas*
Just. *Dial.*	Justin Martyr, *Dialogue with Trypho*
Just. *I Apol.*	Justin Martyr, *First Apology*
Iren. *Haer.*	Irenaeus, *Against the Heresies*
Ter. *Adv. Jud.*	Tertullian, *An Answer to the Jews*
Ter. *Apol.*	Tertullian, *Apology*
Lact. *D. I.*	Lactantius, *Divine Institutes*
Hipp. *Ref. Haer.*	Hippolytus, *Refutation of all Heresies*
Hipp. *C. Jud.*	Hippolytus, *Expository Treatise Against the Jews*
Nov. *Carn. Jud.*	Novatian, "On Jewish Meats"
Orig. *C. Cel.*	Origen, *Contra Celsum*
Athan. *Incarn.*	Athanasius, *On the Incarnation of the Word*
Cyp. *Test.*	Cyprian, *Three Books of Testimonies Against the Jews*
Ps.-Nys. *Test.*	Pseudo-Nyssa, *Selected Testimonies from the Old Testament Against the Jews*
Euseb. *D. E.*	Eusebius of Caesarea, *Demonstrations of the Gospel*
Euseb. *Or. Con.*	Eusebius of Caesarea, *Oration on Constantine*

Euseb. *Vita Con.*	Eusebius of Caesarea, *Life of Constantine*
Euseb. *H. E.*	Eusebius of Caesarea, *Ecclesiastical History*
Chry. *Or. C. Jud.*	John Chrysostom, *Eight Orations Against the Jews*
Chry. *Dem. Jud.-Gen.*	John Chrysostom, *Demonstration to the Jews and Gentiles that Christ is God*
Aug. *Adv. Jud.*	Augustine, *Tract Against the Jews*
Aug. *C. D.*	Augustine, *The City of God*
Aug. *C. Faust*	Augustine, *Against Faustus*
Aug. *Epp.*	Augustine, *Epistles*
Ps.-Aug. *C. Jud., Pag., Ar.*	Pseudo-Augustine, *Against the Jews, Pagans and Arians*
Ps.-Aug. *Alt. Ecc.-Syn.*	Pseudo-Augustine, *Altercation Between the Church and the Synagogue*
Eph. *Rhy. C. Jud.*	Ephrem the Syrian, *Rhythm Against the Jews*
Is. Ant. *Hom. C. Jud.*	*Isaac of Antioch, Homilies Against the Jews*
Did. Jak.	*Teachings of Jacob,* Sargis d'Aberga
Q. Ant. Dux	Pseudo-Athanasius, *Questions to Antiochus Dux*
Aph. *Dem.*	Aphrahat, *Demonstrations Against the Jews*
Jak. Serug	Jacob of Serug, *Homilies Against the Jews*
Max. *C. Jud.*	Maximinus, Arian Bishop of Hippo, *Treatise Against the Jews*
Trop. Dam.	*Trophies Framed Against the Jews at Damascus*
Isid. *C. Jud.*	Isidore of Seville, *Against the Jews*
Prud. *Apo.*	Prudentius, *Apotheosis*
John Dam.	John Damascene, *On the Orthodox Faith* 4.23 "On the Sabbath, Against the Jews"
Dial. J.-P.	*Dialogue of Jason and Papiscus*
Dial. T.-A.	*Dialogue of Timothy and Aquila*
Dial. A.-Z.	*Dialogue of Athanasius and Zacchaeus*
Dial. P.-P.	*Dialogue of Papiscus and Philo*
Dial. G.-A.	*Dialogue of Archbishop Gregentius and the Jew Herban*
Dial. S.-T.	*Dialogue on the Law Between Simon, the Jew, and Theophilus, a Christian* (attributed to Evagrius)
St. Silv.	*Discussion of St. Silvester with Jews at Rome*
Ps.-Cyp. *Mont.*	Pseudo-Cyprian, *De Montibus Sinai et Sion.*

Chapter 4

The Social Incorporation of
The Negative Myth
Of the Jews in Christendom

This chapter will summarize the way in which the negative myth of the Jew, developed in the patristic *adversus Judaeos* tradition, was incorporated into the legal status of the Jew in Christendom. This inferiorized legal status, legislated as a direct interpretation of the Church's doctrine about the Jews, was then passed on to the Middle Ages. This legacy gradually resulted in a loss of all civil rights, as well as an economic role that made the Jew both hated and vulnerable to violence from below and arbitrary action from above, until finally one arrives at that state of total vilification, rightlessness, and ghettoization that was to characterize Jewish life in Western Christendom from the later Middle Ages to the Emancipation. This medieval heritage lasted for the Jew up to our own century, for the Emancipation was not completed in western Europe until 1870, and in Germany full citizenship only came with the Weimar Republic, while traditional ghetto life continued in eastern Europe until Nazism swept away this world in the Holocaust. As the social status and its theological rationale, fashioned for the Jew in Christendom, were dissolving in modern Europe, hatred of the Jew was reasserted in the form of racial anti-Semitism, to become the theoretical argument for the "final solution to the Jewish question" which broke apart the limits of the Christian anti-Judaic theory. This chapter can be no more than a superficial sketch. But for the Christian for whom Jewish history since 70 C.E. is a blank, it may give some guidelines for understanding the links between Christian anti-Judaism and modern anti-Semitism.

The Nazis, of course, were not Christians. They were indeed anti-Christian, despite their ability to co-opt the Church qua "German Christianity." Nevertheless, the Church must bear a substantial responsibility for a tragic history of the Jew in Christendom which was the foundation upon which political anti-Semitism and the Nazi use of it was erected. This chapter will show the stages by which this tragedy unfolded from its original root in the patristic theological image of the Jew. This story cannot be traced in conclusive detail here, for to do so would itself be a book of many volumes and not simply a chapter. Rather, this chapter only offers a sketch that will clarify the way in which the theological doctrine of the Jew interacted with legal, economic, political, and social factors to structure Jewish life in Christian history to its terrible consequences, giving references to the sources and many detailed studies where aspects of this history are pursued in greater depth.

I. *The Jews in the Christian Roman Empire from Constantine to Justinian*

The anti-Judaic arguments, which were examined in the previous chapter, grew to a fixed standpoint between the apostolic period and the fourth century. These arguments were repeated over and over again in every Christian sermon, biblical commentary, or theological tract that touched on the Jews in some way. And since the Church continued to claim Jewish history and the Jewish Scriptures as its own history and scripture, and to understand itself as the heir to the election of Israel, it was difficult to preach or teach anything without touching on the Jews in some way. In the first third of the fourth century, Christianity was transformed from a persecuted faith into the established religion of the empire. What had previously been the hostile tradition of an illegal sect toward its parental faith now became the official creed of the civil religion of the Christian

Roman Empire. In less than fifty years, Orthodox Christianity elevated itself from a position of toleration to that of the exclusive religion of the empire. By the reign of Theodosius I (378–95), the faith and practices of pagans and heretics became illegal. Their temples and churches were destroyed or confiscated. Their very existence was proscribed.[1]

In regard to the Jews, however, the situation was more complicated. Judaism was the only dissenting and non-Christian faith that was to remain legal in Christendom. Its status, both as a pariah religion and as a religion tolerated minimally in this pariah status, was unique. This peculiar status resulted from a combination of the earlier position of Judaism in pagan Roman law and the relation of Judaism to Christianity in Christian theology. As a result of the final compromise between the polytheistic empire and this stubborn monotheistic people, pagan Rome had given Judaism a special protected status. With Caracalla, the Jews became full Roman citizens. Their right to worship and to govern their own communities through their own religious institutions was guaranteed. Their exemption from government service involving pagan worship gave them a privileged status in relation to other groups, although remnants of their humiliation in the Hadrianic laws remained in the form of the *fiscus Judaicus,* the exclusion from Jerusalem, and the prohibition against circumcizing non-Jews. Economically, the Jews occupied variegated roles and were not set apart from the rest of the community by special occupations. The Syrians, not the Jews, were the chief merchants who traveled the trade routes from East to West in the late imperial period until the advent of Islam. Jews occupied an economic range from wealthy to poor, but fell mostly into the lower middle class. They were by no means exclusively an urban group in the Diaspora. Jewish agriculturalists were normal in Spain and Africa. In the legislation that was soon to be decreed against them in the Christian empire, economic grievances are never cited as a motivation.[2] It is solely the theological image of the Jew and the desire of Church and state to reflect this in social segregation that is reflected in these laws.

Christian theology, while it decreed misery for the Jews as their historical status before God, did not advocate extermination. On the contrary, the official view of the Church guaranteed the ongoing existence of Judaism. Although the vituperations of clerics and theologians often fell into language that suggested that the Jews should be killed, the official theory excluded the "final solution" as an option here and now. Judaism was to exist until the end of time, but as an empty religion that had lost its elect status and inner spiritual power. It was to continue to exist in a pariah status in history, both to testify to the present election of the Church and to witness the final triumph of the Church. At the return of Christ, Jews would either finally acknowledge their error or else be condemned to final damnation. The Church should seek the conversion of Jews here and now, but also prevent the influence of Judaism on Christians. The Church felt called upon to enforce this status of reprobation in the form of social "misery," but the "final solution" could not be executed by men, but lay in the hands of God at the time of the final eschatological drama. The legislation of Christian emperors and Church councils on the status of the Jew in Christian society reflects the effort to mirror this theological theory in social practice.

Between 315 and 439 C.E. (from the reign of Constantine to the promulgation of the Theodosian Code), this view of the Jew was enforced through a steadily worsening legal status. The laws of the Theodosian Code, in turn, were incorporated in revised form into the Code of Justinian in a way that further depressed Jewish status. The Theodosian Code also was passed on to the West in shortened recensions, as well as by the incorporation of its laws into canon law. The Theodosian Code thus laid the basis for the position of the Jew in the Byzantine Empire, and also for the further developments of medieval Christendom. The rule of thumb for this development, as J. E. Seaver and James Parkes have summarized it, is as follows: the trend was always one of worsening status (until this trend was actively reversed by a counterdevelopment in the Enlightenment); a right, once lost to the Jews, was never permanently recovered, while the restrictions decreed against them were constantly reaffirmed and extended.[3]

One of the first things to concern the newly Christianized emperor Constantine (a matter which was to be constantly reiterated in later laws in Christian history and in the Nazi anti-Semitic legislation) was the prohibition of Christian slaves (or servants) to the Jews. First this took the form of prohibiting the Jew from circumcizing his slaves.[4] This was a remnant of Hadrianic law, but it was now reasserted to prevent the Jew from proselytizing among the servant class. It was normal for the Jewish family to incorporate their servants into the family religiously. Christianity itself had risen to a large extent through this route. But this prohibition against making slaves Jews soon grew into a prohibition against Jews owning any Christian slaves.[5] This was a law which bishops in the West were particularly concerned to enforce, even after the fall of the Western Roman Empire.[6] The reasons for the large amount of attention paid to this restriction by the Church had nothing to do with a rejection of slavery as such. The Church never took a stand against the legitimacy of slavery as an institution. It was concerned to cut off this potent form of Jewish influence upon Christians. Theologically, it also regarded it as intolerable that the reprobate people, the Jews, should hold in bondage those who had been freed by Christ. But this theological view was never held to imply that Christians should not hold other Christians in bondage. The issue had to do with the reprobate status of the Jew vis-à-vis Christianity. This opposition to Jewish lordship over Christians also meant that a slave could seek emancipation through conversion. Slaves were quick to follow this route to their own freedom, raising the question of compensation of the Jew for this economic loss.[7]

This prohibition of Jewish lordship over Christians had a severe effect on Jewish economic life. In a slave economy, it was impossible to operate any large-scale manufacturing or agricultural enterprise without slaves. Jews would then be eliminated from business enterprises or agriculture through their inability to hold slaves in a Christian society run by a slave (and later a serf) labor force. Jews did continue to be active as slave traders, especially after the advent of Islam, but their traffic was restricted to non-Christian slaves which they brought from pagan or Moslem areas to Christian lands. In a world that was devolving economically to a feudal, agricultural form of life, this legislation made it almost impossible for Jews to participate in the development of latifundia as landholders. Jews were not immediately eliminated from agriculture, but these laws began a trend that was eventually to bias Jewish economic life toward trade and exclude them from their normal participation in land-holding and farming. These laws also interfered in Jewish home and religious life. Non-Jewish servants were commonly used for services such as lighting lamps in the synagogue on the Sabbath. The Apostolic Canons explicitly forbade Christians to perform this service for the Jews.[8]

Another, related, area of legislation prohibited Jews from all proselytizing. At the same time, Jews were strictly forbidden to impede the conversion of Jews to Christianity.[9] It became a crime to become a Jew or to aid in the conversion of anyone to Judaism. The convert to Judaism had his goods confiscated. Later, he lost his testamentary rights. Some laws threatened capital punishment for proselytizing.[10] In a law decreed in 383 C.E., legal suits could be brought against a proselyte or proselytizer up to five years after his death to confiscate the goods inherited by his heirs.[11]

The question of the right of a Jew to return to Judaism when he had been forced to flee to the sanctuary of the Church by persecution also was to become a hotly contested issue. Honorius, in 416 C.E., decreed that a Jew who had fled for sanctuary could return to Judaism.[12] But this right was to be dropped by Justinian.[13] The fixed position of the Church was to forbid a return to Judaism by those who had been forcibly baptized, on the grounds that baptism was valid *ex opere operato*.[14] The forced convert was classified as an apostate if he attempted to return to Judaism, even though the Church generally disapproved of forced baptism, at least officially. Thus, the legal basis was laid in canon and imperial law for the "Marrano," or forced convert, who was forbidden to return publicly to Judaism and had to live his faith secretly, a phenomenon that was to appear continually in Christian history and in great numbers at the end of the Middle Ages. Any effort by the Jewish community to harass the converted Jew, to withhold his testamentary rights, or to persuade him otherwise to return to Judaism was severely proscribed in imperial legislation.[15]

Another area of continued concern to both the imperial and

the ecclesiastical legislator was intermarriage between Christians and Jews. Here, too, the main purpose seems to have been the desire to prevent Judaizing by the Christian partner. In 339 C.E., Constantine promulgated the first of such laws prohibiting Jews from taking to wife women from the weaving factories.[16] Theodosius I passed a blanket decree which made it a crime of adultery for any Christian man or woman to marry a Jew or Jewess.[17] Capital punishment was to be exacted for this crime. The Church also added excommunication to the crime of cohabitation between Christians and Jews.[18]

By the late fourth century, new types of laws began to be added which drastically reduced Jewish social standing. Jews were excluded from all civil and military rank and were gradually excluded from holding any type of public office.[19] Later, they were also excluded from acting as lawyers or judges.[20] Their right to testify in court against Christians was also to be a subject of continual restrictions.[21] This demotion of the Jew from all civic status in the imperial *cursus honorum* was summarized in the Theodosian Code by the principle that a Jew is not to hold any authority over a Christian. For those who are "the enemies of the Heavenly Majesty and the Roman Laws" to "become executors of our laws" or to have authority to judge or decide against Christians is termed "an insult to our faith."[22] We can see this same principle as it operated to forbid the right of the Jew to have Christians as servants. Politically and socially, the Jew was demoted to the bottom of Christian society, while his ability to prosper economically was also being restricted.

In 415 C.E., this demotion of the Jew from all rank or honor in the empire was completed by the abolition of the office of patriarch as a publicly recognized dignitary.[24] Earlier, the *aurum coronarium,* or patriarchal tax, was diverted to the imperial coffers. This patriarchal tax was collected by *apostoli* of the patriarch and was the chief means by which Judaism maintained unified communication throughout the Diaspora. These acts disrupted this ancient means of centralized communication of Jewish religious law. At the same time, the diversion of the *aurum coronarium* to the emperor's treasury renewed the *fiscus Judaicus,* or head tax, which had been levied on every Jew by Hadrian, when he similarly diverted the temple tax to the imperial treasury after the Jewish Wars. The *fiscus Judaicus* had disappeared sometime in the third or fourth centuries, and may have been abolished by the apostate emperor Julian during his brief reign.[25] The Jews, as the only group on whom this special tax was levied, were thus marked out for special economic exactions for the personal treasury of the emperor, a practice that was to continue in the Byzantine Empire and to have a special role in medieval Christendom.

The Jews were also marked for special economic exploitation in other ways in this early imperial law. One of the first anti-Judaic laws under Constantine forced them to accept the role of *decurion,* from which they had previously been exempt. This office of local tax collector was an especially ruinous one in a failing economy, and one which was rapidly driving the middle class of the cities bankrupt. Christians fled from this office by becoming priests and monks. Imperial legislation now forced Jews to accept this office, although, at first, Jewish clergy were exempt from it in the same way as Christian clergy.[26] But gradually this privilege was eroded and Jews of whatever position were forced to accept the decurionate.[27]

Other laws aimed specifically at the interference with Judaism as a religion. In 423 C.E. Jews were forbidden to build new synagogues or repair old ones, a decree that was repeated in the novella promulgating the Theodosian Code.[28] This, too, was a law which was to be reaffirmed again and again, as late as the eighteenth century. After the riots connected with Purim in the early fifth century at Inmester, the right of the Jews to celebrate this festival in the traditional noisy public manner was forbidden. For the first time, we have the idea proclaimed that Jewish rituals aim at sacrilegious mockery of the Christian religion.[29] It was further decreed that Jews must observe Christian laws on marriage, divorce, and consanguinity, a law which hampered considerably traditional Jewish marriage laws.[30] Even the right to conduct religious affairs through their own religious courts began to be restricted in laws which demanded that Jews submit religious questions to Roman law courts.[31] In 425 C.E., Jews were ordered to observe Christian times of feasts and fasts.[32] The practice of forcing the Jewish community to listen to Christian conversion sermons also began in the fifth century.

The Church not only incorporated these imperial laws into canonical legislation, it also added other laws of its own, especially in the areas of sexual relations, sociability, and religious fraternizing. Intermarriage or sexual relations were the subject of continual ecclesiastical prohibitions, beginning with the Council of Elvira, circa 314 C.E.[33] Many kinds of social relations, such as the giving or receiving of gifts or hospitality, invitations to dinner of Jews by Christians or acceptance of Jewish invitations, even, in one canon, the lending of money at interest by clergy, were forbidden by Church councils in this period.[34] But the Church was primarily concerned to rule out any kind of religious fraternizing between Christian and Jews, particularly the participation of Christians in Jewish observances or customs. Despite the Church's efforts in this direction, religious fraternizing continued on the popular level to a remarkable extent late into Byzantine times. Although official antagonism stirred popular hatred in some sectors of the population, it is important to remember that for other groups the line between the two faiths continued to remain blurred. In the early fourth century, the Council of Elvira forbade Christians to have Rabbis bless their fields, a practice which also points to the continuing agricultural character of Jewish life in Spain. Other canons forbid Christians, especially the clergy, from attending Jewish feasts or fasts, celebrating Easter together with the Jewish Passover, attending or praying in synagogues, accepting unleavened bread or other religious gifts from Jews at the times of Jewish festivals, and observing the Sabbath. As we saw earlier, Christian servants were forbidden to light lamps for Jewish synagogues. Christians were to rest on Sunday and work on the Sabbath, and the Judaizing practice of not reading from the Gospel on the Sabbath was prohibited.[35]

The changing attitude of the Church toward the Jews can also be seen in baptismal forms. In the first centuries of the Church, Jews were regarded as monotheists who were already halfway to the Christian faith. Hence the catechumenate was shorter for Jews than for pagans, and their baptismal vows excluded the abjuration of previous demonic worship. But sometime in the fifth century or thereafter, new baptismal forms were introduced that regarded the Jews as more demonic and less open to Christian truth than other converts. This reflected also the experience of the Church with judaizing converts whose conversion stemmed from force or expediency. The catechumenate for Jews is made longer. At their baptism, Jewish converts are made to call down fierce curses upon themselves, if they do not totally renounce all Jewish religious customs, and to curse the Jewish people and their history in the language of Christian theological vituperation.[36] In these baptismal abjurations, we also find the idea that the Messiah expected by the Jewish people is actually the Anti-Christ. The Jewish convert is to renounce this "Anti-Christ, whom all the Jews await in the figure and form of Christ," and to embrace the true Christ.[37]

These anti-Judaic laws, as well as the theological anti-Judaism that continued to be preached by the teachers of the Church, resulted in outbreaks of violence against the Jewish community that went beyond the limits of the law. This reality is reflected in a continual need in imperial law to legislate against vandalism, synagogue burning or confiscation, interference with Jewish celebration of the Sabbath or other religious observances, and even pogroms.[38] Imperial officials occasionally displayed an unseemly zealousness in curtailing legal, economic, or religious activities by Jews.[39] But the chief offenders in this regard were fanatical monks, who stirred up mobs of Christians to pillage synagogues, cemetaries, and other property, seize or burn Jewish religious buildings, and start riots in the Jewish quarter. Bishops also could be found who approved retroactively and even led in this violence and who decreed the forced baptism of local Jewries. Imperial legislation continually admonished against such violence, and demanded compensation for it from the Christian community. But the secular rulers often ran into opposition from the bishops in their efforts to enforce these protective laws.

In the middle of the fourth century, Bishop Innocentius of Dertona in northern Italy destroyed the local synagogue and erected a church on the site. He offered the Jewish residents the option of baptism or expulsion.[40] These incidents of violence and forced baptism were rife in Syria in the late fourth and early fifth centuries. Around 413 C.E., a band of forty monks, led by one Barsauma, swept through Palestine, destroying synagogues and temples. They completed their mission by massacring the Jews who had been allowed to weep at the Wailing Wall in Jerusalem.[41] Although the emperors continually legislated against this violence, their ability to check it became increasingly feeble in the course of the fifth century. They themselves were unwilling to attach any real sanctions to these protective laws similar to the severe sanctions that were typically attached to the anti-Judaic laws. The perpetrators were merely exhorted to make reparations, but punishment of the culprits themselves was not specified. The opposition of prominent churchmen to any reparations to the Jewish community for violence or synagogue destruction also helped to weaken the force of the imperial laws protecting the Jews.

The most famous of these incidents took place in 388 C.E., with the destruction of a synagogue in the frontier town of Callinicum by a mob at the instigation of the bishop. Theodosius ordered the bishop to provide the monies to restore the synagogue. Saint Ambrose, incensed by this order, wrote a long rhetorical letter exhorting the emperor to rescind it. Although Ambrose admits that he had never personally had the opportunity to burn a synagogue, he declares that he would be happy to do so "that there might not be a place where Christ is denied." For a bishop to rebuild a synagogue would be tantamount to apostasy, for it would mean contributing the patrimony of Christ to the maintenance of "vile perfidity." The synagogue is referred to by Ambrose as "a haunt of infidels, a home of the impious, a hiding place of madmen, under the damnation of God Himself." The misfortunes that befell emperors Julian, when he tried to restore the temple in Jerusalem, and Maximius (whose fall Ambrose attributes to the fact that he forced the Christian community in Rome to rebuild a synagogue they had destroyed there) are cited as examples of divine wrath upon emperors who restore Jewish houses of worship. Fearing the wrath of the Church, Theodosius modified this order to a simple restoration of the sacred articles stolen from the synagogue, the actual rebuilding to be financed by the state. But this was not acceptable to Ambrose, who insisted that there be no reparations and no punishment of the culprits at all. When the emperor refused to respond further, Ambrose seized the occasion of the emperor's presence at the Divine Liturgy in the cathedral at Milan to confront him. Coming down from the altar to face him, the bishop declared that he would not continue with the Eucharist until the emperor obeyed. The emperor bowed to this threat of excommunication, and the rioters at Callinicum went unadmonished.[42]

In a similar fashion, the pillar saint, Simon Stylites, intervened to prevent Theodosius II from restoring the synagogues of Antioch when they were destroyed by rioters in 423 C.E.[43] Increasingly violent pogroms and street fighting between Jews and Christians led to the expulsion of the Jews completely from major urban centers in the fifth century. In 414 C.E., the Jews were expelled by Bishop Cyril from Alexandria, a city which had been the center of Diaspora Jewry for seven hundred years.[44] In 418 C.E., Severus, bishop of Minorca, accomplished the forced baptism of all the Jews on that island.[45] Rioting between Christians and the embattled Jewish community took place repeatedly in Antioch in the fifth and sixth centuries, with massacres of Jews. Finally in 610 C.E., the attempt of Emperor Phocas to force the conversion of the remaining Jews resulted in a revolt by the Jews. This revolt was quickly suppressed, many Jews were killed, and the rest were expelled from the city, bringing to an end what had been a second great center of Diaspora Jewry since Hellenistic times.[46] Deprived of all social status by imperial law and left largely unprotected against popular violence, the Jewish community in the Eastern provinces sank into ignominy and looked to the Persian and then to the Moslem empire for deliverance.

In the laws of the Christian emperors enforcing a status of reprobation on the Jewish community, one notes a language of clerical vituperation. The synagogue is referred to in one early law of the Theodosian Code by a Latin slang word meaning "brothel," a word which never before had been used for a place of religious worship in Roman law.[47] The Jews are referred to constantly in the laws as a group hated by God, to be regarded by Christian society as contemptible and even demonic. The laws bristle with negative and theologically loaded epithets. Judaism is called a *feralis secta* and a *Synagoga Satanae*. Their meetings are *sacrilegi coetus*.[48] The very name of Jew is "foul and degrading." To marry a Jew is adultery and to be under their authority is "an insult to our faith." It becomes common to speak of Judaism in the language of pollution, contagion, and disease. The Third Novella, which promulgated the Theodosian Code, calls it a "desperate illness" that is beyond curing. Judaism is called "dangerous," "abominable," "evil teachings," "madness," while Jews themselves are described by such terms as "sly," "shameful," "foul," "insolent," "detestible," "blind," and "perverse."[49] Jews are said to be the "enemies of the Heavenly Majesty and the Roman Laws" and to break the laws against judaizing is equivalent to a crime of *lèse majesté*. In short, the Christian emperors do not legislate as secular rulers. Nor do they act simply as tools of the Church, although churchmen sometimes pushed them further than they wanted to go. Still less are they simply cynical exploiters of the situation for political or economic advantage. Indeed, there was little advantage to be reaped by a weakened empire in such persecution. Rather, the emperors speak here as exponents of the Christian theological view of the Jews, acting in their own right as priest-kings of the Christian theocratic empire.

2. *The Jews in Byzantium and the West from the Sixth Century to the Crusades*

The *Corpus Juris Civilis* issued by Justinian in 534 C.E. discarded over half of the more than fifty laws dealing with the Jews found in the Theodosian Code.[50] The Justinian Code further depressed the status of the Jews by discarding many laws protecting their civil and religious rights, while retaining and extending their restrictions. The immunities of synagogue officials, the rights to internal discipline of Jewish religious courts over members of the synagogue, and the right of a Jew who fled to the Church for sanctuary to return to Judaism were dropped. Restrictions against owning Christian slaves and exclusion from all public office or honors were strengthened. All the old restrictions against building or repairing synagogues, conversion to Judaism, and the duty to serve on the *decurion* were reaffirmed. The death penalty and confiscation of property were decreed for circumcizing a slave or child not of Jewish parentage, and this could be applied even to those who attempted to convert others to Judaism.[51] Justinian added other specifically religious laws, such as that which ordered that the Jewish Passover is never to fall ahead of the Christian Easter, and a remarkable demand that the scrolls of the Law be read in the vernacular, rather than Hebrew, and without the rabbinic commentary, in the synagogue service. This latter law was a direct effort to make the synagogue service itself open to Christian proselytizing by eliminating the rabbinic interpretation of the Scriptures and hence, presumably, making the reading of the Old Testament open to the Christian exegesis. Since Christianity was convinced that its own christological exegesis of the Jewish Bible was self-evident, it was clear to Justinian that once the "blindness" of the rabbinic commentary was removed, the Jews would be able to hear directly the Christian meaning of their own Scriptures. The synagogue seems to have found ways of circumventing this law, which would have eliminated Hebrew and the rabbinic tradition from their liturgy, but it represents a remarkable effort by the Christian emperor to regulate directly the content of Judaism itself.[52]

Justinian's principle, in his legislation on the Jews, is a reflection of the Christian theological view. The Jew is never to enjoy the fruits of any office or labor, but only the penalties thereof.[53] He is to present to Christian society the living proof of the social results of divine reprobation, both to testify to the truth of Christianity, and ultimately to convince the Jews themselves of this truth. Nevertheless, the Jews remained Roman citizens, even though in this restricted condition. Although they were to enjoy no prosperity or social standing in Byzantine society, violence against them was prohibited and their religious institutions were protected. However, Justinian dropped the important law in the Theodosian Code that directly declared that Judaism is a legal religion. This had the effect of making the legitimacy of Judaism a matter for the emperor himself to decide at will, rather than a clearly articulated legal principle.[54]

The position of the Jew in Byzantine society from Justinian to the Crusades represents a case of the Christian theological view enacted into public social policy. The reprobation of the

Jew was institutionalized as exclusion from the *cursus honorum* of Byzantine public life and an economic structuring into the lower class. However, this situation differed considerably from the vilification that was to become the lot of the Jew in the Western Middle Ages, even though the vituperation toward the Jews found in imperial law and theology made this hateful image the official stance of Byzantine church and state. Nevertheless, the violence and popular hatred, the ghettoization and paranoia typical of the late medieval world of the West did not occur. The reasons for this seem to have to do primarily with the fact that in Byzantium the political institutions and economic life of the Roman Empire did not fall, but remained in force. This meant that a centralized enforcement of law and order remained intact. Although the emperors lost control over popular violence toward the Jews in the fifth century, by the time of Justinian imperial control was restored. The emperors were able to enforce the laws which protected Jewish religious institutions and prevented violence against their persons. Although sporadic violence and synagogue burnings continued to take place now and again in Byzantine times, by and large the emperors could prevent this. Pogroms did not become the typical pattern of Jewish life in the East, as they were to become in the West. Moreover, as Roman citizens, the Jews' right to a place in Byzantine society, however restricted, was guaranteed, whereas in the West, where the tradition of Roman law fell into confusion after the fall of the Western Roman Empire, the citizenship of the Jews was forgotten.

Equally important was the fact that in Byzantium the city and a money economy did not disappear, as they did in the feudal West. The official apparatus for a moneyed economy remained in the hands of state institutions, and so the Jew was not structured into a peculiar relationship to commerce in a primarily agricultural and nonmoneyed economy, as was to happen in the West. Religious anti-Judaism was not translated into economic anti-Semitism. The Jew did not become peculiarly associated with trade or money, but remained scattered throughout all economic roles, even farming, although his inability to own slaves prevented him from being a large landholder. Economically, the Jew remained an ordinary person mingling with his fellow citizens in various occupations in the lower echelons of social life. Although singled out as an object of theological hate by official Byzantine institutions, economically this merely meant that he could seldom rise above lower middle class. But he also could not become a special target of envy to his Christian fellow citizens.

The Byzantine emperors erred from the limitations of their own theory chiefly on the side of zealousness toward the conversion of the Jew. Part of the reason for this was political. With the fall of the eastern provinces of the empire to the Arabs, the centers of Jewish religious life were cut off in Moslem lands, and the Jews were suspected of political disloyalty to the Christian empire. This had also been true earlier when the great religious centers of Judaism were in Persia in the Sassanid Empire. Although both the Sassanids and the Moslems were not without their own efforts to enforce a monolithic religious policy for their empires, and treated members of dissenting religions as inferior, by and large the Jews were better treated in these empires than they were in the Christian empire. A wider range of employment was open to them, and the special theological vilification of the Christian tradition was absent. The Jews thus were seen as potential partisans of an Eastern attack against the empire, although this seldom materialized in active disloyalty.

But the emperors were also sincere Christians who regarded the conversion of the Jews as an especially salvific activity. This theological motivation, together with a mistaken notion that the empire would be stronger by being monolithic religiously, caused successive emperors to rescind the legality of Judaism and to order all the Jews to become Christians. Heraclitus in 632, Leo III in 721, Basil I about 870 (and his son Leo IV), and Romanus I in 932 passed such laws ordering all Jews to become Christians. But these efforts always ended in failure, and the efforts to enforce these laws were allowed to become dead letter after a short while. These efforts at forced conversion, however, gave the Byzantine Jew a taste of the political insecurity which was to become the typical situation of the Jew in the West.[55] Nevertheless, when the Western Crusaders seized Byzantium in the fourth Crusade and instituted Western practices, such as forcing Jews to spit on their own circumcision, this was a kind of personal attack on the Jew that was foreign to the Byzantine tradition. In the Eastern Christian empire, where the institutions of public life remained intact, the theological doctrine of reprobation was institutionalized, but its limits were also enforced, and it was not allowed to descend to the same extent into personal Jew-baiting.[56]

In the West, however, these institutions of public life collapsed. Whereas in Byzantium, anti-Judaism was institutionalized in the form of both negations and the limits of these negations, in the West anti-Judaism became erratic and personal. This pattern took some six centuries to emerge in its distinctive form. However, we can summarize here several overall trends. The memory of Jewish citizenship was buried in the recensions of the Theodosian Code made for the barbarian empires, as indeed was the concept of citizenship generally. The collapse of a moneyed economy resulted eventually in the structuring of Jews into a special economic role, while the collapse of law and order meant that Jews could escape the limits of the social ignominy forced on them by imperial law to a somewhat more affluent life, but were also left unprotected against the personal revenge that came to be wreaked upon them by those indoctrinated by the Church's view of the Jew.

Theodoric the Ostrogoth took over the anti-Judaic laws of the Theodosian Code, but was not particularly interested in the matter.[57] Gregory the Great, reigning as Roman pontiff at the end of the sixth century, represents a perfect model of the anti-Judaic theory, as this had been embodied in Christian Roman law and carried on by the Church through Roman law. In contrast to the view of medieval Christians and even medieval popes, Gregory the Great is often cited as a "friend" of the Jews, but this is a misunderstanding of the context in which he himself worked. It is true that Gregory opposed forced baptism and synagogue burning, but he did so as an executor of Roman law which protected Jewish religious institutions and forbade violence.[58] As a churchman, Gregory also knew that the forced-baptized Jew does not make a good Christian but attempts to remain a Jew secretly. It was on these grounds that Gregory decreed that the Jews are not to be forced to the baptismal font by threats, but are to be converted by sweetness and persuasion.

But the pope was not above adding to the spiritual persuasion economic suasions, such as the promise of drastically reduced rents on the Petrine patrimony to those Jews who accepted baptism.[59]

In his letters and decrees, Gregory shows himself the ecclesiastical heir of the emperors, who forbids violence to persons and property. But in his biblical commentaries, he manifests himself as the heir of the Christian *adversus Judaeos* tradition, where the Jew, theologically, is portrayed as the demonic unbeliever whose trail of perfidy and apostasy leads naturally to the killing of Christ and divine reprobation in history.[60] These two are not really in contradiction, however the tone of the two types of writings may appear to differ, for the theory behind Christian imperial law was essentially a social mirror of this theological view. Gregory himself clearly enunciated this theological view, as it had been translated into social policy, when he pronounced his famous "principle" on the Jews, namely, that "just as license must not be granted to the Jews to presume to do in their synagogues more than the law permits them, so they should not suffer curtailment in that which has been conceded to them."[61] This principle was to be republished by Pope Calixtus III in 1120 in the *Constitutio pro Judaeis* and was to be repeated by subsequent popes some fifteen times in the following three centuries, as the foundation of papal policy.[62] Gregory, in his own times, stands forth as the perfect marriage of Christian Rome and the Church. As an imperial churchman, he expressed his theological view of Jewish reprobation in the enforcement of social restrictions against any eminence or authority of Jews in Christian society. But, at the same time, he protected them to the limits of guaranteeing that they would be able to continue to worship as Jews (until they saw the error of their ways) and should not suffer violence to their personal lives or religious institutions. This theory and its social expression, narrow enough in its Christian imperial form, was to appear as a model of enlightenment, compared to the vilification that was to characterize medieval society later.

In Visigothic Spain, the treatment of the Jews took an erratic course. The Arian Visigoths received the anti-Judaic laws of the Theodosian Code in a recension, but were not especially concerned with the matter. But this changed completely when the Visigothic kings were converted to Catholicism. Then all the anti-Judaic laws of the imperial code were revived and the ecclesiastical laws against the Jews were also enacted into civil law. For one hundred twenty-five years (586–711), kings and bishops united in a continuous effort to convert the Spanish Jews by force. In addition to the full force of all the earlier imperial and church laws, the Visigothic kings decreed the abolition of Judaism as a legal religion. Jews who attempted to remain Jews were regarded as apostates, and every method was used to search out those who continued to try to retain Jewish practices. Jews were even ordered to destroy by fire and stoning other Jews who Judaized.[63] The Church itself disapproved of these extreme measures, and they obviously went far beyond any animosity toward the Jews among ordinary Christians. The kings finally ended up attacking the entire Christian populace, including the priests, in an effort to coerce an unwilling people to enforce these laws against the Jews.

Jews were a large, prosperous, and politically powerful group in Spain at this time, while the Visigothic monarchy was weak, faction-ridden, and continually plagued by fears of conquest from the East. In this context, the Jews were seen as a politically subversive element. In a final effort to set the Christian populace against the Jews, the kings ordered the Jews to surrender all property and to engage in no means of economic livelihood. Driven to desperation, the Jews entered into a plot with their coreligionists in Africa to deliver Spain to the Moslems. This plot was discovered, and the Jews were all reduced to the status of slaves *in perpetuum*. Their property was confiscated and their children taken from them to be raised as Christians. But shortly thereafter, the Moslems invaded Spain and delivered the Jewish populace from this final nadir.[64]

With the Arab conquest, a new era began for Spanish Jewry that was to last for six hundred years. Moslems were by nò means without their own laws which inferiorized both Jews and Christians. But relatively speaking, Jews had broader opportunities for advancement in Moslem than in Christian lands. Neither mass massacres, mass expulsions, nor forced conversion took place in orthodox Moslem areas. The Jewish community in Moslem Spain was to rise to unusual creative brilliance, although not always without jealousy from other groups. The eminence of the Jewish community in Spain is illustrated by the fact that in 932, when Romanus I again reiterated the laws of forced baptism against Jews in Byzantium, he was persuaded to call off this persecution by the intervention of the brilliant Jewish courtier-scholar, Hasdai ibn Shaprut, chief minister at the court of the caliph 'Abd al Rahman III at Cordova.[65] For many centuries, the Jews of Spain profited by the religious competition that made it unwise either for the Moslems in the south or for the Catholic kingdom to the north to alienate them and drive them into the other camp by enforcing a monolithic religious policy. As the Catholic kingdom spread southward, it appeared to have learned this lesson even better than its southern rival and extended the benefits of an open society to its Jewish subjects, causing them to prefer the Catholic king to an embattled Moslem rule, which became narrower in its religious policy as its last footholds in Europe were being eliminated in the thirteenth century.

But unfortunately, the lessons of Visigothic Spain had not really been learned by the Catholics. Their efforts to create a monolithic Catholic Spain were merely held in abeyance until the Moslem rival was eliminated. Then Catholic Spain turned on the Jews and from the fourteenth century reinstated all the traditional restrictions. At the end of the fourteenth century, this uniquely assimilated and cultured Jewish community found itself faced with the full force of bloody pogroms, decrees of forced baptism, and the instruments of the Inquisition to search out the secret Judaizers. Hundreds of thousands of Jews accepted baptism. Some of these remained secretly Jews, while those who refused baptism were subject to massacre and confiscation of property. Finally, in 1492, Torquemada persuaded the king to formally expel all Jews who were not baptized, so the Inquisition could settle down to its work of hunting out the secret Judaizers. In Portugal the same tragedy was repeated, only here they were not allowed to leave, but were given only the option of forced baptisms or death.

Spanish Jewish history ends with a phenomenon which approaches racial anti-Semitism. Here we see a formally Christianized Jewish community which is nevertheless hunted down by the Inquisition for being secretly "Jewish." The "laws of purity of blood," which became general in Spanish society by the sixteenth century, were purely racial. They excluded the Jew from public and Church leadership, regardless of whether he was a secret Judaizer or the most sincere Catholic. Those who aspired to positions in public life or the Church had to display their geneological charts to the Inquisition to prove that they had no hidden Jewish ancestry. Such laws remained on the books in Catholic religious orders, such as the Jesuits, until the twentieth century. They are the ancestor of the Nazi Nuremberg laws. They also present us with the ambivalence of the Christian demand for the Jew's "conversion." The individually converted Jew could be assimilated. The mass converted Jewish population, however, was still perceived as a separate "Jewish" community in an ethnic sense. All the diabolism attributed to "Judaism" was still popularly perceived as attached to the "Jew," in this way. Moreover, baptism, even if forced, automatically canceled all the anti-Judaic legislation and thus overthrew the barriers to Jewish advancement in Christian society. Thus, in Spain in the sixteenth century, we have a dress rehearsal for the nineteenth-century European experience. The Jewish community, made to assimilate *en masse,* then is perceived as a shocking invasion of Christian society, and barriers previously thrown up against them on religious grounds are now reinstituted on racial grounds.[66]

In Frankish Gaul, however, a different pattern of development took place. For centuries, it appeared as though the anti-Judaic pattern was to make little serious inroads in these lands of the German heirs of the Western Roman Empire. At first, some of the newly converted Merovingian kings attempted to imitate the policy of forced conversion of their Visigothic cousins. Chilperic in 582 and Dagobert in 629 offered the Jews the options of baptism or expulsion, and many fled to more tolerant regions, such as Marseilles.[67] But these efforts were ineffectual. With the rise of the Islamic empire, the role of the Jews in Gaul took on a new character. The Syrians, who had monopolized trade, were now cut off as Christians in an Arab land. In Gaul, economic institutions had deteriorated to the primitive level. The Jews remained the one go-between who could carry on some modicum of international trade between Europe and the Near East. Thus, in this period, they become uniquely identified as merchants. This does not mean that they completely monopolized trade in Gaul, any more than they ever monopolized moneylending later. The Byzantines also were important traders between East and West. But the Jews, with their base in communities of coreligionists scattered from England all the way to China, had a unique opportunity to provide the catalyst for the revival of trade at the very moment when it was fading to its lowest ebb in the West. In this role, they became favored and protected by the Frankish kings, who gave them special charters to reside in Gaul and carry out trade between Gaul and the East.[68]

In Gaul, therefore, it became primarily the Church which attempted to maintain the old theory of Jewish reprobation and to insist on all the old laws that restricted Jews from office holding, possession of Christian slaves, or any other type of eminence or authority over Christians, while the Carolingian kings found it inexpedient to adhere too closely to these laws of the Christian state. In this situation, the institutionalization of Jewish reprobation was eased. The Jewish community was able to emerge into prosperity and favor, and even to make Judaism itself attractive enough to win converts, among them the minister to the court of Louis the Pious[69] and a prominent ninth-century Italian bishop.[70] The discipline and communal ethics of Judaism contrasted favorably with the corruption of the Church. But this meant that the Church, in attempting to maintain a theory of Jewish reprobation that was falling into legal neglect, appealed much more directly to the possibilities of envy and hatred in the Christian population. It indoctrinated in its sermons a viewpoint that it temporarily could not enforce.[71] With the development of liturgical drama at the turn of the millennium, the possibilities of inculcating hatred for the Jew through popular representation of him as the enemy of salvation was greatly extended.[72] The Jewish community prospered in the towns of France and Germany at the end of the Dark Ages, thanks to its ability to play the middleman in reviving commerce. But the theological image taught by the Church to the Christian populace was preparing a terrible revenge for this temporary escape from repression.

3. *From the Crusades to Emancipation: The Age of the Ghetto*

In the high Middle Ages, the Church's struggle to reassert the theologically required status of "misery" upon the Jews was rewarded a thousandfold. The medieval period ended with the Jewish community reduced to political servitude, social ignominy, and ghettoization, economic ruin, vulnerability to violence from below, and arbitrary exploitation and expulsion from above, until finally the Jewries of England, France, Spain, Portugal, and much of Germany had been disseminated, expelled, or forced to practice their religion in hiding. Above this whole development, there reigned the theological image of the Jew, both shaping developments and then serving as the explanation and excuse for them, the image itself growing constantly more evil, until it culminated with the virtual identification of the Jew with the Devil. How this development took place is an exceedingly complex story with many of the connecting points of different factors uncertain, although the overall trend is ever downward. We can do no more than make the barest summary of the various elements here.

The great turning point of Jewish status in the Western Middle Ages, a turning point itself expressive of the success of the Church's indoctrination of popular religious hatred for the Jew, was the Crusades. Like a great underground stream of enmity, the Crusades burst upon the prospering Jewish communities along the Rhineland from the lower levels of medieval society, catching both ecclesiastical and secular leaders by surprise and leaving them quite helpless to protect the victims. Although the Church and all Christian society agreed in principle that the Jews were a vile people hated by God, the social consequences of this in massacres ever eluded their understanding. The fine points of the Church's theory that the Jews, though damnable, are to be physically preserved to the end of time, although in a state of "misery," to witness the triumph of the Church, eluded the comprehension of the mobs. The Church, in turn, proved incapable of understanding that the mob merely acted out, in practice, a hatred which the Church taught in theory and enforced in social degradation whenever possible. Moreover, the Church offered neither political rights nor means of livelihood to the Jews. Therefore, the Church's theory that the Jews should be physically "preserved," but in a state of "misery," itself contained the basic contradiction that the Church could offer them no concrete protection or means of existence in practice. These had to be won by the Jews themselves by allying themselves with secular princes to contravene the Church's laws against usury, thus placing themselves in the additional jeopardy of being defined as sinners, heretics, and doubly carnal men.

The mobs that pillaged and massacred the Jewish communities along the Rhine in 1096, and again in each successive Crusade, were generally not the armies of nobles recruited by the Church, but the armies of the poor that arose spontaneously to take the cross, led by popular religious fanatics.[73] The Church did not oppose this popular "enthusiasm," and indeed encouraged it by its teaching that anyone who takes the cross automatically has all his debts in moratorium. But popular fanaticism added to this other ideas, such as the claim that anyone "who kills a Jew has all his sins forgiven" and that "it is preposterous to set out on a long journey to kill God's enemies far away, while God's worst enemies, the Jews, are dwelling at ease close at hand."[74] Although religious rather than economic motives dominated the minds of the mobs, the fact that many of the Crusaders, individually and as expeditions, were in debt to Jews doubtless had an additional effect. The Crusades also opened the door for European international trade. The Crusader's path was converted into the path of commerce. The trade routes which had been pioneered by Jewish traveling merchants since the rise of Islam now became unsafe for Jewish merchants, for Jewish caravans found on the routes to the East would automatically be slaughtered by Crusaders. So the rise of the Crusades corresponds to the expropriation and retreat of the Jew as merchant, who had kept the trade routes between Europe and Asia open during the Dark Ages.[75]

The pogroms of the Crusades were met with stoic heroism by the Jewish communities of the Rhineland. Refusing the baptism offered at sword's point by the Crusaders, they regularly submitted to death or committed mass suicide rather than be baptized. A martyr ethic was forged in European Jewry. The Christian doctrine of the Trinity was regarded as polytheism and its view of Jesus' divinity as idolatry. To resist baptism was comparable to the witness of the ancient martyrs of Israel, who resisted to the death the assaults of paganism at the time of the Maccabees. Jews died uttering the *Shema'* as witnesses to the unity of God's Holy Name.[76] This resistance of the Jews to baptism was inexplicable to Christians. Christian theology had deprived Jews of inner spirituality and defined them as people of mere legalism and "carnality." This encounter with Jewish faith then could not bring about repentance in Christians. It resulted instead in a compensatory wave of new anti-Judaic myths to justify this gratuitous slaughter of an unoffending group of people. The myths of ritual murder, well poisoning, and host profanation arose in the wake of Crusader violence to provide an image of the Jew as an insidious plotter against Christianity and to justify fanaticism.[77] These libels had not existed before. They arose as a reaction and an attempt to justify the violence of the Crusades, after the fact.

The Crusades also showed the Christian masses the vulnerability of the Jewish community, something they had not realized before. Now they saw that this prosperous group, seemingly under the protection of powerful princes, actually could be attacked by any mob with impunity. The weak forces of law and order were helpless against such mob violence. After this lesson had been learned, the pogroms never ceased for many centuries. The Crusades also helped to redefine the political status of the Jew. It was a crime to kill a Jew, placed under the king's peace. But since the prince protected the Jew, the Jew himself was now forbidden to bear arms. In a chivalric society, this worked to redefine the status of the Jews as serfs. But this result was itself dependent on the theological view of the Jews.

Clergy were unarmed and protected as sacred persons "for their honor." But the Jews, being ignominious persons, could not be defined as protected for this reason. So there remained only one other option in feudal law. This was that the Jews were unarmed and protected because they were serfs, not free men.[78]

This political redefinition of the Jews as personal serfs of the prince only became clearly defined when it interacted with ecclesiastical law, which, in the early thirteenth century, was systematically working to reduce all Jewish social privileges. The basic theory that underlay Church law on the Jews was the doctrine of *Servitus Judaeorum,* or the perpetual servitude of the Jews, i.e., their reprobate place in history as punishment for killing Christ. Through interaction with this idea, which was the theoretical principle of canonical anti-Judaic legislation beginning with the Epistle of Innocent of 1205, German law came to define the Jews as persons without citizenship or civil rights who are classed in the unique status of *servi camerae* or "serfs of the royal chamber."[79]

This idea has often been traced to the earlier status under German law of the Jewish merchants as "strangers," who are given rights of residence for trade only by special charter by the prince and are regarded as persons to be protected by the prince, since they have no other "lord."[80] This helped to shape the special relation of the Jews to the princes. But this did not itself create this special status, for the special charters were normal procedure for all foreign merchants, and not just Jews. In a corporative society, there was no general concept of citizenship in which everyone is "equal" before the law. Each group is equal only to its peers. Groups then have specific contractual relations to each other. It was thus inevitable that the Jews would be seen as a special corporate group. But their status in relation to other groups long remained undefined. It was only with the interaction between their status as a special group, that is, to be protected by the prince, and the ecclesiastical theory of *Servitus Judaeorum,* that the political status of the Jews became redefined as that of the king's serfs and their previous status as free men was lost. Now, for the first time, a special political status was created for the Jews qua Jews regardless of occupation. The defining principle for this was exclusively religious.

It was as Jews religiously, not as a distinct racial, ethnic, or national group, that they were so distinguished. This status disappeared as soon as a Jew was baptized.[81]

The canonical legislation of the Church in the thirteenth century effected a systematic social degradation of the Jew. The Church struggled to reimpose all the old canonical and imperial anti-Judaic legislation back to Constantine. But it went beyond this in forbidding even Christian servants or nurses to the Jews under pain of excommunication.[82] The Church's basic position was that the Jew should occupy no place of eminence or power in Christian society which would ever put him in a position of authority over a Christian, however modest. The basic principle for this, as we have indicated, was that of the *Servitus Judaeorum,* as the reprobate status of the Jew in history. The imagery of Sarah, as the Church, whose children are free, and Hagar, as the Synagogue, whose children are in bondage, was the standard one for popular imagery, Church sculpture,[83] and sermonizing, as well as canonical legislation. It is an expression of the salvation wrought by Christ for Christians (and his corresponding reprobation of those who rejected him) that the "sons of the freed woman" (the Church) are never to serve the "children of the slave woman" (the Synagogue), but rather are always to be served by them.[84] This meant that any position of authority of the Jew in society, from minister of state to employer of a nurse in his home, was to be challenged by the Church on theological grounds. The Jew is always to be under, not over, Christians.

In addition to this theological degradation of the Jew to the status of servitude, Christian society was to be rigidly protected from Jewish "contamination." Any social contact, living together, eating together, sexual relations, personal conversation, especially on religious matters, was to be prevented, lest Jewish "unbelief" contaminate Christian faith. This notion of "Jewishness" as a kind of contagion that one might catch by any kind of association was to become a virulent source of notions such as "well poisoning." It also provided the stock imagery of racial anti-Semitism, which was always to depict the presence of the Jew as a kind of dangerous or insidious "contagious disease."

The final expression of the Church's effort to segregate the Jew from any social contact with Christian society was the ghetto and the wearing of Jewish dress, conical hat, and "Jew badge" (usually a yellow circle, symbolic of the Jew as betrayer of Christ for "gold," an image which fused religious with economic anti-Semitism). These regulations were passed at the Fourth Lateran Council (1215), although the Church only succeeded in enforcing them universally after the Council of Basel (1434).[85] These marks had the effect of making Jewish ignominy visible and singling the Jew out for physical attack as never before, destroying further the ability of the Jew to travel the open roads as a merchant. Other canonical rules, such as those that insisted that the synagogue must be a low and miserable building, that Jews must not enter churches or come into the streets on holy days, especially during Passiontide, or work on Sunday, were intended to enforce the visible superiority of Christianity.[86] But it also reinforced the popular idea that Jews secretly desired to mock and profane Christian symbols, even though the popes officially tended to discount the myths of ritual murder and host profanation. Finally, the Talmud itself was declared illegal. Successive inquisitions condemned it, despite the defense put up against Christian accusations by talmudic scholars.[87] The Talmud and Jewish works were burned publicly in France in the mid-thirteenth century, bringing to an end an important center of talmudic scholarship. Like Justinian, the Church seems to have believed that without the rabbinic exegesis, the Jews would quickly come to acknowledge that the christological exegesis of the Church was the correct one.

The final element that shaped the status of the Jew in medieval society was the economic one. Deprived of normal participation in agriculture, first by their inability to hold Christian servants and then by outright prohibition of landowning; trade constricted by the new dangers of hostility; and most crafts closed off by the religious character of trade guilds—the Jew had no place in medieval economy except moneylending. Unfortunately, moneylending had no place in the Church's concept of economy. In the face of a reviving commercial society, the Church clung to a fundamentally agricultural concept of economics which had no place for monetary processes. Moneylending was thought of as a charity extended to the poor, not as an enterprise that generated new wealth. Interest-taking was, therefore, forbidden. The Church clung to this outdated notion until the sixteenth century and exerted every ounce of its moral energies in attempting a futile battle against the rise of a money economy. More and more stringent penalties were attached to usury until finally usury was defined as a heresy and placed under the Inquisition. In practical terms, this effort was a total failure, since the Church itself was a part of this rising money economy, and so its own officials constantly evaded these laws. The result of the Church's crusade against usury, therefore, had as its chief effect the attachment of an enormous stigma to the moneylender and the forcing of this necessary practice into subterfuge, where interest rates became far more exploitative than would have been the case if a monetary policy had been regularized.[89]

This stigma which the Church placed upon usury ended by attaching itself primarily to the Jews. This was not because the Jews were the only usurers, or because the Church made any exception for the Jews to its general prohibition. Agents of the Church, tax collectors, and merchants were the three groups that possessed liquid capital in a still largely agricultural society, and all engaged in usury. The Church could control the first two better than the third. But among the merchant group, the Italians, who retained Eastern contacts and traditions of an urban economy from Roman days, soon rivaled the Jews.[90] The Church condemned all usurers, Jew or Christian, and attempted to cut off Jewish usury by excommunicating Christians who dealt with them. But the princes, who needed money for their operations, opposed the Church and protected Jewish usurers. In popular thought, Jewish usury was excusable, either because the Bible allowed one to give money at interest to the "stranger," or else because the Jews were damned anyway, so it made no difference if they sinned. However, the Jews had come to be understood as property of the prince, which automatically meant that their money was his personal property also. To rob a Jew was to rob a prince. To kill or convert a Jew was to deprive a prince of his property. The moneymaking capacity of the Jews became the personal assets of the princes. On these grounds, the princes protected Jewish usury, granted Jews rights of residence, prevented mobs from attacking them, and even prevented the

Church from converting them! The Jews were changed from free economic actors into subjects of the economic policy of the princes. They became the personal usurers of the princes.

This role as royal usurers of the princes allowed the Jews to survive, but only on the most precarious basis. Socially, they were degraded as figures of ignominy in every town. Protected from attack by the princes, they became the objects of boiling hatred which the exploited classes felt against both the political power and the economic exactions of the rulers. Since the Jews were the buffers and expressions of both of these kinds of power between the princes and the people, this hatred became diverted on to the Jews. The Jews themselves had no intrinsic political rights. Their very rights of residence depended on the grants of kings who admitted them in defined numbers to serve as their economic tools, but revoked this right of residence, confiscated their property, revoked debts owed them, and expelled them, whenever it suited their purposes. As economic tools of the prince, they survived by exacting from the people the money he needed for his activities and, in turn, became the objects of the hatred which the people felt at this economic extortion. While this role lasted, leading Jews appeared wealthy to the people, but their wealth was ephemeral, most of it flowing into the coffers of the king. At any point, they could be ruined and expelled when popular protest, often taking the form of charges of ritual murder and other religious charges, made things too hot for the prince, forcing him to accede to the demands of townsmen or nobles against whom the feudal prince struggled for power. The Jews were caught in the middle of this power struggle and ultimately became its victims.[91]

The expulsions of the Jews from Spain and Portugal in the fifteenth century reflect the mingling of religious fanaticism with a new concept of nationalistic absolutism. The expulsions of the Jews from England in 1290, from France in 1390, and from most German cities in the mid-fourteenth to sixteenth centuries also had economics as their sub-theme, although the charges brought against them usually featured trumped-up accusations of ritual murder, host profanation, and the like. Luther, who began his reformation with pro-Jewish sentiments, ended by turning against them when they failed to convert. His work "The

Jews and Their Lies" was a compendium of the most virulent medieval anti-Semitism and ended by calling for the expulsion of the Jews from Germany. It had great influence in promoting such expulsion. This tract was revived in modern times as a textbook for modern anti-Semitism. The Jews fled eastward, piling upward against the Russian wall in Poland. By the end of the Middle Ages, Western Jewry was ruined. Most major areas had no professing Jews, although huddled communities of Marranos clung to the memories of the old ways in secrecy. Where Jewries survived, they were broken economically, socially degraded, reduced to pawnbroking and dealing in second-hand goods to make a bare living at the dregs of society.

As the Jewish role as moneylender was being broken in a Christian society (which was also expropriating this role for itself, often in a much more exploitative way), religious fanaticism grew all the more virulent. The late Middle Ages became not only the age of the ghetto, but the age of the Devil. The outbreak of the Black Plague in the mid-fourth century, which took the lives of a third of the population of Europe, and other factors unhinged the mind of Europe. Everywhere witches, devils, and death danced together through a cloud of sulfur and ashes, and the mingled figure of all these evils was stamped by the mythical face of "the Jew." The fact that Jews were prominent as physicians, especially to the princes, and the more hygienic character of Jewish life occasionally spared it somewhat from the ravages of the plague, only added to the paranoia. It was believed that a conspiracy of Jews and lepers had poisoned the sources of water with magically cursed bags of excrement and menstrual blood, which, through secret tunnels, flowed through all the wells of Europe. Again we see the image of the Jew as an insidious disease secretly poisoning the life systems of Christian Europe, an image which was to be revived in such potent form in racial mythology. All over Europe, pogroms broke out against the Jewish community, adding the corpses of the slaughtered to those dying from the plague.[92] The image of the Jew deteriorated in the minds of Christians to that of a deformed monster, with horns, tail, cloven hoofs, and sulfuric odor to betray his fundamentally diabolic character. At the moment when drama, woodcuts, and printing were enormously increasing the range of popular communication, it was this image of the Jew that was stamped on the popular minds of Europeans, and it remained the basic image of the Jew up to its use by Nazism.[93]

4. *From the Enlightenment to the Holocaust: The Failure of Emancipation*

For the Christian, the "Middle Ages" is thought of as a period of about a thousand years, lasting from about the sixth century to the Renaissance and Reformation. From the perspective of Jewish experience, this medieval period looks quite different. The "Middle Ages" for Judaism coincides with Christendom itself! Legal disabilities of Jews in Western society lasted from Constantine to the nineteenth century, when the liberal revolutions dissolved the legal structures of Christianity as the established state religion. The age of the ghetto lasted, for Jews, into the nineteenth century in western Europe and into the twentieth in eastern Europe. The French revolutionaries disbanded the anti-Judaic laws in France in 1789, and Napoleon carried this revolution with him during his wars of conquest. But during the reaction and restoration, anti-Jewish restrictions were reinstated in many places. It was only between 1848 and 1870 that the ghetto was disbanded and full citizenship attained generally in western Europe. All disabilities were not dropped in Germany until the Weimar Republic! In eastern Europe, the pogroms of the late nineteenth and twentieth centuries mingled the old religious with the new racial charges against Jews. The ghetto was dissolved with the Russian Revolution, but for much of eastern Europe, the world of the ghetto was swept away, not by emancipation but by the Holocaust![94] When looking at European history from the perspective of the Jews, we must adjust fundamentally our sense of periodization. What for Christians is the "medieval world," abandoned centuries before Nazism, contained no such "breathing space" for Jews. The medieval world, for Jews, lasted until the revival of anti-Semitism in racial form.

When we realize the continuation of the medieval status of

the Jew down into the modern period, the imagined discontinuity between medieval anti-Judaism and Nazism narrows to uncomfortable proximity. We begin to realize that what Nazism revived was not a long-dead set of attitudes and practices, but a world only recently dissolved in the West, still maintained in the East, whose myths were still live, glowing embers easily fanned into new flames. Moreover, the very processes of the emancipation, the arguments on which it was based, the price it demanded of Judaism revivified anti-Judaism in new forms, translating the basis for contempt from theological to nationalist and then racial grounds. Where the Middle Ages was intolerant of the religious alien, the modern state was intolerant of the person of alien national identity. It had no place for Jewish self-government, such as was possible in the medieval corporate state. The Jew in the modern state became the representative of the "outsider" to nationalist identity. But the same stereotypes, the same set of psychological attitudes were preserved in this change of theoretical grounds. Philosophical liberalism provided the theoretical basis for emancipation, but at the same time suggested the basis for this transition from religious to nationalist anti-Semitism. Protestant theology and biblical studies absorbed and deepened this cultural anti-Semitism.[95]

Emancipation began earliest in the home of European rationalism, England. The expulsion of the Jews in the thirteenth century meant that their readmission in Cromwell's time allowed for the building of different relationships. Puritanism regarded the Jews as the people of the Old Testament, but its own revival of Hebrew prophetic religion gave the Jewish tradition in Christianity a much more positive evaluation than was the case with Lutheranism, with its antithesis of Law and Gospel. The laws of the ghetto were not revived for returning Jews, who were allowed to live anywhere. Insofar as they suffered disabilities, they were the same as were suffered by all dissenters from the established Church, and so linked them with Catholics and dissenting Protestants.[96] Efforts to remove disabilities upon the Jews began in England among rationalist thinkers in the seventeenth century. The American colonies, that were founded in this English Protestant tradition and later fused this tradition with the heritage of the Enlightenment, were able to make a fresh start, carrying with them the relatively more liberal traditions of England toward the Jews.

In eastern Europe the pogroms in Poland in the mid-seventeenth century and the continual oppression of Russian Jews from the eighteenth to the early twentieth centuries drove eastern Jewry again westward, seeking admission to areas where they had previously been expelled. The great pogroms of late nineteenth century Russia drove a large community to America. But in western Europe, in those places where Jews were allowed to reside or were readmitted, the laws of the ghetto remained fully intact until the mid-eighteenth century and only slowly began to dissolve thereafter. The first to emerge from the ghetto were the "court Jews," the wealthy Jews who were given additional privileges of residence, extra-ghetto housing, the right to discard the Jewish dress, to marry, to pass on their privileges to their children, all restricted for ordinary Jews. In turn, they acted as special financial agents for princes, especially in German principalities. This role of the court Jew was simply a continuation of the traditional status of the Jews as "serfs of the prince," put to extended use in the age of absolutism. These very rights granted to court Jews illustrate the disabilities of most Jews, for they were simply rights of ordinary existence, which the court Jew had to purchase as special privileges by bribery and regular payment of protection money.[97]

The court Jew was also the emissary between the Jewish community and the gentile world. Whole Jewish communities often slipped into an area under the cover of the privileges of the court Jew. The court Jew protected the Jewish community and sought to win for them extended rights of residence and means of existence. But he also exploited them, made them dependent on him, and sought to differentiate himself from them in order to prove to the world of the court that he was "different" from the "other Jews." Thus the court Jew prefigures the identity conflict that emancipation was to bring to the Jew. On the other side, there were the Jewish vagabonds, with no rights of residence or means of existence, who eked out a precarious existence as peddlers and often were pushed into the underworld of robbers. This wide range of status created intense problems of discipline and self-image for the Jewish community which was held collectively responsible for any crime done by any Jew.

The chief occupation allowed Jews was still moneylending. Court Jews translated this into a new, creative role as agents of the financial and organizational needs of the growing modern state. For a third time in European history, Jews pioneered a new development needed for the expansion of society, turning a necessity into a virtue. But Christian society, in turn, turned this virtue into a vice by stigmatizing this role as "carnal" and conspiratorial. Jews as bankers, diplomats, and agents of international communication between states played these roles for their masters, the princes, who were its primary beneficiaries, while the court Jew himself often ended his life on the gallows as the victim of jealousy.[98] Some Jews grew rich and were able to buy their way out of the ghetto, while their children made haste to depart from the financial and commercial life to more "respectable" professions. The role of the court Jew gave birth to the Jewish banker-diplomat, which found its apex in the House of Rothschild. But this also became the basis for the revival of economic anti-Semitism. No myth was more widely believed in the late nineteenth and early twentieth centuries than the myth that "the Jews" controlled international banking and trade and were the secret government of the world. But this attack on "Jewish money" took place at a time when this development had been almost entirely expropriated by non-Jews. Just as in Crusading times and in the late Middle Ages, the attack on this pioneering Jewish development took place when the actual role of the court Jew was at an end; vilification and ruin were heaped on Jews whose role had already been replaced.[99]

However, even the liberalism with which Jews allied themselves in their struggle for emancipation harbored fundamental ambivalences toward Jews. The price of emancipation was also seen as one of cultural assimilation. Most liberals actually thought of this as paving the way for Jewish conversion to Christianity. All liberals took it for granted that ghetto Judaism represented a bad moral, spiritual, and intellectual condition. Talmudic Judaism, as the religious basis of the self-governing Jewish community, must be relinquished. The price of emancipation was the destruction of Jewish self-government and autonomous corporate identity. It was this autonomous corporate identity, possible in the medieval corporate state, which had allowed the Jews to keep a sense of peoplehood within Christian society. It was this sense of autonomous corporate identity and peoplehood which the modern nationalist state could not tolerate and which became the basis of modern anti-Semitism. Now Jewish identity in an ethnic sense was seen as intrinsically evil. It must be dissolved so the Jew could become a "German," or else it was seen as indissolvable, and so the Jew must be expelled. In any case, the Jew must pay for emancipation by ceasing to be a Jew in a corporate sense.

To be sure, the Jews themselves wanted emancipation too. They wanted full access to modern cultural and economic life and were ready to pay for this by sacrifice of their political autonomy. However, the narrowness from which the emancipated Jew fled in the ghetto had little to do with that "materialism" of Christian anti-Judaic polemic. Indeed, the classical spirit of the ghetto resembled nothing so much as a rather austere monastery, resolutely turned away from the Christian world, where men in long black garb studied with profound reverence every word of Torah, seeking to penetrate every time and place of daily life with the fire of the Divine Presence.[100] But Christian liberals had no knowledge or perception of any such riches underneath the outwardly alien image of the ghetto. Indeed, it is fair to say that Christianity throughout this whole history never really engaged in dialogue with Judaism itself or entered into Jewish history or perspective, but only used it as a foil and antithesis to Christianity. This anti-Judaic left hand of the Christian redemptive self-image continued to be basically the stance of nineteenth-century liberal theology and philosophy. Talmudic Judaism, even the Old Testament, was seen as a retrograde, bigoted, immoral, and fossilized religion, without inward spiritual or ethical principle, which had to be overcome, both here and now and in world history, in order for mankind to "progress."

This view also penetrated to the liberals' understanding of Christianity, leading them to deny that Christianity and Jesus were in any way intrinsically "Jewish." Christianity was seen as the universal religion of nature or reason, which arose as the antithesis and negation of Judaism. It was this universal, natural religion which was the basis on which the Enlightenment sought the unity of all men beneath their religious differences. The Christian rationalists identified this with the "essence" of Christianity. The anticlerical deists rejected Christianity also for the religion of reason which must supersede it. But, in either case, what was hated in biblical revealed religion was stereotyped as "Jewish," while all positive values of spirituality, rationality, and universality were the characteristics of Christianity or philosophy that were antithetical to "Judaism." Jews were offered an ideology of emancipation which was itself based on a rationalist version of anti-Judaism.[101]

Jewish liberals responded by proposing Judaism itself as a better candidate for the religion of reason, a religion based on ethics which did not demand the conversion of others. Out of this fusion of Judaism and rationalism grew Reform Judaism. But no Christian liberal took seriously this viewpoint, or bothered to examine the possible credibility for this view in talmudic tradition. For them, rabbinic thought was a closed book and Judaism the antithesis of every value of mind or depth of spiritual feeling.[102]

For liberals, what was "wrong" with the Jews was regarded as cultural. Jews could be emancipated if they ceased to be Jews culturally, becoming secular or, as most liberals secretly expected, Christian. For conservative Christians, what was wrong with the Jews was intrinsic to Jewish "character." Bigotry, immorality, legalism, carnality, materialism, and lack of inner spiritual or ethical principles were regarded as intrinsic traits that expressed the "nature" of the Jews. In the seventeenth century, a tradition of anti-talmudic scholarship was developed which distorted and gathered out of context negative statements throughout Jewish tradition on Gentiles and idolators. Out of this was created a polemical caricature of Judaism that was presented as its teachings against Christians. This anti-talmudic tradition was exemplified by J. A. Eisenmanger's *Judaism Revealed* (1700). Here, Judaism was represented as a religion of bigotry and immorality, filled with hatred for Christians and giving license for any kind of immoral dealings with them. These views were reprinted continually from the eighteenth century to the Nazi era and became an integral part of the arguments for and against emancipation. Liberals believed that the Jews would get over these evil traits by dissolving the identity created by rabbinic thought. Conservatives believed that they could never get over these traits because it was their unchangeable "nature." But both sides took the basic stereotypes of Judaism for granted.[103]

Emancipation did not depend on who won these arguments, but on the processes of secularization that shaped the modern state and which could not tolerate self-governing groups apart from the monolithic organization of the nation-state.[104] It was on these grounds that the Jews had to either be drawn into a secular definition of citizenship, based on nationalism, or else be regarded as incapable of assimilating into this national identity and eliminated by expulsion (or extermination). It was here that liberal philosophy and theology also played an ambivalent role. Their definition of religion, either as the universal, natural religion of reason, or else as profound inwardness, made Judaism the antithesis of the concept of "religion." Since Judaism was not a religion, according to either Christian rationalist or Christian romantic theories, Judaism came to be defined in this tradition of thought in nationalist, quasi-racial terms. Judaism was said to be, not a religion, but the laws of a nation. Jews were not a religious group, but a foreign nation. The antithesis of Judaism and Christianity was translated into an antithesis between Jews and Europeans, or Jews and Germans.[105] But the fundamental stereotypes of Judaism as the antithesis of Christian salvific values persisted underneath this secular translation. Now the Jews were unassimilable because they represented a perverse and alien "foreign essence" which was the opposite to all that was spiritual, noble, and true in the "Germanic spirit." The German spirit was that of *"Innigkeit, Gemütsleben, Glaube, Idealismus,"* while the "Jewish spirit" was that of *"Skeptizismus, Sarkasmus, Spott, Materialismus."*[106] It was not until the advent of racist anthropology in the late nineteenth century that this view recieved its full-blown racial theory. But the grounds for a secular translation of anti-Judaism into racial anti-Semitism were laid in the philosophy of the Enlightenment and then deepened in the philosophers of Romanticism.[107]

Since the emancipated Jew left the ghetto by accepting, in large measure, these stereotypes of talmudic faith and taking for granted the possibility of a neutral national culture and society where he could become "like the others," this meant that he was largely unable to correct these stereotypes, having made haste to bury any deeper understanding of the roots of the world he was leaving. The emancipated Jew thus became a self-contradiction who must prove his right to be accepted "as a Jew," by proving that he was not at all "like the Jews." Accepting the ideology of the secular national state at face value, he remained baffled by his own continuing rejection, unable to overcome the ways in which all positive values were still regarded implicitly as "Christian," while he, as a Jew, was still assumed to possess the characteristics of "evil Judaism" under his apparently assimilated exterior. The emancipated Jew thus became an unwilling Marrano. It was not that he secretly practiced talmudic Judaism, while feigning assimilation; now he actively sought assimilation on secular grounds, but still had projected upon him, by Christian society, all the alien features of the ghetto which are presumed to be still hiding under his good bourgeois appearance as his "real" identity! The ghetto Jew of Christian mythology remained the screen through which western Europe continued to view the emancipated Jew. In vain did the Jew escape the ghetto and dissolve its life, because the myth of the ghetto Jew remained firmly fixed in the minds of Christians as his real "nature."

The processes of emancipation coincided with traumatic changes in European society in the revolutionary era which dissolved the old Christian order for secular, liberal industrialized society. Thus the processes through which Jews entered mainstream society also created a traumatic reaction in those classes —clerics, landholders, and lower-middle-class artisans—who were deeply threatened by the new secular industrial society. The secular Jews were hardly the creators of these new forces. Indeed, they formed only about one percent of the population in Germany and France, and only a small part of them were actually secularized, and even fewer were leaders in the commerce and culture of the new society. Yet they were concentrated in urban areas and in professions that made them highly conspicuous. As the beneficiaries of secularism, the secular Jews became the symbolic representatives of the dissolution of Christendom. Secular Jews came to be fantasized as a kind of "insidious disease," flowing into the veins of "Christian Europe," sapping its spiritual, moral, and economic energy. They were imagined to be the creators and secret managers of all the forces represented by the new secular industrial state. The traditional stereotype of the Jew as "carnal man," which mingled religious and economic anti-Semitism, ever conspiring against both the faith and the wealth of Christendom, was brought into play to create the new myth that everything which these threatened groups hated in the new society was intrinsically "Jewish."[108] Even socialists, especially Christian socialists, bought into this myth by identifying the Jews with capitalism, while conservatives identified Jews with the forces of scepticism, secularism, and democracy that were dissolving the old order, religiously and socially. Contrary as these two positions may appear, they often made common cause with each other in the anti-Semitic parties that arose in the late nineteenth century.[109] The infamous *Protocols of the Elders of Zion* was a chief instrument of this myth. Produced by the Russian secret police in the late nineteenth century, its roots lay in Russian anti-Judaic mysticism. It built the ancient Christian claim that the Messiah whom the Jews expect is the Anti-Christ into a fantasy wherein a Jewish secret government, in existence since the time of Christ, plots the overthrow of Christendom and the establishment of the reign of the Devil over the world in the last age of world history. The *Protocols* thus provided a clear link between Christian anti-Judaism and modern anti-Semitism.

Nazism arose as the final repository of all this heritage of religious and secular anti-Semitism, making Jews responsible for capitalism and communism simultaneously! The racial theory was new, but the stereotypes of hatred were old. The mythical Jew, who is the eternal conspiratorial enemy of Christian faith, spirituality, and redemption, was being shaped to serve as the scapegoat for all the things in secular industrial society which the middle class had created and now feared and hated for their dissolution of traditional religion, culture, social hierarchy, and life style. But the middle class could not challenge this new society without challenging the basis of their own wealth, and conservatives did not want to liquidate the economic affluence of this society—only its social results. So the way to be against modern society without upsetting bourgeois power was to do so in a purely ideological way, diverting all the pent-up fear and unrest of the dissolution of Christendom onto the Jews. European society was primed to undergo a gigantic "purge" of the dangerous infection that it felt was threatening its inner health, wealth, and wisdom. The mythical Jew had long been fashioned in Christian history to serve as the symbol of this "disease" from which the Christian must purge himself in order to save himself. Under the slogan "the Jews are our misfortune," mass paranoia again gripped the soul of the European heartland, but in the language of racism and deliberately engineered by gangsters of mass communication.

In 1933, when Hitler came to power, there began the systematic reassertion of anti-Jewish laws which reversed the gains made by the emancipation. Jews quickly were again reduced to persons without rights, citizenship, or means of existence. First, Jews were excluded from all civil offices, including teaching and judgeships. Then, they were expelled from the army; then, from the legal profession and, as much as possible, from medicine. Then, they were denied citizenship altogether and forbidden to intermarry with Aryans or employ them in their homes. Finally, the Crystal Night of 1938 saw a coordinated attack on Jewish businesses, homes, and synagogues throughout the Reich. Nazi propaganda flooded every means of communication. Even little children were held up for ridicule and abuse in school. Jews again were forced to wear the yellow badge and began to be rounded up for places of detention. The Talmud and Jewish learning again went up in flames. The Jews were being marked down for final elimination, although the decision to exterminate them, rather than expel them, only came about when all doors to Jewish emigration were closed with the war.[110]

The Christian background to the Aryan laws is illustrated by an incident reported in Hitler's *Table Talk*. Here, he reports that two bishops came to confront him on the issue of Nazi racial policy. Hitler replied that he was only putting into effect what Christianity had preached and practiced for 2000 years.[111] Even the Confessing Church proved peculiarly unable to confront the issue of anti-Semitism itself, theologically or practically. It took its stand instead on opposition to German Christianity in the name of "pure doctrine."[112] Even the great figure of the resistance, Bonhoeffer, displays an element of this myopia. In his lectures of 1934, one of his few references to the Jewish issue, Bonhoeffer remarks that the Jews should never be expelled from Europe. They must remain, for Christians, as a negative witness to Christ, the exemplification of divine wrath. He is oblivious to the fact that it is this very myth that lies behind the history that shaped anti-Semitism.[113] For most churchmen, Protestant and Catholic, the fact that the Nazis declared themselves anti-communist, anti-liberal, and anti-Semitic was enough to guarantee that they were on the side of Christianity and the restoration of Christendom, despite their worship of Wotan.[114]

But nationalist, racial anti-Semitism contained a crucial element that went beyond the framework of Christian anti-Judaism. It was now Jewish *peoplehood* that must be destroyed before the monolithic nationalism of the modern state. This meant that the massacres conducted in the name of racial anti-Semitism now came from the state itself, whereas, in Christendom, violence had always come from the mob, while the state had been the protector of Jewish continued existence. This perhaps helps to explain the paralysis of the European Jews before the phenomenon of Nazism. Pogroms from the mobs were well known. But state-engineered genocide was heretofore unknown. Christian religious anti-Judaism had demanded the misery of the Jews and the containment of Jewish "unbelief," leaving the "final solution" in the hands of God. Racial anti-Semitism could stop at no such limitation. A disease of the body, unlike that of the will, cannot be cured by conversion. Hence, even assimilation was viewed as a trick by which the "Jewish disease" infiltrated the Aryan bloodstream. Master of its own eschatology and creator of its own millennium, the Third Reich took in hand that Last Judgment which Christianity had reserved for the returning Christ. In Hitler, the Führer empowers himself with the ultimate work of Christ to execute the "Final Solution to the Jewish question."

Today, European Jewry is gone, swept away by the Holocaust. To be sure, some Jews continue to live in Europe. But European, especially German, Jewry, as a cultural phenomenon, which made such brilliant contributions to modern culture and scholarship, has been destroyed. In North America, the promise and the ambivalences of the emancipation are still intact. In Russia, the condition of ghetto Jewry mingles with the totalitarianism of the modern revolutionary state. It is in Israel that the myth of Christian anti-Judaism comes to an end. Here, the dispersion is overcome, and the Jewish people regathered into the ancient homeland, contrary to that Christian theory that denied this possibility. The Zionist messianic vision of the Return confronts the Christian doctrine of eternal misery and dispersion of the Jewish people to the end of history. Yet, the hope for a people "at ease in Zion" still eludes the Jewish state, as it struggles with the effects of Western imperialism which, now, set one victimized people against another.

Chapter 5

Theological Critique of
The Christian Anti-Judaic Myth

We have seen that the anti-Judaic myth is neither a superficial nor a secondary element in Christian thought. The foundations of anti-Judaic thought were laid in the New Testament. They were developed in the classical age of Christian theology in a way that laid the basis for attitudes and practices that continually produced terrible results. Most Christians today may seem more than willing to prune back the cruder expressions of these attitudes and practices. But to get at the roots from which these grew is a much more profound problem. The wheat and the tares have grown together from the beginning, and so it may seem impossible to pull up the weed without uprooting the seed of Christian faith as well. Yet as long as Christology and anti-Judaism intertwine, one cannot be safe from a repetition of this history in new form. The end of Christendom may seem to have brought an end to the possibility of legislating theological anti-Judaism as social policy. But we witnessed in Nazism the ability of this virus to appear in even worse form in secular dress. Yet I believe that this is actually a critical moment when a deep encounter with the structures of anti-Judaism is not only necessary to atone for this history, but may be essential to revitalizing the original Christian vision itself.

The end of Christendom means Christianity now must think

of itself as a Diaspora religion. On the other hand, the Jewish people, shaken by the ultimate threat to Jewish survival posed by modern anti-Semitism, have taken a giant leap against all odds and against their two thousand years of urban Disapora culture, and founded the state of Israel. The Return to the homeland has shimmered as a messianic horizon of redemption from the exile for the Jewish people for many centuries. But Christianity dogmatically denied the very possibility of such a return, declaring that eternal exile was the historical expression of Jewish reprobation. Now this Christian myth has been made obsolete by history. But the Jewish hope that gave messianic ultimacy to the Return is also in difficulty. When viewed from the perspective of oppression in the exile, the Return to Israel is indeed a liberation movement and a salvific event for Jews. But in the Middle East conflict, it manifests its historical ambiguity. In Israel the Jewish people face seemingly irreconcilable demands: Jewish nationalism versus Palestinian nationalism, national security against equality and social justice for all. This struggle takes place in a land with a heritage of communal and imperial conflicts, from ancient times to modern colonialism and neocolonialism.

Every criticism of Israel is not to be equated with anti-Semitism. Yet there is no doubt that anti-Zionism has become, for some, a way of reviving the myth of the "perennial evil nature of the Jews," to refuse to the Jewish people the right to exist as a people with a homeland of its own. The threat to Jewish survival, posed in ultimate terms by Nazism and never absent as long as anti-Semitism remains in the dominant culture of the Diaspora, lends urgency to the need for the Israeli state. But the religious interpretation of Israel, as the Promised Land given by God and as a land whose restoration was regarded as a messianic event, impedes the search for that pluralism that is necessary for peaceful coexistence with indigenous Arab peoples, both Moslem and Christian. Stuck between a religious orthodoxy forged in the Diaspora and secular nationalism, Israel awaits the rebirth of that prophetic tradition that can transform Zionism into a language of self-criticism in the light of that ultimate Zion of justice and peace which is still to be achieved. In Israel, the Jewish people have tasted salvation. Yet, they must now take their stand on this, not as an ultimate but as a new historical foundation from which to continue the struggle for that final redeemed earth which still eludes both Jew and Christian. The collapse of Christendom and the founding of Israel, then, provide Christians and Jews with a new historical situation from which to rethink their relationship.

This concluding chapter will examine the basic theological structures of the Christian anti-Judaic myth. The more virulent anti-Judaic myths of the sort which most modern Christians would reject are not the problem. At the most fundamental level, the problem is the presuppositions which are still affirmed by Christian theologians as basic to Christian theology, long after they have repudiated the more fanciful mythic projections. We must be frank about the risks of this undertaking. Possibly anti-Judaism is too deeply embedded in the foundations of Christianity to be rooted out entirely without destroying the whole structure. We may have to settle for the sort of ecumenical goodwill that lives with theoretical inconsistency and opts for a modus operandi that assures practical cooperation between Christianity and Judaism. Certainly, most Jewish thinkers assume that this is the best that can be done. Nevertheless, this study has made clear that the anti-Judaic structure of Christian thought is not only a problem for Jews, but rests on forms of thought that are troubling to Christians as well. Rethinking these modes of thought has become as necessary for Christian identity as it is for improved relationship with Jews. Each of the basic antitheses which were used to vilify the Jews also appears as an antithesis that has retarded Christian theological maturation. Anti-Judaism was originally more than social polemic. It was an expression of Christian self-affirmation. So now rethinking anti-Judaism has become more than an external task. It has become an internal task of Christian theological reconstruction.

1. *The Schism of Judgment and Promise*

If we wish to reaffirm the gospel without this anti-Judaic left hand, we must analyze and reconstruct the basic dualisms which shaped early Christian self-understanding. These dualisms, which make Judaism their negative side, are so deeply ingrained in Christian language that modern critical theology and liberal sermonizing still remain largely oblivious to their implications. "Christian" sincerity and authenticity are, as a matter of course, contrasted with so-called "Pharisaism." "Christian" inwardness is explicated over against something called "Jewish legalism." The good news of the gospel is proclaimed as a fulfillment which discards as obsolescent that which is "Jewish." These antitheses, presumed to be an accurate description of Judaism, both then and now, remain a basic mode of Christian thinking and preaching. Seldom does it occur to Christians to ask if these judgments have anything to do with real Judaism, either in Jesus' time or today, much less if these negations have anything to do with a history that led to Auschwitz. As a young student, I questioned teachers and preachers who used such language, asking them if such language was not "anti-Semitic." Usually I received a shocked response and a denial of any connection between the two. Christians have generally suppressed a knowledge of their own history on this matter and preserve an obliviousness to the results of their anti-Judaic language.

The schism of judgment and promise in the exegesis of the historical and prophetic books of the Old Testament was originally fundamental to the Christian anti-Judaic argument. This type of exegesis hardly has any currency today. Old Testament scholars at Christian seminaries generally have abandoned christological for historical interpretation of their texts. Yet, seldom is the contradiction between an "Old Testament," interpreted in its own terms, and a "New Testament," which presumes a christological interpretation of the Old Testament, really brought out in the open. One slides over from one to the other without ever grappling with the implications of the fact that the bridge that once linked the two has broken down. Having classified this collection of texts as "Old Testament," one continues to assume that the "New" somehow "fulfills" the "Old," despite the fact that the entire midrashic structure that once supported this claim has mostly been scrapped by Old Testament scholars themselves. Moreover, by failing to refer to Jewish biblical scholarship or to study the traditional Jewish line of interpretation, Christians sustain the illusion that the New Testament is the natural successor to the Hebrew Scriptures. Basic to this illusion is a scornful ignorance of the talmudic tradition.

The Church Fathers interpreted the Jewish Scriptures as though they spoke of "two peoples," a people who were sinful and condemned, the Jews, and the people of the Promise, the Church. No Christian Old Testament scholar today would interpret these texts this way, as far as I know. Reinterpreting New Testament texts to purge them of their anti-Judaism is still more difficult. The New Testament also assumes a christological and anti-Judaic reading of the Old Testament; here, the schism between the Christian "good guys" and the Jewish "bad guys" is explicit and intentional. Today, we must see this division of prophecy into anti-Judaic judgment and christological hope as a profound misappropriation of the dialectics of prophetic religion. Prophetic religion is a religion of self-criticism. Election and messianic hope stand as principles of discernment by which the shortcomings of the present community are judged. Messianic hope is not an escapist device that allows the community to deny or cover up its present faults. Rather, it is the reality principle that illuminates the clash between what is and what ought to be. The prophetic dialectic works properly only if one sees both sides of the dialectic to be directed at the same people, their hope and their historical actuality. The judgmental word is valid only when spoken by a prophet who speaks from within his identification with this community. His identification with it and suffering with its failures is the basis for his becoming the spokesman for its hopes and the divine demand.

The meaning of the prophetic dialectic of judgment and promise is destroyed when its cohesion in a single people is pulled apart. By applying prophetic judgment to "the Jews" and messianic hope to "the Church," Christianity deprived the Jews of their future. They also denied to the Jews the record of their greatest moral accomplishment, the breakthrough from ideological religion to self-critical faith. By the same token, the Church deprived itself of the tradition of prophetic self-criticism. The revolution of the prophets was undone by the Church. Prophetic faith was converted into self-glorification and uncritical self-sanctification. Judgment was projected upon "the Jews" from an ecclesiological stance of transcendent righteousness.

Anti-Judaism and the ecclesiastical infallibility complex, which regards any questioning of the Church as an attack on its essence, arise as two sides of the same error. The Church can read the prophets rightly as scriptural texts only by appropriating the judgmental side as well and applying this, not to some "other people," but to that same people which affirms its hope.

This hermeneutical translation is much more difficult to accomplish with the Christian Gospels, for here the schism is explicit, whereas it is accomplished only by a distortion of the real context of the prophetic texts. Yet, here too the same hermeneutical principle must be applied. To do this, we must think ourselves back into a framework in which Christianity was within, not outside of, Judaism. The "Jews," the "leaders" who are being attacked, do not represent some "other people," but one's own people, one's own "Church" leaders, who are perceived as antithetical to authentic faith. The schism is not one that divides Christian from Jew, but one which divided Jew from Jew then and which today divides Christian from Christian. This is unquestionably the framework in which Jesus' own criticism took place, a criticism which has been translated into sectarianism and then total estrangement in the course of development within the apostolic period. Insofar as this criticism is still usable, it must be used today to criticize the "hypocrisy" and "legalism" of one's own people and Church leaders, and not to characterize the "nature" of another people with whom the Church no longer identifies. Such a recovery of valid prophetic critique in the New Testament will require conscious translation, both new translations of the actual texts, as they are popularly used, and a conscious translation as one reads and interprets them. One can no longer use a terminology shaped by sectarian strife against the leaders of official Judaism. However much the condemnation of "Pharisees" by such terms as *hypocrites* may have appeared valid at the time, it was onesided as a historical judgment and today can be read only as a false vilification of that group which founded the talmudic tradition. One must find words, such as *teachers, scholars,* even *theologians,* which suggest the scribal leaders of one's own community tradition as well, rather than the vilification of the teachers of another people and religion.

This will be very difficult to do, requiring a demythologizing of the literal text and a concerted hermeneutical training of the Christian preacher in the seminary. Some texts may simply be unusable and will have to be put aside or relativized historically, not unlike other scriptural texts which condone practices which modern Christians no longer accept, such as slavery. There is as yet little evidence that Christian seminaries are sufficiently exercized about this issue or aware of how offensive ordinary Christian language is to Jews to undertake the profound textual and hermeneutical reconstruction that would be necessary. Some may be inclined to despair. What can be done, when such sentiments have become canonical Scripture? But scriptures do not exist as timeless facts. They exist as they are read and interpreted in the Church. A retranslation and a systematic application of these critical hermeneutical principles would purge much of the anti-Judaic results and restore greater prophetic integrity to the use of the Christian Scriptures.

When Christians were still Jews, operating as a Jewish sect that still hoped to be accepted by its parental faith, it might have seemed meaningful to rail against those "hypocrites and blind guides." However onesided these judgments appear in retrospect, they did express the deep disappointment of early Christian experience. But once Christianity moved outside of Judaism, these judgments ceased to carry prophetic integrity. Whatever is valid in them (as ethical principles, not as literal history) is now usable only when they are reintegrated into a self-criticism which is applied to the legalism and institutional rigidity of that group which now utters them. But this demythologizing of the anti-Judaic side of Christian prophecy must remain explicit. That is to say, in explicating its prophetic meaning, one must explicitly combat its anti-Judaic formulation, as this appears in the literal text. In so doing, one may also criticize any new tendency simply to project the negative side of our judgments on new "enemies" who are not ourselves or for whom we do not take responsibility. Only when prophecy is read as self-criticism can the Church's use of Scriptures cease to carry that tinge of anti-Semitism, and the Church recover the power of prophecy from the ideology of ecclesial triumphalism.

2. *The Schism of Particularism and Universalism*

Perhaps the most difficult schism for most Christians to criticize is that which makes Judaism a "particularism" over against a Christian "universalism." Catholic Christianity regarded itself as the universal messianic fulfillment of the election of the Jews. Some of the verisimilitude for this perspective on the Church, as the fulfilled messianic ingathering of the nations to Zion, rested on its later fusion with the ecumenical empire. Christianity having become the established religion of this empire, Christian theologians came to imagine that the religion of the biblical God had literally conquered all peoples and all lands. This perspective was possible only within that geographical myopia that imagined the boundaries of the ecumenical empire to be coterminous with the "civilized earth."

It was the Jews who struggled against this same ideological universalism in antiquity. This was not a matter of refusing to coexist politically or assimilate elements of Greco-Roman culture, for the Jews did both. The heart of the Jewish struggle against the empires was a struggle against a pseudo-universalism which assumed that the culture of the dominant group was a universal culture, the culture of true civilization, against which all else was barbarism. On the basis of this ideological interpretation of its own culture, the Greco-Roman Empire especially assumed the right to incorporate all other peoples into the culture of the conquering imperial power. Many of the conquered peoples chaffed under this imperial ideology. But the Jews held out against it in principle and struggled to be recognized as a people who defined their own identity independently of this imperial ideology, challenging thereby its universality. Even when the Jews accepted a client status in the empire or assimilated aspects of its culture, they insisted on doing this on their own terms, not on its terms. What they rejected at all costs was an assimilation that subsumed their own identity. For this reason, the Jews stood out against imperial ideology as the unassimilable element. After much conflict, they won a grudging acknowledgement of their differences from the dominant group.

Christianity, however, took the universalism of the messianic hope and fused it with the ideological universalism of the ecumenical empire. The result was a doctrine of the Church as the one Catholic faith for all mankind which could no longer tolerate the concessions to particularism possible for a polytheistic empire. One God, one faith, and one Church for all mankind invalidated the rights of other people to exist in other ways before God. There was only one path to God, that of Christian revelation. There was only one society of salvation, the Church, founded on this revelation, the cultural and political vehicle for which became the Roman Empire. Historically, from this time on, the missionary and the conquistador went hand in hand to realize the manifest destiny of the Church's mission to become the one faith through which all men are to be saved.

Today this universal mission of the Church seems to be on the wane in religious form, although it still lives on in Western imperialism and neocolonialism. The Church's identification with the empire ended in delimiting a Christian cultural particularism. Although there were Oriental forms of Christianity outside the empire, they have died out or survive as shrunken groups. These are not the expressions of Christianity which have had the greatest historical impact. Developed cultures outside the Greco-Roman sphere have resisted Christianity and identified it with Western imperialism. Even in antiquity, the areas that tried to develop an indigenous Christianity, separate from this political vehicle, were regarded as schismatic (African Donatists, Egyptian Monophysites, Oriental Nestorians), and these areas became dominantly Moslem. Christianity became the dominent religion only of areas which belonged to or were conquered completely by the political and cultural heirs of the Greco-Roman Empire. It has been able to take root only to a limited degree in areas with alternative cultural traditions. Thus, the culture of the Greco-Roman Empire has ended in defining a Christian particularism. But even if one attempted to create a totally non-Western, non-Greco-Roman Christianity, making a new cultural "incarnation" of Christianity in African, Indian, or Asian thought forms, as the Jesuit missionaries tried to do in China, this does not erase Christianity as a particularism, so long as Christianity still claims to be a historical religion resting on historical revelation. Resting on a particular salvific experience appropriated by a particular group in a particular context, the very meaning of which can hardly be understood without making oneself a cultural adopted-child of the West, Christianity confronts other cultural heritages which proclaim other ways to the ultimate.

The modern world has seen the wane of Christian influence (if not Western influence) and the reaffirmation of the other cultural traditions of mankind, as an intimate part of the rise of the non-Western world against Western imperialism. Some of the Christian missions in these areas are surviving this leap and becoming genuinely national churches. But huge areas, such as China, have rolled back the earlier Christian missionary thrust. Missionary theology is itself in crisis, and the dogma that all men must be Christian to be saved is being rethought on the missionary front. Missionaries now seek to provide only human solidarity and service, rather than conversion, and even here it is often hard to separate "service" from Western acculturation. Christianity, having lost its own political establishment in the West, also has all but lost, except for fundamentalists, the notion that all men should become Christians. Today, for the first time, Christianity must come to terms with itself as a particularism among other particularisms, one language among other languages. This forces a rethinking of Christian universalism and its historic negation of the ongoing validity of Jewish particularism.

Christian scholarship has often spoken misleadingly of an oscillation in Judaism between particularism and universalism. The former was assumed to be bad, whereas the latter was an anticipation of that catholicity to be realized in Christianity. In rabbinic thought, there was a spectrum of viewpoints that ranged from exclusivistic nationalism to liberalism which maintained that both the Jews and the nations would share in redemption. With its sense of pluralism of standpoints, the tradition preserves both views, but indicates that it is the latter which is to be followed. But this second viewpoint is not one of generalized universalism which waters down Jewish election. Rather, it affirms a universalism which is the corollary to Jewish particularism. Benjamin Helfgott, in his *Doctrine of Election in Tannaitic*

Literature, traces this dialectical relationship between particularism and universalism in the Rabbis of the first and second centuries C.E. Helfgott believes that this relationship between universalism and Jewish election was affirmed and clarified in this period as a conscious refutation of the Christian claim to be the universal ingathering of the nations that inherits the election of Israel. For Judaism, universalism and particularism were not to be seen as mutually exclusive alternatives, but two sides of a relationship between Israel and the other peoples. In this relationship, the other peoples retain their own identities. The Jews define their identity as the people elected by God and called to an especially exacting relation to his will. They, in turn, have been wise (or foolish) enough to accept this election, with its extraordinary burdens, as well as its special love relation with God. Other peoples are not called to this specific identity necessarily. What identity they are called to Judaism does not define in detail, for the term *Noachide* does not try to define the intrinsic identity of other peoples. It only refers to that generalized humanity which allows for the affirmation of the brotherhood and salvation of the others. The righteous of all nations are said to have a share in the world to come. Good deeds are what saves, and not a particular historical revelation. Jews become righteous by obeying that way mediated by their revealed commandments. The others become righteous through that conscience which can be formed in other traditions. The Noachian laws affirm the bare minimum standards for this. It does not presume to say what Torah is for others.

God is the God of both Israel and the other peoples, each in their own histories and contexts. "Blessed be Egypt my people, and Assyria the work of my hands, and Israel my heritage" (Isa. 19:25). Man is one because God and his creation are one. Israel is to be a light to the nations to bring all men to a knowledge of the one God who created us all. All may join Israel, but all need not join Israel or adopt its specific identity to be saved. For all peoples, out of their own traditions and ethical insights, can come to know the basic way of righteousness and so be saved. Idolatry is not a necessity outside of biblical revelation. The specific content of other peoples' way remains largely undefined, because Israel does not overstep the limits of its own identity, either to define itself as a universal necessity for all, nor to define in detail that "universalism" for "all men." We are left with the unstated conclusion that Israel knows what righteousness is for itself. Other peoples have to discover for themselves what God demands of them. Looking beyond its specific identity and divine commands, Israel sees what is general to all people in the Noachian laws. What is comparable to Torah for others is not knowable or definable from within the context of Israel's revelation.

Man is one because God is one and will finally gather all mankind together at the messianic fulfillment of history. Sometimes it is assumed that all peoples will embrace Judaism at that time. But this does not alter the belief that the righteous of all nations will have a share in the world to come. It does not become a mandate for a universal mission that declares that all people can be saved only by becoming Jews. The gap between the two is not closed and cannot be closed, nor the way of bridging it defined before the final redemption. This unresolved gap between Israel, other peoples, and the future messianic unity of man expresses the effort to set universalism in tandem with Jewish particularism in a way that violates neither side; i.e., which neither makes Judaism an ideological universalism nor tries to define the content of a "larger universal" in a way that waters down the specific identity of Israel.

Such a concept of particularity is not the antithesis of universalism. Rather, it accepts its own limits, leaving room for an authentic, i.e., nonideological, universalism which does not demand political or cultural uniformity or the conquest of all the others by "our" salvific language. Its particularism may become ingrown and ask only to be left alone in its proud exclusivity, especially when pressed upon by surrounding imperialism. Or it may have palmy days of humanitarian liberalism. But its universality is not a platform for world conquest. Rather, its universalism rests on the universality of God as Creator and Redeemer of mankind and the universe, not on the universality of its historical revelation and way of salvation. Universalism is based on particularisms which accept their own distinctiveness and so leave room for the distinctiveness of others.

Christianity, however, was founded on the belief that the

unity of all peoples, which was to be established by God at the end of history, has already been established, in principle, in the Christian historical revelation in Christ. Faith in Christ is then seen as the launching pad for a universal mission which does not say merely that all peoples can become Christians, but that all peoples must become Christian to be saved. Only through Christ does anyone come to the Father. In the post-Nicene Fathers, there was a disposition to regard this universal mission as already achieved in the establishment of Christianity as the religion of the ecumenical empire. Fulfilled messianism then became the new foundation for the ideological universalism of the Christian Roman Empire. Faith in Christ is the last word on the unification of all mankind, giving the Church here and now the right to conquer all peoples in the name of its given revelation. The particularity of its historical revelation is regarded as a "universal particularity." This particular historical revelation is the only true way for all peoples, to which all nations should submit, obliterating their previous identities and histories thereby. Christianity imported the universalism of messianic fulfillment into history as its own historical foundation, and later united it with the ideology and political vehicle of the empire, to reestablish a Christian version of imperial universalism. This claim to catholicity has functioned as the religious justification for that union of mission and imperialism characteristic of Christian history.

To criticize this Christian imperialist impulse, we must question fulfilled messianism which regards the final perspective of God's sovereignty over the world as already revealed, incarnate, and available in history as the basis for the assimilation of all people into the final messianic unity of mankind. This viewpoint does not take seriously the independent histories and identities of other peoples, in its own missionizing, much less accept these as autonomous ways of salvation. This does not mean that Christianity, and indeed each particular language about the ultimate, does not have a language which truly speaks about and connects us with that which is ultimate and universal. But we must recognize that this is our particular language about the universal, and not the one universal language about the universal which all people must use in order to speak validly about the ultimate. There are many languages which are more or less adequate to speak about the universal. But there is no universal language. Nor are these languages themselves simply interchangeable, even though one who becomes deeply bi- or tri-lingual can discover profound commonality among them. Each is the product of a people, its history and revelatory experiences. A universal language which can unify all mankind, taking account of each of these traditions, cannot be the already established possession of any one of these traditions. Nor is it yet known how they can all come together at some future point of true unity. This future point of unity exists now only in the transcendent universality of God and his original work as Creator, which gives us the basis for affirming universal human kinship. But this unity of God as Creator and Redeemer cannot be said to be incarnate in one people and their historical revelation, giving them the right to conquer and absorb all the others. The only universality which can be truly said to be "of God" is one that transcends every particularity, guaranteeing the integrity of each people to stand before God in their own identities and histories (Mic. 4:5).

3. *The Schism of Letter and Spirit*

Christian anti-Judaic exegesis used the language of both Jewish and Hellenistic dialectics to express its belief in its supersession of Judaism. What was dialectical in each of these traditions becomes dualistic in Christian usage, dividing into "two peoples" what was originally the dialectics of historical existence. Just as Judaism becomes a negated particularism, left behind by a Christian universalism, so too Judaism is seen as that which is trancended temporally, morally, and ontologically. Christianity is the "new," over against Judaism as the "old." Christianity is the ultimately new, so it itself can never become old (although successive Christian sectarianisms and revolutionary movements would use the same dualisms to negate the previous Christian Church as that "old humanity" which is now being superseded by the new newness, presumed to stand for the final messianic newness). Christianity is the inward and authentic over against a Jewish hypocrisy and outwardness. Since Christianity sees itself as posessing the incarnation of fulfilled Being, against Judaism, which is mere shadow and anticipation, Judaism is also, in some sense, mere "seeming" over against "true Being." It is the "outward figure of the good things to come," which now truly "is" in Christ. These modes of thought fuse messianic sectarian dualism (the two eras) with the Greek dualisms of the body and the spirit, Becoming and Being, the phenomenal and the noumenal. Judaism is seen as both the "old man" and the "carnal man." Moreover, this judgment is not allowed to remain in the past, as a judgment about some presumed bad state of official Judaism in New Testament times. It becomes Judaism's ongoing historical identity to the end of time. The Jews were relegated both to a past and to a morally and ontologically inferior status of existence as their ongoing identity from the time of Jesus to the end of history (which was then projected back on their identity in Old Testament times as well). Christianity transcends Judaism historically, morally, and ultimately. It is the fulfillment of that which Judaism merely "foreshadowed" in the "fleshly way." This perspective came about, as we have seen, by subsuming Philo's Platonic dualisms into the messianic sectarian dualism of the historical and the eschatological. But since Christianity assumes that the Messiah has already come, this allows it to apply to itself the characteristics of the "eschatological era," rendering schismatic what was dialectical in Philo. By historicizing the eschatological, the "two eras"—the historical world and the messianic age to come—become the Christian historical era, over against Judaism as the type of unredeemed humanity. The line between history and eschatology is imported into history as though it were a line dividing history, at the time of Jesus, into a premessianic and a postmessianic era (B.C. and A.D.). Judaism (and all that is not Christian) not only then but now becomes the unredeemed, "carnal" mankind over against the Christian "eschatological" man. The common use of B.C.E. and C.E. by both Christians and Jews would be one way of overcoming this tradition.

This translation of the Philonic dialectic of letter and spirit into a messianic sectarian dualism between the old historical humanity and the new messianic humanity falsified the Church's ability to see either Judaism or itself as they really were. Judaism was reduced to mere outwardness and moral turpitude, while the Church remained docetic about its own bodily, institutional, and historical existence. This seems to be a key to the reason why Christianity has had such difficulties with its own historical body. Certainly, Christianity has spawned as many institutions and laws as any religion in history. Yet, it has oscillated between sectaran spiritualist docetism and Catholic institutional absolutism. The one rejects the validity of institutional vehicles of the Spirit; the other reifies the institution as an extension of the incarnate "Body of Christ."

Judaism was never a religion of "legalism," but a religion of revealed commandments which seeks thereby to concretize God's presence in everyday life. For Judaism, there can be no such antithesis of law and grace, letter and spirit, for the Torah is itself God's gift and mediates the presence of the Spirit. Since Judaism does not accept the Pauline doctrine of original sin, it believes that people are capable of responding to God out of their natural powers. But this is also because Judaism does not accept the quasi-Gnostic dualism of "nature" and "grace" that demonizes Creation, making grace alien to nature. Judaism believes that nature was created by God, not by demons, and so man's ability to respond to God is itself God's gift. Man, to be sure, remains in tension between the "two impulses," good and evil choice, response and nonresponse to God. Someday there will be a time when this evil impulse will be overcome. Then there may be no more need for the outward commandments, for each will obey God from the heart. Paul's dualism of "letter" and "spirit" really assumes that this eschatological transcendence of the tension between the "two impulses" has already taken place with the death and resurrection of Christ. The messianic covenant of Jeremiah 31:31 has already arrived. Christians are the people reborn to this spiritual obedience founded on Christ's redemptive act, relegating Torah to mere outward letter.

This Pauline view fatally distorts Judaism's understanding of the Way of Torah. Judaism is not letter without spirit, but a way of life which knows the unresolved tension of letter and spirit. But the Pauline dualism also fantasizes Christian historical existence. In Christianity, this tension between the inward and the outward has not really been resolved. To declare that it is already overcome, and that this victory founds a new possibility of existence, in some ways merely reinstitutes the tension in a more contradictory way. The more one proclaims the supersession of the "Law," the more one tends to generate a problem of "legalism." The dualism used to negate Judaism is used to negate past forms of the Church. Luther negates Catholicism with the same dualisms used by Paul to negate Judaism, and, in turn, generates new revolts of spiritualism against legalism.

Christian ecclesiology oscillates between a messianic sectarian negation of the past and an idolatrous institutional incarnationalism which divinizes the historical body of the Church, making its appointed forms and leaders infallible and irreformable. Messianic sectarianism and incarnational triumphalism are the two sides of a religious position that must either suppress or constantly negate its historical actuality in the name of an eschatological identity that is its already established foundation. The claim that the eschatological Body of Christ is one's institutional foundation, the charter for one's historical existence, is read with a literalism that renders the Church unable to account for the imperfection of its historical existence. An imperfect past is repudiated as "fallen" and hence "not Christian," or else it is absolutized as perfect. This is merely to say that a messianic sect turned historical church cannot account for its premessianic or unredeemed historical existence.

Only with great difficulty has the Church come to terms with the idea that it carries its spiritual treasure in earthen vessels. As earthen, it is finite, inadequate, and so ever reformable. But, because we are "of the earth," this is quite necessary for making God's Spirit concrete and present to us in space and time. The corrective to messianic sectarianism cannot be an incarnationalism that divinizes the vehicles of God's presence, but a sense of the unresolved tension between outward and inward. Particular historical vehicles are both necessary and finite. No vehicle is itself absolute, yet one must provisionally commit oneself to some vehicle in order to experience miracles and make God's Spirit present.

This same conflict also is the basis of the unresolvable problem of the "two natures of Christ." On the one side, early Christian theology tended to a docetism that made Jesus "pure spirit" without any body. On the other, it tended to an incarnationalism which divinizes his body as divine. The divinizing of the body of the Church is simply an extension of this divinizing of Jesus' historical being. The Chalcedonian doctrine of the two natures in one divine person is only a poor compromise indicative of the Church's inability to sort out the duality between Jesus' historical existence and his mediation of eschatological presence. As soon as this eschatological presence is regarded as already realized in his historical existence—i.e., he already *was* the Messiah—then the historical Jesus as a human person must be abolished. The Church could not resolve the duality of Jesus' "two natures" without recognizing that, as a historical person, he can only be nonfinal in himself, not only in the sense that he becomes a mediating presence for some but not for others, but also in the sense that he himself is not "the One," but points beyond himself to the "One who is yet to come."

This dualism between the outward and the inward, the historical and the eschatological, is not overcome for him or for us. The New Covenant of Jeremiah goes beyond Christian existence as much as it goes beyond Jewish existence. Our existence too is one of unresolved conflict between a somatic finitude that both mediates and limits our access to the eternal. To say that "Christ is the Way," rather than that "Torah is the Way," does not resolve the tension in fact. It simply holds up the ultimate standard by which to radicalize the tension or else to pretend that it is solved by fiat, but "invisibly," i.e., in a way that makes no outward perceptible difference. The reality of unredeemed existence continues despite these tricks of realized eschatology played upon history.

Those trained in traditional Christian theology will be pained by this discussion and declare that "Christ's coming" has made an ultimate difference. What this means is that we know that we are "ultimately accepted." We do not have to depend for our salvation upon our own efforts. But we have only to recall all the contradictions which have been produced by the efforts to make sense of this proposition. Either this means that everyone is finally accepted no matter what they do, obliterating any difference between good and evil. Or else it means that some are accepted and others are rejected no matter what they do, which makes God an amoral tyrant. In an effort to bring righteousness and election into tandem, one declares that the elect are known by their righteousness. Election is the basis of righteousness and not vice versa. We then embark on that all-consuming Puritan "legalism," which seeks perfect righteousness, not to earn but to *prove* one's election. Ordinary Christianity constantly abdicates from this whole discussion in practice and assumes the view that we are already loved by God, and yet must also *do* something to become what we are supposed to be. For such an ethic does one need a Messiah? It would seem that Creation, covenant, and commandments would be sufficient.

The Church's historical existence constantly evidences its premessianic actuality, while the proclamation that it is founded on the "new being" of Christ serves as much to hinder as to give it any perceptibly superior way of existing. Christian actuality has not transcended the human historical, i.e., unredeemed conditions known to Judaism. Yet, its messianic faith has made it a kind of mirror-opposite of Judaism. Judaism believes it has the commandments, can obey the commandments well enough to be in friendship with God, and yet the final resolution of the tension of letter and spirit is not yet. Christianity holds up the final redeemed moment of the "end" as its already established foundation. Yet it proves no more capable than Judaism of producing that final eschatological transfiguration of existence in practice, while losing the commandments that assured Judaism that it had the "way" to the "end." For Christianity, there can be no "way" to the "end," because the "end" (Christ) is the "way." For Judaism, which had Torah without the Messiah, Christianity substitutes the Messiah without Torah. But the effort to deal with the finite as though one were already based on the Final produces myriad self-delusions; either one constantly rejects the finite qua finite, or else attempts to absolutize a particular givenness as final.

In practice, Christianity constantly tends to boil down to a religion of grace and good deeds structurally identical to Judaism in its assumptions about the unredeemed nature of man and history, except that it is far less sure what good deeds are commanded and is impenetrably obscurantist about the meaning of the word "Christ." In the light of this, we must analyze the pyschopathology represented by Christian anti-Judaism. The assertion that the Jews are reprobate because they did not accept Christ as having already come is really a projection upon Judaism of that unredeemed side of itself that Christianity must constantly deny in order to assert that Christ has already come and founded "the Church." The Jews represent that which Christianity must repress in itself, namely the recognition of history and Christian existence as unredeemed. In this sense, the Jews do indeed "kill Christ" for the Christian, since they preserve the memory of the original biblical meaning of the word *Messiah* which must judge present history and society as still unredeemed. For Judaism, Jesus cannot have been the Messiah, because the times remain unredeemed and neither he nor anything that came from him has yet altered that fact. In short, Judaism, in rejecting Jesus' messianic status, is simply reaffirming the integrity of its own tradition about what the word *Messiah* means. Once the true nature of Judaism's objection to Christian faith becomes clear, it becomes necessary to reappraise the meaning of Judaism's Great Refusal. If Christian anti-Judaism is the suppression of the unredeemed side of itself and its projection of this upon Judaism, then Judaism's negation of Christian faith must be recognized as a prophetic critique refused. Judaism's Great Refusal stands for its recognition of the critical theological error in the heart of the Christian gospel which rendered its message nonnegotiable for Judaism from the beginning. As long as this critical insight is refused, the revelatory work of Judaism on behalf of its messianic offspring could only be seen by Christians as "obduracy" and "hardness of heart," i.e., the externalization of a truthful criticism rebuffed. Christianity can lose its anti-Judaism only when it is able to hear and internalize the message from Judaism which heretofore it has repressed and projected back as the sin of Judaism in "rejecting Christ."

4. *The Key Issue: Christology*

Our theological critique of Christian anti-Judaism, therefore, must turn to what was always the other side of anti-Judaism, namely Christology. At the heart of every Christian dualizing of the dialectics of human existence into Christian and anti-Judaic antitheses is Christology, or, to be more specific, the historicizing of the eschatological event. Realized eschatology converts each of the dialectics we have examined—judgment and promise, particularism and universalism, letter and spirit, history and eschatology—into dualisms, applying one side to the "new messianic people," the Christians, and the negative side to the "old people," the Jews. The message of messianic expectation is imported into history and reified as a historical event in a way that makes it a reality-denying, rather than a reality-discerning, principle. Evil is declared to have been conquered once-for-all by the Messiah. His victory has been established as the Catholic Church. Let anyone who fails to discern the Kingdom of God in the Christian imperium be anathema. The destruction of the enemies of the Christian empire is now tantamount to the defeat of the minions of Belial by the messianic hosts. Christ becomes the vengeful instrument to persecute that people who hoped for his coming and who fail to recognize in such a Christ their own redemption. But is it possible for Christianity to accept the truth of this refusal without at the same time rejecting totally its own messianic experience in Jesus? Is it possible to purge Christianity of anti-Judaism without at the same time pulling up Christian faith? Is it possible to say "Jesus is Messiah" without, implicitly or explicitly, saying at the same time "and the Jews be damned"?

The most fundamental affirmation of Christian faith is the belief that Jesus is the Christ. He is that Messiah whom the prophets "foretold" and the Jews "awaited." On this affirmation, everything else in Christian theology is built. To ask about this affirmation is to ask about the keystone of Christian faith. For Judaism, however, there is no possibility of talking about the Messiah having already come, much less of having come two thousand years ago, with all the evil history that has reigned from that time to this (much of it having been done in Christ's name!), when the Reign of God has not come. For Israel, the coming of the Messiah and the coming of the Messianic Age are inseparable. They are, in fact, the same thing. Israel's messianic hope was not for the coming of a redemptive person whose coming would not change the outward ambiguity of human and social existence, but for the coming of that Messianic Age which, as Engels was to put it, is "the solution to the riddle of history."

Earliest Christianity believed that Jesus was the Messiah in the context of a lively expectation of the imminent end of the world. Jesus was the one who was shortly to reappear on clouds of glory to bring in redemption. It is now "in his name" that this coming redemption is announced. It was only gradually that a gap opened up between the experience of Jesus as messianic proclaimer and this expectation of his imminent return. The Church settled down into the new historical era that had opened up between Jesus' historical coming and his future return. The return in glory was pushed off into an indefinite future, while his historical life was invested with the borrowed glory of the eschatological advent. With the growing wordly success of the Church, the Church came to see its own times as the "Christian era," no longer simply as a time of proclamation of repentance and suffering anticipation, but as a new historical era which itself realized the conditions of the millennium. The Church's era became the thousand-year reign of Christ on earth. This was still to be distinguished from the final eschatological era of eternity after the "end of history," to be inaugurated by the Second Coming. But the Church's era nevertheless came to be seen as "messianic times." The ultimate crisis of human existence, the crisis that divides the historical from the eschatological, was thus imported into history as itself a "historical event." All history "before Christ" could then be regarded as the era of "unredeemed man" —which is still the identity of those outside Christian faith, i.e., Jews—while Christian times take on the aura of messianic glory. Messianic hope, instead of illuminating the crisis between the historical and the eschatological, now becomes the tool of false consciousness, allowing the Church to dress historical ambiguities in the dress of finality and absolute truth. This new historical era and people are seen as standing, not merely in a relative but in an absolute supersessionary relationship to Judaism and to all human possibilities "before Christ."

This view rests on an illegitimate historicizing of the eschatological. This is a false reifying of the experience of the eschatological in history. Within a particular historical experience, such as that which characterized Jewish history from the Maccabees to the Jewish Wars, a period filled with alienation from evil power structures and laden with ultimate expectations, one may experience the eschatological horizon impinging on history. This is the experience expressed by Jesus in the proclamation that "the Kingdom is at hand." When and where this eschatological expectation occurred, the person who exemplified it may then be remembered as a paradigm of that final hope which has not yet been accomplished, but still lies ahead of our present possibilities. This memory may then be reexperienced as a paradigm again and again, in that community which preserves this memory, providing the pattern for experiencing the eschatological in history. But this experience and person in the past does not become the final eschatological event of history, placing all history before that time in an obsolescent and morally inferior relation to itself or invalidating the access to God of those who go forward on other grounds.

The ultimate eschatological event, the ultimate "coming" of the Messiah, must still signify that final future when "every tear will be wiped away." This clearly has not taken place, nor has Christianity appropriated its message in a way that has been a very convincing means to this "end." The attribution of an absolute finality to the heightened expectations surrounding the life and death of Jesus must be regarded as a flawed way of appropriating the real meaning of eschatological encounter. This historicizing of the eschatological has most serious consequences. Both Christian anti-Semitism and the patterns of totalitarianism and imperialism that have appeared in Christendom (and its secular revolutionary stepchildren) find their root in this error.

The idea that the final messianic Advent has already happened in Jesus must be reformulated through an empathetic encounter with the way this idea originally arose in its Jewish context. Here we discover a historical Jesus as a faithful Jew within the Mosaic covenant, who did not set out to replace Judaism by another religion, but who lived in lively expectation of the coming of God's Kingdom and judged his society in its light. This expectation drove him to Jerusalem and to his death at the hands of hostile Roman and Jewish collaborationist officials. To reaffirm Jesus' hope in his name, then, is not to be able to claim that in Jesus this hope has already happened, albeit in invisible form. Nor does it mean that it is now only in his name that this hope can be proclaimed. It is simply to say that, for those who were caught up with him in that lively expectation, it is now in his memory that they reaffirm his hope. They are sure that his death was not in vain. Ultimately, God will vindicate his hope, by revealing that victory over all the oppressive forces of evil for which he lived and died. It is now in his name that *we* (those who inherit the memories of this first community of Jesus' companions) reaffirm this hope, and it is in his name that this victory will be finally manifest for us; viz., he has been seated on the right hand of God and will come again in glory. This is the theological content behind the proclamation of Jesus' resurrection. As the recent Theology of Hope has put it, the Resurrection is not the final happening of the eschatological event, but the proleptic experiencing of the final future. In this proleptic experiencing of the final future of mankind in advance, we reaffirm Jesus' hope in his name. He becomes the mediator of this hope to us and to our descendants. But this hope was not finally fulfilled either in his lifetime or in his death. The Resurrection reaffirms his hope, in the teeth of historical disappointment, that evil be overcome and God's will be done on earth. The messianic meaning of Jesus' life, then, is paradigmatic and proleptic in nature, not final and fulfilled. It does not invalidate the right of those Jews not caught up in this paradigm to go forward on earlier foundations.

Like the Exodus, the Resurrection represents an experience of salvation that is remembered by the heirs of that community which experienced it. For those who incorporate themselves into this experience, it becomes their foundation for continued and ultimate hope. But the fulfillment of that hope, the closing of the gap between what is and what ought to be, remains as much in the future for the Church as it does for the Jewish people. The Resurrection experience gives the Church a foundation for this hope, a paradigm for the dynamics of reexperiencing this hope—i.e., death and resurrection—and a foretaste of its realization. But these are not the final accomplishment of this hope. The final happening of the messianic Advent must still be referred to that final goal of history when evil is conquered and God's will is done on earth. It is in the light of this final horizon that we can then recognize the redemptive moments when they happen to us here and now, beginning with our experience of Jesus.

I believe that this paradigmatic and proleptic view of the messianic work of Jesus is the only theologically and historically valid way of interpreting it consistent with biblical faith and historical realism. It is the only way we can reconnect Christianity with the context of this event in its original Jewish setting and so rediscover the real historical Jesus, who must ever elude an anti-Judaic Christianity. It represents the way we should have read the New Testament, if apocalyptic imminentism had not confused the early Christian sense of history. It is the way we needed to appropriate this apocalyptic expectation once its immence had faded from sight, rather than transposing it into that messianic absolutism which generated Christian totalitarianism and imperialism. Only by reading the Resurrection in a paradigmatic and proleptic way can the Church avoid making the absolutistic claims about itself which are belied by its own history.

But this proleptic and paradigmatic reading of the meaning of the eschatological experience in Jesus also requires a relativizing of it vis-à-vis other communities of faith who have not incorporated themselves into the memory of this paradigmatic experience. The cross and the Resurrection are a paradigm for Christians, not for "all who would be a part of Israel" or necessarily for "all men." That is to say, it is a paradigm for those for whom it has become a paradigm. Those who have not chosen to make it their paradigm, because they have other paradigms which are more compelling to them from their own histories, are not to be judged as false or unredeemed thereby. This contextual view of the significance of the cross and the Resurrection takes seriously the diversity of peoples and their histories, out of which they hear God through the memory of different revelatory experiences.

5. *Toward a New Covenantal Theology*

The question of a new covenantal theology cannot be solved or even adequately discussed from one side alone. It would be the area where Christians and Jews would have to enter into discussion of their contrary traditions about the nature of covenantal peoplehood. Each of the traditional positions proves inadequate before the facticity of the other people. It is also the area, I believe, where there might be interesting and fruitful dialogue.

Traditional Judaism knew what Israel was intended by God to do. Beyond the horizon of its own identity and revealed Way, it spoke of the others only as "Noachides." As indicated earlier, this term does not define the identity of the others; it simply refers to that minimal commonality that assures the possibility of universal salvation. What the specific identity of others is, what is comparable to Torah for them, Israel does not discuss.

When faced with the phenomenon of a "second people from among the Gentiles," a people who had learned and adopted this Jewish identity, claiming to be the true Israel that supersedes Israel, traditional Jewish categories were at a loss. At first this group was seen as Jewish heretics. When the Church became predominantly gentile, the way was open for looking at the Church simply as "goy." Yet, what does one do with Gentiles who claim to be the "true Israel"? One can think of them alternatively as Jewish heretics or pagan idolators, a people who mix idolatry (the divinity of Jesus) and polytheism (the Trinity) with Jewish heresy (false messianism, antinomianism). This is traditional Judaism's basic view of Christians. But through association with Christians it became clear that this view was inadequate, as Jacob Katz has shown in his study *Exclusiveness and Tolerance*. The roots of Christian identity—its view of God—was too biblical to be simply regarded as pagan. Christians fall in some indeterminate status between Jewish messianic hereitcs and incompletely converted gentile proselytes. Seen as gentile semiproselytes, Christians can even be viewed more benignly as one way in which Judaism carries out its mission to spread the true concept of God to "the nations." These options more or less exhaust the traditional Jewish categories for understanding Christianity. One thing it cannot be and that is the "true Israel."

Christians, on the other hand, are hardly content to be regarded as "good Noachides," much less as pagans. They have regarded themselves as the true heirs to the covenant of God with Israel. They are, in fact, the final universal destiny of this covenant, surpassing its "Jewish stage." They are the people of the final messianic covenant which now achieves, through Christ, that inner righteousness which Judaism sought in vain through the outward commandments. This Christian New Covenant supersedes the covenant of God with Israel in the Jews in a way that can leave no room for a continuing covenant of Israel in Judaism. The Christian New Covenant must deny the legitimacy of ongoing Jewish covenantal existence. It can grant them only that negative space in which the Jews are to be preserved until the end of time, when they finally have to admit their error and join the true covenant of Israel, now passed on to its destined heirs, the Christians.

Should we try to replace the Christian concept of the New Covenant and the Jewish concept of the second, Noachian covenant with a plural concept of "separate but equal" covenants of God with each people? Should we say that God has made a covenant with each people in their own context and history and given them each a way to salvation? This would seem to be implied by what we have said earlier about contextualism and relativism. But it is also tinged with an assumption that we can transcend our own context and see everyone as God sees them. A student of mine tried to solve this dilemma by suggesting that there are two covenants: a particularist covenant to the Jews and the universal covenant of the Church for the other peoples. The two are parallel, not supersessionary. This view relativizes the patristic doctrine of the "two peoples." But this translation distorts Jewish and Christian historical reality. It assumes that everyone is supposed to be Christian, except the Jews! It fails to see that Jews in the Diaspora have long since ceased to be identifiable as descendants of a local Semitic tribe. Even the

Nazis were never able to describe the Jews genetically as a "race." In fact, Jews today are gathered from as many different peoples as are Christians. The multiregional and multiracial character of the Jews in Israel should demonstrate this fact. The Jews, as much as the Christians, have become a people gathered out of many peoples. They are a people only because they have all adopted the Jewish covenantal identity.

On the other hand, the Christian concept of the New Covenant did not originally signify simply a second covenant which, in a relative and historical way, can be paralleled with a still valid covenant to the Jews. Rather, the New Covenant is the one covenant of God with Israel in its final and ultimate form. This New Covenant is the messianic destiny of the covenant with Israel of Jeremiah 31:31, which overcomes the ambiguities of historical existence and human self-alienation. Christians saw themselves as the people of the New Covenant, in the sense of being the beginning of the final messianic covenant that unites mankind and Israel. Must we not say today that this messianic covenant lies as much ahead of the historical reality of Christianity as it does that of Judaism? Before God, must we not see the Christians as being in the same historical situation as the Jews? Christians are not yet encamping in the Promised Land. Still less does their hope give them the right to usurp access to it altogether. The Christian, as much as the Jew, is still on the way through the desert between the Exodus and the Promised Land, with many a golden idol and broken tablet along the way.

The idea of election is not really original with Israel, although Christians know this idea primarily through Jewish identity. Most ancient peoples tended to see their own identity as being the umbilicus of the universe. A certain concept of election, in this sense, is found among any people who have a sense of identity that links them with heaven. Most ancient peoples also confused their own particular identity with the ultimate and made it the standard for judging humanness in general. Judaism took a step beyond this parochial ideology with the concept of the distinction between the covenant to Israel and the covenant to Noah, recognizing, on the one hand, their own particularism, but also its limitation by the humanity of others. Christianity obliterated this limitation by its fusion of messianic universalism

No, God's act in Jesus (handwritten)

and imperial ideology, making its own identity the one true way for all men. It identified the fulfillment of the covenant to Israel with an already realized covenant to all men, so destroying the delicate balance which Israel had created between the two.

Christianity today might learn a version of the Jewish concept of particularism, which accepts the general humanity and possibility for salvation of others, without trying to define their identity for them. This works for peoples whom Christianity has not known from the inside, such as Hindus or Buddhists or even Moslems (whom Jews must regard as a second offspring of biblical faith). But Christians cannot look at Jews simply as people of another "world religion." Each has known the other from within the same household of faith. Christianity, however gentilized, remains rooted in the Jewish identity of Jesus and the apostles. It is through them that it inherits its claim to identify with the Jewish past as its own past. Judaism may come to speak more benignly of Christians as semiproselytes. In this form, it was able to tolerate Christians in the synagogues. But this view conceals the earlier, more intimate, and angrier knowledge of Christians, not as gentile semiproselytes, but as Jewish heretics, trying to proselytize the synagogue. As such, Christians could not be tolerated in the synagogues. As the gentile adopted descendants of these Jewish heretics, Christians inherit from them their claim to be the true heirs of the Jewish past and identity, appropriating it through the medium of fulfilled messianism. Both remain in unresolved relation to each other, each claiming to carry on the one covenant of God with Israel. The elder brother carries it on through an exegesis still based on the original "cornerstone" of Abraham and Moses. The younger claims it through a foreshortening of history on one side, and a foundation upon the Jew Jesus, who is the aperture through which it inherits Jesus' Jewish identity.

The crisis of the first century produced, then, two ways of carrying on the biblical inheritance. Using Jesus' parable, we might see the Jews as the faithful elder brother who remains tending the father's flocks in the ancestral house. The younger son goes off chasing his vision. Today he can neither renounce that vision that drove him out of the father's house, nor can he renounce his claim to be a son and heir of the same household of faith. Should we declare that the nonappearance of his fortune —i.e., Jesus' *parousia*—must finally force him to admit that inheritance of the covenant rests solely on its original cornerstone, i.e., Abraham and Moses? There is nothing to prevent any Christian from accepting this option and using Christianity as a way to full conversion to Judaism. But, for most, the story cannot become simply a circular one. The younger son refuses to see his adventure simply under the rubric of a "prodigality," calling for repentance and return. This is because a development took place which Jesus did not anticipate when he told the story. Jesus' faith rested on the original cornerstone, the Mosaic covenant. He did not become for himself a "new cornerstone." But the Christian cannot return to Jesus' Jewish identity before the Easter experience. The vision which drove Christians into separation from the parental faith, however unrealized, still determines our religious consciousness and the way we appropriate the older stories. However much we may repent of having pursued this vision falsely, we cannot forget *our own story*. The messianic encounter which originally inspired us continues to be our foundational paradigm, through which we appropriate the earlier stories and out of which our history flows. Jesus, as the new cornerstone, continues to divide the two brothers, giving Christians a different way of appropriating the biblical past and relating to its future hope.

We have seen that this Christian paradigm tends to double back on itself constantly, oscillating between new messianic sectarianisms and the absolutizing of what has been actualized out of it. Yet, in the very dialectic between these two errors, Christianity again and again proves its ability to mediate new breakthrough experiences. By bringing history into constant collision with eschatology, it makes history itself dynamic. The Christian paradigm has been the foundation of the Western revolutionary tradition, which constantly rediscovers the imminent eschatological horizon from out of its past immanences. This is the paradigm through which Christianity mediates encounter with God and constantly reawakens messianic hope, projecting again upon the future what has been absolutized in its past moment of experience. When we are able to see those past places of experience, beginning with Jesus, as proleptic, rather than final and fulfilled, then we may be able to validate messianic hope in Jesus in a way that is no longer anti-Judaic. This also means that we can use this paradigm to mediate new breakthrough experiences in a way that need not demonize the past of the "others" who are the antagonists of the experience.

Before it was anything else, the Christian messianic experience in Jesus was a Jewish experience, created out of Jewish hope. As an experience of messianic ecstasy, born of the dream of biblical faith, it becomes paradigmatic and foundational for reaffirming this hope in the final coming of God's Kingdom that is definitive for the heirs of that community which experienced it. But others remember this history quite differently, as a time when no Messiah came, although many frantically hoped for his coming. This people survived by continuing to base their hope on the original stories of Abraham and Moses. For them, the Exodus continues to be the breakthrough experience that founds their hope for ultimate salvation. The messianic experience, which happened to a small group of companions of Jesus, failed to become paradigmatic for most Jews. Those who loved Jesus could not mediate this gap between their own vibrant encounter with the messianic horizon through Jesus and the nonexperience of other Jews. Each then comes to invalidate the experience of the other by his own experience or nonexperience. The two rapidly become incapable of living in the same house.

When we find a way of accepting the situational validity of these differing experiences, which give different communities different foundations for their faith, then the Christian story can cease to be an assault on the right of Jews to continue to exist. Christians must be able to accept the thesis that it is not necessary for Jews to have the story about Jesus in order to have a foundation for faith and a hope for salvation. The story of Jesus parallels, it does not negate, the Exodus. It is another story, born from Abraham's promise, which becomes the paradigm of salvation for Christians. In each case, the experience of salvation in the past is recounted as the paradigm for continued hope experienced in the present and pointing to that final hope which is still ahead of both Jews and Christians. When Easter is seen, not as superseding and fulfilling the Exodus, but as reduplicating it, then the Christian can affirm his faith through Jesus in a way that no longer threatens to rob the Jew of his past, eliminate his future and surround his present existence with rivalrous animosity. ⌉

6. *Education for a New Relationship*

In order to give this acceptance of ongoing Jewish convenantal existence flesh and blood, Christians must learn the story of the Jews after the time of Jesus. Christians must accept the oral Torah as an authentic alternative route by which the biblical past was appropriated and carried on. This requires the learning of a suppressed history. Learning history is never really an act of "detached" scholarship, as academicians like to think. Learning history is, first of all, a rite of collective identity. Christians learn who they are by learning the story of the Jews from Abraham to the time of Jesus and, through Jesus, carrying down a history created by the Christian Church and society. The history of the Jews disappears at the time of Jesus. This testifies to the Christian claim that it is the true Israel which alone carries on the biblical legacy. This Christian way of learning history negates ongoing Jewish existence. If we learned not only New Testament, but rabbinic midrash; if we viewed the period of the Second Temple, not merely through the eyes of early Christianity, but through the eyes of the disciples of Rabban Yohanan ben Zakkai; if we read Talmud side by side with the Church Fathers; if we read the Jewish experience of Christendom side by side with the Christian self-interpretation, this Christian view of history would fall into jeopardy. For this reason, Jewish history "after Christ" is not merely unknown, but repressed. Its repression is essential for the maintenance of Christian identity.

For Christians to incorporate the Jewish tradition after Jesus into their theological and historical education would involve ultimately the dismantling of the Christian concept of history and the demythologizing of the myth of the Christian Era. It would mean the opening of the mind to the other side that must provide the decisive critique at each stage of development of this myth. If, when the Christian student, especially the seminarian, studied the Hebrew Bible through Christian exegesis, both ancient and modern, he also had to know something about rabbinic midrash and modern Jewish biblical studies, the myth of Jewish Scripture as "Old Testament" would have to be taken apart. The seminarian would have to deal seriously with a second line, other than "NewTestament," through which this legacy was appropriated. If, in studying New Testament, the Christian student also studied rabbinic thought in Jesus' time, he would have to see Jesus in his Jewish setting in a new way. The myth of Pharisees as hypocrites and Judaism as "dead legalism" would be exploded. He would also have to see the crucifixion in the context of Roman imperialism and Jewish messianism and resistence. These things are sometimes mentioned in biblical courses in liberal seminaries. But real entry into the perspective of those who salvaged Judaism after the fall of the temple is not undertaken. So this criticism remains abstract and without flesh and blood. The old anti-Judaic myths live on in attenuated forms.

Because the anti-Judaic myth and its social workings in Christendom is almost never taught in Church history or "Western civilization," the questionableness of Christendom and the roots of anti-Semitism remain buried. The vital key for understanding an aspect of Western history is thus lost. Avoidance of this knowledge also allows the Christian theologian to continue to turn out Christologies which are implicitly, if not explicitly, imperialist and anti-Judaic. The dilemma of messianic ideology and its career in Western history also remains mostly untouched or is not connected with Christian theology. This selective ignorance is then passed on in the teaching and preaching of Christianity in the churches in a way that continues to inculcate the myth of the carnal, legalistic, and obsolete "Jew." This very suppression of Jewish history and experience from Christian consciousness is tacitly genocidal. What it says, in effect, is that the Jews have no further right to exist after Jesus. We repress the memory of their continued existence and our dealings with them so that it appears that "after Christ" Jews disappear, and only Christians remain as the heirs of Jewish history and the people with a future.

The Christian anti-Judaic myth can never be held in check, much less overcome, until Christianity submits itself to that therapy of Jewish consciousness that allows the "return of the repressed." This means establishing a new education for a new consciousness, the sort of new consciousness that would make us grapple with the need for a new way of formulating Christian identity that allows space for the Jewish brother to live—live not on our terms, but on his. To a committee of the American Association of Theological Schools, I recently proposed the following reforms of current theological curricula:

1. Christian biblical scholarship must learn and teach the Jewish line of commentary and interpretation of Hebrew Scripture in midrash, questioning thereby the treatment of Judaism as something fulfilled and made obsolete by Christianity, to which the Hebrew Scriptures are assigned the status of "Old Testament."

2. New Testament scholarship must import into its teachings the rabbinic context of the thought of Jesus and Paul and correct the stereotypes of the Pharisees and the Torah which occur in the New Testament. Christians must grapple especially with the myth of Jewish "blood guilt" and seek ways of overcoming the anti-Judaic implications of Christian Scriptures for preaching.

3. Church historians should teach the history of the legal and social persecution of Jews in Christendom by ecclesiastical and political rulers, inspired by the myth of Jewish reprobation, and make Christians aware of the responsibility of Christianity for the translation of theological anti-Judaism into social anti-Semitism.

4. Christian theology must question the anti-Judaic side of its redemptive language and ask itself how these formulations can be eliminated from its interpretation of the gospel.

5. Christian seminaries should cultivate face-to-face conversation between faculty and students and the living Jewish religious consciousness, so that Christians can become aware of the conflict between the way in which Christians perceive the "Judaeo-Christian tradition" and the way this history has been experienced and appropriated by Jews. Field education courses should establish contact with rabbinic leadership and Jewish

community agencies and work out internships where insight into Jewish concerns may be gained first-hand.

6. Above all, courses on preaching and Christian education must work conscientiously to overcome anti-Judaic language in its hermeneutics and in the educational and liturgical materials which teach Christianity to the people.

Such material is in no way intended to substitute for courses in the history of Jewish thought and society which should go on in departments of Jewish studies and which Christians also should study. It is the repressed side of a history which Christians, especially seminarians, presently study as their own tradition.

These concrete steps toward a new consciousness do not mean that Christians can now claim this Jewish history and tradition as their own. The very content of this tradition precludes such easy appropriation, for it makes it necessary for the Christian to understand the Jew, not as the Christian has seen him, but as the Jew sees himself. This would strike the anti-Judaic myth at its root, establishing Jewish consciousness in its autonomy and its rejection of the Christian appropriation. But since the Christian anti-Judaic myth has been not only a means of hating Jews, but a means establishing Christian identity as the "true Israel," this Jewish consciousness means also a rethinking of Christian identity in such a way as to accept Judaism as still the "true Israel." What this will mean for Christian identity, we do not yet know. It means at least a certain relativization of Christian absolutism which can accept the independent salvific validity of the Jewish tradition, the authenticity of this alternate way of appropriating the biblical heritage. Perhaps, for some, it may become a real mutuality, an imaginative appreciation of each other's revelatory stories, an interpenetration of each other's identities. It is doubtful that these two streams will soon merge. It is, more importantly, not necessary to anyone's salvation that they should. Today, the tyranny of unity needs to be replaced by a valuing of the enrichment of dialogue that happens when various traditions cultivate their distinct perspectives. Perhaps Christianity needs a separate Judaism to keep it honest! God, who creates the many peoples, also can allow for many ways to the Father, which only become one at that end of history which is truly "final." The fratricidal side of Christian faith can be overcome only through genuine encounter with Jewish identity. Only then might a "Judaeo-Christian tradition," which has heretofore existed only as a Christian imperialist myth, which usurps rather than converses with the Jewish tradition, begin to happen for the first time.

1. See Alan Davies's valuable study, *Antisemitism and the Christian Mind* (New York: Seabury,1969), for a careful analysis of the Christian theological literature dealing with the Jewish people after Hitler's persecution and genocide.

2. The revised edition of *Jésus et Israel,* published in 1959, was translated into English and published under the title *Jesus and Israel* (New York: Holt, Rinehart and Winston, 1971).

3. The book, published by Newman Press, New York, 1961, was slightly revised and republished under the title *Is the New Testament Anti-Semitic?* (New York: Paulist, 1965).

4. E.g., *Is the New Testament Anti-Semitic?* pp. 148, 174.

5. Cf. Walter Abbot, ed., *The Documents of Vatican II* (New York: Associated Press, 1966), pp. 660–68.

6. Ibid., p. 665.

7. Ibid., p. 662.

8. Ibid., p. 666.

9. This expression is taken from "The Dogmatic Constitution on the Church," n. 16, ibid., p. 34.

10. Ibid., p. 665.

11. Fortress Press, Philadelphia, 1964, pp. 27–30. The full account of the visit I have learnt from private conversation with the author.

12. Paul Démann, "Israel et l'Unité de l'Eglise," *Cahiers Sioniens* 7, 1 (March 1953), pp. 1–24; Karl Thieme, *Biblische Religion Heute* (Heidelberg: L. Schneider, 1960).

13. *The Conflict of the Church and the Synagogue* (New York: Atheneum, 1969).

14. For a brief discussion of Tillich and Niebuhr with appropriate references to their work, see Alan Davies, *Antisemitism and the Christian Mind,* pp. 145–46.

15. "The Two Covenants and the Dilemmas of Christology," *Journal of Ecumenical Studies* 9 (1972), 249–70.

16. *Theological Investigations,* vol. 5 (Baltimore: Helicon, 1966), pp. 115–134.

17. "Judaism and Christianity," *Harvard Divinity Bulletin* 28 (Oct. 1963), pp. 1–9, and new series 1 (autumn 1967), pp. 2–9; "Jesus and the Kingdom," *The Alumni Bulletin* (Bangor Theological Seminar) 42 (April 1967), pp. 6–14.

18. "In What Sense Can We Say That Jesus Was 'The Christ'?" *The Ecumenist* 10 (Jan.–Feb. 1972), p. 22.

19. Ibid., pp. 19–20.

20. "The Decree on Ecumenism," n. 6, *The Documents of Vatican II,* p. 350.

NOTES TO CHAPTER ONE

1.   Edward Flannery declares that the sources of Christian anti-Semitism are either pagan hate or a misreading of Christian herme-neutics under the pressure of social competition. He denies that there is any root of anti-Semitism in the "legitimate anti-Judaism of ortho-dox Christian doctrine" (*The Anguish of the Jews* [New York: Mac-millan, 1964], pp. 60–61); see also G. Baum, *Is the New Testament Anti-Semitic?* (New York: Paulist, 1965), p. 328, n. 40.
2.   Marcel Simon, *Verus Israel* (Paris: Boccard, 1948), p. 237ff.; also J. Juster, *Les juifs dans l'empire romain* (Paris: P. Geuthner. 1914), vol. 1, pp. 45–48, summarizes the kinds of charges made against the Jews by pagans and the appearance of these charges in patristic anti-Judaic literature.
3.   Victor Tcherikover, *Hellenistic Civilization and the Jews* (Phila-delphia: Jewish Publication Society, 1959), pp. 357–77. See also Philo, *Embassy to Gaius*, 132–36 C.E. and *Flaccus* on political con-flicts between Jews and natives in Alexandria.
4.   *Contra Celsum* 3,5.
5.   Josephus *Contra Apionem* summarizes anti-Judaic charges by various Hellenistic writers beginning with Manetho.
6.   See Philip Deever, *Anti-Judaism of the New Testament in the Light of Its Biblical and Hellenistic Context* (New York: Th.D.. Union Theological Seminary, 1958), chap. 1. Also Robert Wilde, *The Treatment of the Jews in the Greek Patristic Writers of the First Three Centuries* (Catholic University Patristic Studies, no. 81 [Wash-ington: Catholic University, 1949]), and Dora Askowith, *The Toler-ation and Persecution of the Jews in the Roman Empire* (New York: Columbia University, 1915), chap. 3.
7.   Josephus *Jewish Wars* I, 38 wrongly places the alliance at the time of Judas Maccabeus, giving it maximum authority thereby. His account of the siege of Jerusalem (V, 362–428) is geared to pro-Roman apologia.
8.   Philo *Vita Mosis* II, 17–24 shows the admiration for things Jewish among pagans. Clement of Alexandria *Strom.* I, xxv pre-serves the Jewish apologetic view that Plato derived his philosophy from Moses.
9.   *Aristeas* 143–48.
10.   The Septuagint legend is found in Aristobulus (Eusebius, *Prae. Ev.* 13.12.2) and Aristeas and in Philo (*Vita Mosis* II, 25–44) and was accepted by the Church Fathers (Moses Hadas, *Aristeas to Philocrates* [New York: Harper, 1951], pp. 73–78). The Rabbis accepted it until Christianity made the LXX its text. Then they re-jected it and declared that the day that the Scriptures were translated into Greek was as hard a day for Israel as the day on which the

264 § *Faith and Fratricide*

golden calf was made (*Massakhet Soferim* 1.7–10; see Hadas, *Aristeas*, pp. 80–81 and n. 110).

11. "Laws, Noachian," *Jewish Encyclopedia*, 12 vols. (New York, 1901–06), vol. 7, 648–50.

12. Josephus, in his *Antiquities* and *Jewish Wars*, habitually depoliticizes Jewish religion, while concealing the religious character of the Zealot movements. Philo conceals the messianic tradition, except for two veiled references; see E. R. Goodenough, *The Politics of Philo Judaeus* (New Haven: Yale University, 1938), pp. 21–22.

13. Simon, *Verus Israel*, 250ff.

14. Josephus *Contra Apion* I, 229, 290; II, 125ff. and 137.

15. Ibid., II, 89.

16. See chap. 4, below, p. 189f.; also Robert L. Wilken, "Judaism in Roman and Christian Society," *Journal of Religion* 47 (1967), 313–30.

17. Marcel Simon, *Jewish Sects at the Time of Jesus* (Philadelphia: Fortress, 1967), pp. 110ff. Simon recognizes that Hellenistic Judaism belongs in a different category from the "sects."

18. Hadas, *Aristeas*, p. 65.

19. Saul Liebermann, *Greek in Jewish Palestine* (New York: Jewish Theological Seminary, 1942), and *Hellenism in Jewish Palestine* (New York: Jewish Theological Seminary, 1950).

20. C. H. Dodd, *The Bible and the Greeks* (London: Hodder & Stoughton, 1935), pp. 3–95.

21. *Opif. Mund.* 13–16 and 89–129 on the first and seventh days of Creation; also *Vita Mosis* II, 209ff.

22. *Aristeas* 128–70; for Moses Hadas's dating of Aristeas, see his introduction, p. 54.

23. *Aristeas* 150–61; also Philo *Spec. Leg.* IV, 106–8 and *Agr.* 145.

24. Deut. 10:16; Jer. 4:4; see Philo *Spec. Leg.* I, 8–11; *Q.G.* III, 48 (*Mig.* 92).

25. A. S. Kapelrud, "Temple Building: A Task for the Gods," *Orientalia* 3 (1963), pp. 56–63; Mircea Eliade, "Sacred Spaces: Temple, Palace, Centre of the World," *Patterns in Comparative Religion* (New York: Sheed and Ward, 1958), p. 367ff.

26. Philo *Vita Mosis* II, 88ff.; *Q.E.* II, 55–91.

27. Josephus *Ant.* III, 180ff., 123; *Jewish Wars* V, 212ff.

28. E. R. Goodenough, *By Light, Light: The Mystic Gospel of Hellenistic Judaism* (New Haven: Yale, 1935), p. 108.

29. Philo *Som.* I, 215. See Sidney Sowers, *The Hermeneutic of Philo and Hebrews* (Zurich: EVZ-Verlag, 1965), pp. 62–63.

30. Sowers, *Philo and Hebrews*, p. 64ff.

31. Philo *Spec. Leg.* I, 271.

32. *Spec. Leg.* I, 144ff.

33. Montgomery Shroyer, *The Alexandrian Jewish Literalists* (Philadelphia: Jewish Publication Society, 1936).

34. *Mig.* 89–94. See J. Lauterbach, "The Ancient Jewish Allegorists in Talmud and Midrash," *JQR* (1910).

35. See Louis Ginzberg, *The Legends of the Jews,* vol. 5 (Philadelphia: Jewish Pubn., 1909–38), p. 187, n. 51. Also below, n. 65. The idea that Abraham kept the Torah, including the oral Law, appears to be a late view, although it appears in the *Book of Jubilees.* Authoritative Tannaim and Amoraim leaned to the view that Abraham observed only the Noachian laws plus circumsicion, or only the moral laws of Torah. The view that Abraham kept the whole Torah plus the oral Law, however, is found in b. Yoma 28b. See J. Neusner, *Aphrahat and Judaism* (Leiden: Brill, 1971), pp. 185–86.

36. *Mig.* 127ff.; *Abr.* 276; Sowers, *Philo and Hebrews,* pp. 44–49.

37. R. P. C. Hanson, *Allegory and Event* (London: SCM, 1959), p. 25ff.

38. Ibid. See also Krister Stendahl, *The School of Matthew* (Philadelphia: Fortress, 1954), p. 183ff.

39. Gerhard von Rad, *Old Testament Theology* (New York: Harper and Row, 1965), vol. 2, pp. 21ff., 165. The remnant idea as a religious category is fully developed only in post-Isaic prophecy: Isa. 4:3; 10:20; 11:11,16; 28:5.

40. The discovery of sectarian scrolls at Masada confirms a common literature read by the Zealots and the Qumran sectarians; see Y. Yadin, *Masada* (New York: Random House, 1966), chaps. 12–14. Qumran may have been occupied by sectarian supporters of Bar Kochba in the 133–36 C.E. war; see Yadin, *The Message of the Scrolls* (New York: Simon and Schuster, 1957), p. 65.

41. John MacDonald, *The Theology of the Samaritans* (Philadelphia: Westminster, 1964), pp. 14–32 and passim.

42. Bertil Gärtner, *The Temple and the Community in Qumran and the New Testament* (Cambridge University, 1965), p. 14.

43. The dates of occupation of the Qumran site have led to a dating for the founding of the community in the reigns of John Hyrcanus or Alexander Jannai. A. Dupont-Sommer, *The Jewish Sect of Qumran and the Essenes* (New York: Macmillan, 1956), pp. 38–57, and H. H. Rowley, "The Teacher of Righteousness and the Dead Sea Scrolls," *BJRL* 40 (1957), pp. 114ff., would argue for later and earlier dates.

44. *Manual of Discipline* ix, 10, and *Zadokite Document* viii; *Manual of Discipline for the Future Congregation of Israel,* ii.

45. R. Travers Herford, *The Pharisees* (New York: Macmillan, 1962 edition), p. 29ff.

46. J. Neusner, "Qumran and Jerusalem," *Fellowship in Judaism* (London: Vallentine, Mitchell and Co., 1963), chap. 1; also "The Pharisaic Fellowship in the Second Commonwealth," *HThR* 53 (1960), pp. 125–42.

47. W. H. Brownlee, "John the Baptist in the Light of the Ancient

Scrolls," *The Scrolls and the New Testament*, ed. K. Stendahl, p. 36ff.; see H. H. Rowley, "Jewish Proselyte Baptism," *HUCA* 15 (1940), pp. 313–34.

48. Dupont-Sommer, *Jewish Sect of Qumran*, pp. 62–64.

49. *Zadokite Document* iii, 12–iv, 6.

50. Ibid. vi, 9; viii, 21 (T. H. Gaster, *The Dead Sea Scriptures* [New York: Doubleday, 1956], p. 72).

51. *The War Between the Sons of Light and the Sons of Darkness* i, 1–17 (Gaster, *Dead Sea*, pp. 181–82).

52. Acts 2:22–40; 3:16–21.

53. H. Odeberg, *Third Enoch or the Hebrew Book of Enoch* (New York: Ktav, 1973).

54. G. Scholem, *Jewish Gnosticism, Merkabah Mysticism and Talmudic Judaism* (New York: Ktav, 1960).

55. G. Scholem, *Major Trends in Jewish Mysticism* (Jerusalem: Schocken, 1941), pp. 40–79 and passim.

56. Hans Jonas, *The Gnostic Religion* (Boston: Beacon, 1958), pp. 17–28.

57. Ibid., pp. 29ff. and 26off.

58. See Col. 2:8–23; 1 Tim. 1:4; 4:1–3, 7; 2 Tim. 2:18; Titus 1:10, 12; 3:9; also 1 John 2:22; 4:2–3; Jude 1:8; 2 Peter 2:10–11; R. McL. Wilson, *Gnosis and the New Testament* (Philadelphia: Fortress, 1968), pp. 31–59.

59. Jean Doresse, *The Secret Books of the Egyptian Gnostics* (London: Hollis and Carter, 1960), pp. 197–218.

60. Adolf von Harnack, *Marcion: Das Evangelium von fremden Gott* (Darmstadt: Wissenschaftliche Buchgesellschaft, 1960).

61. For a text, translation, and commentary of one of the pre-Christian Gnostic writings which displays this fundamental Genesis myth, see R. A. Bullard, *The Hypostasis of the Archons* (Berlin: W. de Gruyter, 1970). A somewhat less developed form of the same myth is found in the untitled work from Codex II of Nag-Hamadi, edited by H. M. Schenke under the title "Vom Ursprung der Welt," *ThLZ*. 84 (1959), pp. 243–56.

62. See 2 Cor. 3:7ff.; Gal. 3:19, 24–25; 4:3, 21–31; and Rom. 7.

63. Ellis Rivkin, *The Shaping of Jewish History* (New York: Scribner, 1971) pp. 42ff.

64. J. R. Brown, *Temple and Sacrifice in Rabbinic Judaism* (Evanston, Ill.: Seabury-Western Theological Seminary, 1963), p. 26ff.

65. The rabbinic traditions declare that God taught Moses the whole oral Law, including the contents of the Mishnah and the Talmud (Tanh. B., Ki Tissa 58n.; C. J. G. Montefiore, *A Rabbinic Anthology* [London: Macmillan, 1938], 159–60). See Rivkin, *Jewish History*, pp. 51ff.

66. Max Kaduskin, *Organic Thinking* (New York: Jewish Theological Seminary, 1938), pp. 219–28.

67. Rivkin, *Jewish History,* pp. 68–69.

68. Tanh. B., Wayikra 2a–2b; Sifra 91a; Sifre, Num., Beha'-aloteka 72, f. 18b (Montefiore, *Rabbinic Anthology,* pp. 570–71).

69. For the role of Protestant liberal theology in the nineteenth century in translating traditional Christian theological anti-Judaism into secular anti-Semitism, see David C. Smith, *Protestant Attitudes Toward Jewish Emancipation in Prussia* (Yale Ph.D., 1971).

70: Sifra 86b; Bab. K. 38a (Montefiore, *Rabbinic Anthology,* p. 564).

71. Emil Fackenheim, "The Human Condition after Auschwitz," B. G. Rudolph Lectures in Judaic Studies, Syracuse University (April 1971), p. 1.

72. Arthur Cohen, *The Myth of the Judaeo-Christian Tradition* (New York: Harper and Row, 1963), p. xx.

73. Ben Zion Bokser, *Judaism and the Christian Predicament* (New York: Knopf, 1967), p. 43n.

74. Travers Herford, *Christianity in Talmud and Midrash* (London: Williams and Norgate, 1903). Herford has collected the possible references to Jesus in rabbinic traditions.

75. Jer. Taanith iv; fol 68d; Emil Schürer, *A History of the Jewish People at the Time of Jesus* (New York: Schocken, 1961), p. 299ff. For a summary of the contemporary messianic tradition and the Pharisaic preservation of it, see G. F. Moore, *Judaism in the First Century of the Christian Era: The Age of the Tannaim* (New York: Schocken, 1971), vol. 2, pp. 323–76.

76. Mekilta of R. Simon ben Yohai, p. 1f.; see Brown, *Temple and Sacrifice in Rabbinic Judaism,* pp. 24–26.

77. Sotah 17a.

78. On the earliest of these traditions see J. Neusner, *A Life of Rabban Yohanan ben Zakkai* (Leiden: Brill, 1962), pp. 130–46.

79. Ibid., chap. 6.

NOTES TO CHAPTER TWO

1. Douglas R. A. Hare, *The Theme of Jewish Persecution of Christians in the Gospel According to Matthew* (Cambridge University Press, 1967), p. 84.

2. J. Rendel Harris, *Testimonies* I, II (Cambridge University Press, 1916–20); also D. Plooij, *Studies in the Testimonies Book* (Amsterdam, 1932). For a critique of the testimonies book thesis, see Barnabas Lindars, *New Testament Apologetic: The Doctrinal Significance of Old Testament Quotations* (Philadelphia: Westminster, 1961), p. 13ff.

3. *Sab.* 31a (C. J. G. Montefiore, *A Rabbinic Anthology* [London: Macmillan, 1938], p. 173).

4. Mekilta *Ki Tissa'*, Shab. I (Montefiore, *Rabbinic Anthology*, p. 711).

5. See Montefiore, "The Importance of Motive or Intention," *Rabbinic Anthology*, pp. 272–94 and 127.

6. Zech 9:9. For the original locus of the procession in the New Year's ritual of Davidic times, see Sigmund Mowinckel, *The Psalms in Israel's Worship* (New York: Abingdon, 1962), vol. I, p. 62; and *He Who Cometh* (New York: Abingdon, 1954), pp. 76–77.

7. For the idea of the suffering prophet in first-century Judaism, see H. A. Fischel, "Martyr and Prophet," *JQR* 37 (1946/7), pp. 265ff. and 363ff.

8. For the tradition of the dying Messiah ben Joseph, see *Jewish Encyclopedia*, vol. 8, pp. 511–12.

9. C. H. Dodds, *According to the Scriptures: The Substructure of New Testament Theology* (London: Nisbet, 1952) showed that Old Testament exegesis is a key to the earliest Christian theological reflection. The use of Ps 110:1 is discussed in its Christian context in Lindars, *New Testament Apologetic*, pp. 45–51. The rabbinic refutation of this Christian use of the psalm is discussed in Benjamin W. Helfgott, *The Doctrine of Election in Tannaitic Literature* (New York: King's Crown, 1954), p. 86.

10. Bertil Gärtner, *The Temple and the Community in Qumran and the New Testament* (Cambridge University Press, 1965).

11. See Jacob Neusner, *From Politics to Piety: The Emergence of Pharisaic Judaism* (Englewood Cliffs, N.J.: Prentice Hall, 1973), pp. 71–72.

12. Matthew Black, *The Scrolls and Christian Origins* (New York: Nelson, 1961), pp. 118–24.

13. Rabbinic tradition makes sharp fun of the various kinds of hypocrisy into which the "observant" may fall. There are seven kinds of Pharisees: the "shoulder Pharisee" (who wears his good deeds on his shoulder); the "wait-a-while" Pharisee; the "bruised" Pharisee (who knocks his head on a wall to avoid looking at a woman); the "pestle (mock-humble) Pharisee," and the "bookkeeping (virtue-calculating) Pharisee"; then there is the Pharisee who obeys God out of fear, and the Pharisee who obeys God out of love. Only this last is a true Pharisee (Montefiore, *Rabbinic Anthology*, pp. 487–89).

14. J. C. O'Neill, *The Theology of Acts in its Historical Setting* (London: SPCK, 1961), pp. 95ff.

15. Bernard J. Bamberger, *Proselytism in the Talmudic Period* (New York: Ktav, 1968), pp. 135–38.

16. The traditions about James in the New Testament are found in Matt. 13:55; Mark 6:3; Luke 8:19–21; Matt. 12:46–50; Mark 3:31–35; John 7:3–7; Acts 1:14; 15:13ff.; Gal. 1:19; 2:9. The two chief sources outside the New Testament are Hegesippus' fifth

Memoir from Eusebius *H.E.* II, 23, 4–18 and Josephus *Ant.* XX, 200.

17. See Hans Joachim Schoeps, *Jewish Christianity,* trans. Douglas R. A. Hare (Philadelphia: Fortress, 1964), pp. 19–20 and passim. An interesting effort to reconstruct the theology of Jewish Christianity is found in an article by Shlomo Pines, "The Jewish Christians of the Early Centuries According to a New Source," *Israel Academy of Sciences and Humanities,* vol. 2, no. 13 (Jerusalem, 1966).

18. See the essays on Jewish sectarianism and early Christianity in J. Neusner, ed., *Religions in Antiquity* (E. R. Goodenough Memorial volume; Leiden: Brill, 1968); especially the essay by Robin Scroggs, "The earliest Hellenistic Christianity," pp. 176–206. Also M. Simon, *St. Stephen and the Hellenists* (London: Longmans, 1958), pp. 31–38.

19. Paul Winter, *On the Trial of Jesus* (Berlin: Walter de Gruyter, 1961); also E. Bammel, ed., *The Trial of Jesus* (Naperville, Ill.: Allenson, 1970), and S. G. F. Brandon, *The Trial of Jesus* (New York: Stein and Day, 1968).

20. Stephen's death appears to have been due to a popular riot rather than a judicial decision of the religious court. James, the son of Zebedee, was executed by Herod on political grounds, for Zealot connections, and James, the brother of Jesus, seems to have died in a purge of the personal enemies of the new high priest Annas against the strong disapproval of the "observant," i.e., the Pharisees, in Jerusalem. Hare, *Theme of Jewish Persecution,* pp. 20–43, regards the theme of persecution and especially the motif of "killing" in the Gospels as a theological a priori, rather than the result of experience of such a "pattern" in the Church's relation to the synagogue. This expectation of persecution "to the death" carried over into an exaggeration of the role of the Jews in the accounts of the deaths of Christian martyrs. See S. Zeitlin, *Who Crucified Jesus?* (New York: Bloch, 1942).

21. Ben Zion Bokser, *Judaism and the Christian Predicament* (New York: Knopf, 1967), pp. 217–28; cf. Hugo Mantel, *Studies in the History of the Sanhedrin* (Cambridge, Mass.: Harvard University, 1965), pp. 54–101.

22. B. S. Easton, *Early Christianity: The Purpose of Acts and Other Papers* (London: SPCK, 1955), pp. 33–118.

23. For example, see Dominic Crossan, "Anti-Semitism and the Gospels," *Theological Studies* 26, 2 (June 1965), pp. 189–215; also Gregory Baum, *Is the New Testament Anti-Semitic?,* pp. 40–52, 78–87. A careful study of the way in which Matthew uses the symbols of the Jewish "leaders," in contrast to the "crowds," in their reaction to Jesus is found in Sjef van Tilborg, *The Jewish Leaders in Matthew* (Leiden: Brill, 1972).

24. Lindars, *New Testament Apologetic*, pp. 88ff.
25. Hare, *Theme of Jewish Persecution*, pp. 83–4, 137–41. Hare cites Joachim Jeremias's study, *Heiligengräber in Jesu Umwelt* (Göttingen: Vandenhoeck, 1958), pp. 118–21, for the view that Herod was the originator of such tombs and the rabbis probably opposed them; cf. H. J. Schoeps, *Die jüdischen Prophetenmorde* (Uppsala, 1943).
26. Fischel's article contains abundant documentation on the various aspects of the idea of the suffering prophet-martyr (see n. 7 above) in rabbinic, apocryphal, and Christian literature in the period from the second century B.C.E. to the second century C.E. See also Sh. H. Blank, "The Death of Zechariah in Rabbinic Literature," *HUCA*, 12–13 (1937–38), pp. 327–46.
27. Peter Richardson, *Israel in the Apostolic Church* (Cambridge University Press, 1969), chap. 5.
28. Günther Bornkamm, *Paul*, trans. D. M. G. Stalker, (New York: Harper and Row, 1969), pp. 52, 54, 57, 91, 106.
29. See Alan Davies, *Anti-Semitism and the Christian Mind* (New York: Seabury, 1969), pp. 92–107.
30. Sidney Sowers, *The Hermeneutic of Philo and Hebrews* (Zürich: EVZ Verlag, 1965), pp. 79–88.
31. Ibid., pp. 64–74.
32. C. H. Dodd, *The Interpretation of the Fourth Gospel* (Cambridge University Press, 1963), pp. 86, 297.
33. See Brandon, *Trial of Jesus*, pp. 134–35; also Haim Hermann Cohen, *The Trial and Death of Jesus* (New York: Harper and Row, 1971), pp. 186–87.
34. On excommunication from the synagogue as a disciplinary measure and the *Birkath ha-Minim* (malediction of the sectaries inserted in the Eighteen Benedictions), see Hare, *Theme of Jewish Persecution*, pp. 39, 48–56. Hare concludes that Christians were never excommunicated for profession of faith in Jesus per se. The *Birkath ha-Minim* would detect primarily a sectary trying to lead the service. Use of an actual ban was exceptional and was not used for doctrinal reasons, but as a reaction to specific cases of disturbances of worship.
35. See Philip Deever (above, chap. 1, n. 6); also Edward Flannery, *The Anguish of the Jews*, (New York: Macmillan, 1964), p. 30; and Baum, *Is the New Testament Anti-Semitic?*, pp. 138–44.

NOTES TO CHAPTER THREE

1. *Ante-Nicene Fathers* 5, pp. 507–57 (*PL* 4, cols. 703–810). A summary of the *adversus Judaeos* writings of the patristic and medieval periods can be found in A. L. Williams, *Adversus Judaeos* (Cambridge University Press, 1935).

2. *PG* 46, 194–234.
3. *PG* 28, 589–700.
4. *PL* 83, 449–538.
5. *ANF* 5, pp. 645–50.
6. *ANF* 3, pp. 151–74 (*PL* 2, 633–82).
7. J. Neusner, *Aphrahat and Judaism* (Leiden: Brill, 1971). Also F. Gavin, "Aphraates and the Jews," *Contributions of Oriental History and Philology* 10 (Toronto, 1923).
8. *ANF* 5, pp. 219–21 (*PG* 10, 787–94).
9. *PG* 48, 813–38 (*Fr: Oeuvres complètes de S. Jean Chrysostome* 1 [Paris, 1865]).
10. Text edited by C. H. Turner in *JThS* 20 (1919), pp. 289–310.
11. *The Fathers of the Church* 27 (1955) (*PL* 42 [Augustine viii], 51–64).
12. *Eight Homilies Against the Jews: PG* 48, 843–942; *Fr: Oeuvres complètes de S. Jean Chrysostome* 1, pp. 500–580; *ET:* C. Mervyn Maxwell, *Chrysostom's Homilies Against the Jews* (University of Chicago, Ph.D. Thesis, 1966).
13. *Library of the Fathers*, J. B. Morris (Oxford, 1847), pp. 61–83.
14. A summary of Isaac of Antioch and the anti-Judaic writings of Jacob of Serug and Dionysius bar Salabhi, in the context of Syrian Christianity, can be found in essays by Stanley Kazan, *Oriens Christianus* 45, pp. 30–53; 46, 87ff.; 47, 89ff.; and 49, 57ff.
15. *ET:* I. K. Cosgrove in unpublished ms. at the University of London.
16. Robert A. Kraft, *The Apostolic Fathers: The Didache and Barnabas* (New York: T. Nelson, 1965) (*PG* 2, 727–81).
17. Frags. in *PG* 5, 1277–86.
18. F. C. Conybeare, *The Dialogues of Athanasius and Zacchaeus and of Timothy and Aquila* (Oxford: Clarendon, 1889).
19. *Dialogue of Athanasius and Zacchaeus.* Trans. F. C. Conybeare, *Expositor* 45 (1897), pp. 300–20, 443–63.
20. *PG* 86, 621–784.
21. *PL* 20, 1076–1166.
22. *PL* 20, 1165–82.
23. A. C. McGiffert, intro. and trans. (Marburg, 1889).
24. *PG* 121, 521–40.
25. *PG* 40, 847–60.
26. Greek text with French trans., G. Bardy, *Patr. Orient.* 15, 2 (1920).
27. A. B. Hulen, "Dialogues with the Jews as Sources for Early Jewish Arguments Against Christianity," *JBL* 51 (1932), pp. 55ff.; also A. C. McGiffert's introduction to the *Dialogue of Papiscus and Philo* (see n. 23, above).
28. *ANF* 1, pp. 194–270 (*PG* 6, 471–799).

29. *PL* 42, 1117–30 and 1131–40. See also E. N. Stone's trans. in *University of Washington Publication in Language and Literature* (Seattle, 1928). For its use in medieval drama, see Karl Young, *The Drama of the Medieval Church* 2 (Oxford, 1933), pp. 125–71.

30. *Teachings of Jacob, Sargis D'Aberga,* Ethiopic with French trans. by F. N. Nau, *Patr. Orient.* 3,4 (1909) and 13,1 (1919).

31. *ANF* 6, pp. 395ff. For the kinds of questions discussed by Jews and Christians from the point of view of a defender of classical paganism, see Julian's *Against The Galilaeans* in W. C. Wright, *The Works of Julian* (Library of Classical Literature) 3, pp. 313–428.

32. Eusebius, *Preparation for the Gospel,* trans. E. H. Gifford (Oxford, 1903); *Demonstration of the Gospel,* trans. W. J. Ferrar, (London: SPCK, 1920).

33. *The City of God,* especially XVI, 16–XVIII, 46.

34. John of Damascus, "Against the Jews, Concerning the Sabbath," *On the Orthodox Faith,* iv, 23 (*Fathers of the Church* 37 [1958], pp. 389–92; *PG* 94, 1201–6).

35. Prudentius, *Apotheosis,* 321–551 (Loeb), vol. I, pp. 116ff.

36. *Divine Institutes* IV, 10–21 (*ANF* 7, pp. 108–24); also Athanasius, "Against the Heathen," bk. 1 (*Nicene and Post-Nicene Fathers* 4, pp. 1–30).

37. Irenaeus, *Against the Heresies,* especially III, 21 and IV, 7–26 (*ANF* 1, pp. 451–54, 469–98).

38. The recent study by Robert L. Wilken espouses all the same tenets of the *adversus Judaeos* tradition through a study of the exegetical commentaries and theological writings of Cyril of Alexandria: *Judaism and the Early Christian Mind* (New Haven: Yale. 1971).

39. Just. *Dial.* 71; Aug. *C.D.* XV, 13; *Dial. T.-A.* foll. 117–19; Orig. *Hom. in Jer.* 16, 10 See S. Krauss, "The Jews in the Works of the Church Fathers," *JQR* 5 (1893), pp. 122ff. and 6 (1894), pp. 225ff. Also Salo Baron, *A Social and Religious History of the Jews,* vol. 2 (New York: Columbia University, 1952), pp. 141–47.

40. A preliminary attempt at doing this has been made in Jacob Neusner's *Aphrahat and Judaism* (Leiden: Brill, 1971), pp. 150–95.

41. Chrysostom uses the same phrase (*Or. C. Jud.* V, 9 [*PG* 48, 898]) reading Dan. 9:24, where seventy weeks are given to "put an end to sin" as though this meant seventy weeks were given to "fill up the measure of the sins" of the Jews to the point of final reprobation, i.e., Matt. 23:32.

42. Cyp. *Test.* I,2; cf. Just. *Dial.* 39.

43. Lact. *D. I.* IV,11.

44. Euseb. *D. E.* I,6,17.

45. Aph. *Dem.* 15,4.

46. Cf. Ezek. 16:31; 23:3; Chry. *Or. C. Jud.* VI,2 (*PG* 48,906).

47. *Ep. Barn.* 4,8.

48. Orig. *C. Cel.* II,75; cf. Chry. *Or. C. Jud.* VI,2 (*PG* 48,906).
49. Cf. Iren. *Haer.* IV,14; Just. *Dial.* 34.
50. In the LXX translation: Rom. 2:24; Just. *Dial.* 17; Ter. *Adv. Jud.* 13.
51. Rom. 10:21; *Ep.* Barn. 12,4; Just. *Dial.* 24.
52. Just. *Dial.* 20; Ps.-Nys. *Test.* 4.
53. Chry. *Or. C. Jud.* I,2 (*PG* 48,846).
54. Ibid., I,7 (*PG* 48,853).
55. Eph. *Rhy. C. Jud.* 12.
56. Isa. 1:9; cf. Rom. 9:29; Aph. *Dem.* 11,1; cf. Chry. *Or. C. Jud.* IV, 6 (*PG* 48,879); Cyp. *Test.* I,6.
57. Orig. *C. Cel.* II,75.
58. Isid. *C. Jud.* I,18. Cf. *Dial. S.-T.* (*PL* 20, 1179C).
59. Chry. *Or. C. Jud.* IV,2; VI,6–7, and passim.
60. It is characteristic of the *adversus Judaeos* tradition to read the "enemies" of the Davidic king in the Psalms and of the prophet in Isaiah as "the Jews," while the spokesman is seen as Christ; cf. Chry. *Or. C. Jud.* VI,5 (*PG* 48,911); *Ep.* Barn. 6, 6–7; Hipp. *C. Jud.* 3.
61. Cyp. *Test.* I, 19 and 21; *Ep.* Barn. 13, 2–4; Ter. *Adv. Jud.* 1; Iren. *Haer.* IV, 21, 2; Max. *C. Jud.* 1 and 5; Aug. *Adv. Jud* 7, 9; *C. D.* XVI, 35, 37; Is. Ant. *Hom. C. Jud.* (Kazan, *Oriens Christianus* 45, pp. 32 and 41); Ps.-Aug. *Alt. Ecc.-Syn* (*PL* 42, 1134–35); *Dial. S.-T.* (*PL* 20, 1173); *Trop. Dam.*, (*Pat. Orient.* XV, p. 237).
62. Chry. *Or. C. Jud.* I,7; *PG* 48,853; in *Or. C. Jud.* VIII, however, Chrysostom used Cain as the image of the Judaizer marked by his sin, while the Jew himself appears to be beyond the pale of even his divine protection for sin.
63. Aug. *C. D.* XV,7; *Reply to Faustus* (*PL* 42,210–11).
64. Aug. *Adv. Jud.* 5 (6); also Max. *C. Jud.* 1 and Cyp. *Test,* I,20.
65. Aug. *Adv. Jud.* 5 (6); Max. *C. Jud.* 5.
66. Cf. Just. *Dial.* 134; Iren. *Haer.*, IV,21,3; Max. *C. Jud.* 5; *Did. Jak.* (*Pat. Orient.* 3, p. 633).
67. See chap. 4, below, p. 209.
68. Neusner *Aphrahat*, p. 63; cf. *Dial. S.-T.* (*PL* 20,1177).
69. Cf. Williams, *Adversus Judaeos*, pp. 326–36. The text, written in the fifth century, reflects the laws of the Theodosian Canon forbidding the Jews public office in the empire (see chap. 4, below, p. 189). These laws are interpreted by our text as proof of God's reprobation of the Jews.
70. Rom. 4:11; cf. *Ep.* Barn. 13, 7; Just. *Dial.* 119; Ter. *Adv. Jud.* 2; Euseb. *D. E.* I, 2, 15; Cyp. *Test.* I, 5; Aph. *Dem.* 11, 4; 13, 8; 16, 1; Iren. *Haer.*, IV, 7, 2; Max. *C. Jud.* 5; Prud. *Apo.* 363–5; *Dial. A.-Z.* (Conybeare, *Expositor* 45, p. 447).
71. Kazan, *Oriens Christianus* 45, pp. 45–47.
72. Cf. Just. *Dial.* 130–31; Aug. *Adv. Jud.* 1 (2), 5 (6), 6 (7), 7

(8, 9), 9 (12, 13); Iren. *Haer.* IV, 7–8; Lact. *D.I.* IV, 11, 20; Ter. *Apol.* 21, and Ter. *Adv. Jud.* 12, 13; Cyp. *Test.* I, 21, 23; Ps.-Nys. *Test.* 16; Euseb. *D.E.* II, 3ff.; Eph. *Rhy. C. Jud.* 19; Aph. *Dem.* 16; Is. Ant. *Hom. C. Jud.* II (Kazan, *Oriens Christianus* 45, pp. 38, 52); Orig. *C. Cel.* II, 78; *Dial. T.-A.*, foll. 113ff; *Dial. G.-H.* (*PG* 86, 694f.); *Did. Jak.* (*Pat. Orient.* 3, pp. 617, 622; and 13, pp. 34–39); Prud. *Apo.* 364–67, 506–07; Isid. *C. Jud.* II, 1, 2, 4, 8; *Q. Ant. Dux* 137, 3 (*PG* 28, 637); *Dial. A.-Z.* (Conybeare, *Expositor* 45, p. 317).

73. Cf. Euseb. *Or. Con.* 16, 8; *Dial. A.-Z.* (Conybeare, *Expositor* 45, p. 455).

74. Especially his treatise, "That Christ is God, Against the Jews and Gentiles"; also Prud. *Apo.* 365–510; *Did. Jak.* 18 (*Pat. Orient.* 3, p. 581ff).

75. Cf. Cyp. *Test.* I,20; Ter. *Adv. Jud.* 7.

76. Just. *Dial.* 31–33, 52, 110–12; Lact. *D. I.* IV, 16; Aph. *Dem.* 21,9–10; Orig. *C. Cel.* II,29.

77. Chry. *Or. C. Jud.* IV, 3 (*PG* 48, 874).

78. Cf. Just. *Dial.* 16; Just. *I Apol* 47; Ter. *Adv. Jud.* 13; Cyp. *Test.* I,6; Euseb. *D.E.* II,3, 24–35; Chry. *Or. C. Jud.* VI ("The Cross is the Cause of their Woe"); also *Or. C. Jud.* V,1, etc.; Orig. *C. Cel.* II,8; *Dial. P.-P.* 16; Aug. *Adv. Jud.* 5 (6); *C. D.* XVIII,46; Eph. *Rhy. C. Jud.* 13–17; Aph. *Dem.* 19, esp. 2–5; Ps.-Nys. *Test.* 16; Isid. *C. Jud.* II,9–13; *Dial. A.-Z.* (Conybeare, *Expositor* 45, 449).

79. A standard text taken as prophesying the new Christian worship; cf. Just. *Dial.* 117; Euseb. *D. E.* I, 6,19; Chry. *Or. C. Jud.* V,12 (*PG* 48, 902); Ter. *Adv. Jud.* 5; Aph. *Dem.* 16,3; Aug. *Adv. Jud.* 9,12; *C. D.* XVIII,35; Ps.-Nys. *Test.* 16; *Did.* 4,3; Isid. *C. Jud.* II,17; *Did. Jak.* (*Pat. Orient.* 3, p. 615).

80. Chry. *Or. C. Jud.* III,3 (*PG* 48,865–66), citing Deut. 16:5–6; also *Or. C. Jud.* VI,5–7; a favorite text for this is Jer. 2:12–13, comparing the synagogue to a broken cistern which will not hold water; cf. Ter. *Adv. Jud.* 13; *Ep.* Barn. 11,2; Just. *Dial.* 19; Cyp. *Test.* I,3.

81. Chry. *Or. C. Jud.* V,10–11.

82. Lact. *D. I.* IV,11, 18; Hipp. *C. Jud.* 6; Aph. *Dem.* 19; Orig. *C. Cel.* II,8; IV,22; *Dial. P.-P.* 17; Chry. *Or. C. Jud.* V,1,5; VI,12. Chrysostom traces three captivities; the 400-year Egyptian one, the 70-year Babylonian one, and the three-and-a-half-year captivity under Antiochus Epiphanes from Daniel, thus making the *fourth* the endless captivity.

83. A LXX mistranslation of Ps. 69:22–24 (the Hebrew reads "may their loins quiver"). It addresses the foreign enemies of the Davidic kings, which the Church reads as "the Jews." A favorite patristic text for Jewish servitude; Aug. *Adv. Jud.* 5 (6), 7 (10); *C. D.* XVII,19; XVIII,46.

84. Just. *Dial.* 16; cf. Ter. *Adv. Jud.* 3; Iren. *Haer.* II,16,1.

85. Aug. *C. D.* XVIII,46 and XX,29; see chap. 4, below, p. 200.

86. Hipp. *Ref. Haer.* IX,25.

87. Chry. *Or. C. Jud.* V,9–10; Aug. *C. D.* XVIII,34; Euseb. VIII,2; *Trop. Dam.* 4 (*Pat. Orient.* 15, pp. 262ff.); *Did. Jak.* 22, *Pat. Orient.* 3, pp. 591ff.; *Dial. P.-P.* 17.

88. Ter. *Adv. Jud.* 13.

89. See chap. 4, below, p. 192.

90. Isid. *C. Jud.* II,2; *Did. Jak.* (*Pat. Orient.* 13, pp. 64–66); *Dial P.-P.* 7.

91. Cf. Chry. *Dem. Jud.-Gen.* 11.

92. Euseb. *D. E.* I,2,16,17; cf. Ter. *Adv. Jud.* 2; Iren. *Haer.* IV,15; Nov. *Carn. Jud.* 3; Jak. Serug. *Hom. C. Jud.* II; *Did. Jak.* 35 (*Pat. Orient.* 3, p. 612).

93. Aph. *Dem.* 15.

94. However, Noachian law was seen as positive law also, and was not identified with the Stoic concept of Natural Law by the rabbis. Philo linked Jewish Law and Natural Law in a positive, not an antithetical, way; see above, pp. 26, 264, n. 11, and p. 34.

95. *Ep. Barn.* 9,6–9; Just. *Dial.* 19, 23; Iren. *Haer.* IV,16; Ter. *Adv. Jud.* 2,3; Euseb. *D. E.* I,6 (146); *Dial. S.-T.* (PL 20, 1172).

96. Just. *Dial.* 20; Iren. *Haer.* IV,15; Nov. *Carn. Jud.* 3; Euseb. *D. E.* I,3; *Dial. S.-T.* (PL 20, 1179–80); Aph. *Dem.* 15,3.

97. Just. *Dial.* 22; Chry. *Or. C. Jud.* IV,6 (PG 48, 882); Aph. *Dem.* 15,6; Euseb. *D. E.* I,3.

98. Aph. *Dem.* 13,1,9.

99. Ps.-Nys. *Test.* 13; cf. John Dam. 4,23.

100. Just. *Dial.* 21.

101. Aph. *Dem.* 11,4; Jak. Serug. *Hom. C. Jud.* II; Isid. *C. Jud.* II,16; *Dial. A.-Z.* (Conybeare, *Expositor* 45, p. 461).

102. Just. *Dial.* 16; Ter. *Adv. Jud.* 3.

103. Ps.-Aug. *Alt. Ecc.-Syn.* (PL 42, 1134–35); Isaac of Antioch repeats Paul's declaration that those who want to keep on circumcizing themselves should go all the way and castrate themselves (Gal. 5:12; Is. Ant. *Hom. C. Jud.* II [Kazan, *Oriens Christianus* 45, p. 46]).

104. Just. *Dial.* 23; Max. *C. Jud.* 6.

105. Just. *Dial* 22; Iren. *Haer.* IV,15; Aph. *Dem.* 15,8.

106. Jer. 31:31 (a basic text for the Christian concept of the "new covenant"); cf. Just. *Dial.* 11; Cyp. *Test.* I,11; *Dial. T.-A.*, foll. 113; *Dial. A.-Z.* (Conybeare, *Expositor* 45, pp. 460, 462–63); Aug. *Adv. Jud.* 6 (8); *C. D.* XVII,3; XVIII,33; *Did. Jak.* 11 (*Pat. Orient.* 3, p. 569; *Pat. Orient.* 13, p. 57); Euseb. *D. E.* I,4,8; 6,22; 7,29, etc.; *Ep.* Barn. 6,14; Aph. *Dem.* 11,11; 12,11; Ter. *Adv. Jud.* 3; Iren. *Haer.* IV,9,1; 32,14; Isid. *C. Jud.* II, 14, etc.

107. Deut. 18:15; Lact. *D. I.* 4,17; Ter. *Adv. Jud.* 6; Cyp. *Test.* I,10,18; Euseb. *D. E.* I,3,60; *Did. Jak.* (*Pat. Orient.* 13, pp. 21ff).

108. Exod. 17:8–15; cf. *Ep.* Barn. 12,2–7; Just. *Dial.* 90; Ter. *Adv. Jud.* 10, etc.

109. *Dial. T.-A.*, foll. 130; Ps.-Cyp. *Mont.*; Lact. *D. I.* IV,17; Cyp. *Test.* I,10; Euseb. *D. E.* I,4,8d.

110. Just. *Dial.* 96; Euseb. *D. E.* I,16,18; Chry. *Or. C. Jud.* II,2 (*PG* 48, 859).

111. Chry. *Or. C. Jud.* IV,3–4 (*PG* 48, 876).

112. Deut. 10:16; Jer. 4:4; 9:26; Rom. 2:25–29; Gal. 5, etc.; *Ep.* Barn. 9, 1–5; Just. *Dial.* 24; Ter. *Adv. Jud.* 3; Cyp. *Test.* I, 8; Ps.-Nys. *Test.* 11; *Dial. A.Z.* (Conybeare, *Expositor* 45, pp. 460–62); Chry. *Or. C. Jud.* II, 1 (*PG* 48, 857); Aph. *Dem.* 11; Jak. Serug. *Hom. C. Jud.* II; *Dial. T.-A.* II, 8; *Dial. S.-T.* (*PL* 20, 1172–74); Isid. *C. Jud.* II, 16.

113. Aug. *Adv. Jud.* 2.

114. John. Dam. IV, 23.

115. Lact. *D. E.* IV,17.

116. See above, n. 101.

117. Josh. 5:2; *Dial. Z.-A.* II,8; *Dial. A.-Z.* (Conybeare, *Expositor* 45, pp. 456–57, 462); *Dial. S.-T.* (*PL* 20,1173); Ter. *Adv. Jud.* 9; Cyp. *Test.* I,8; II,16; Just. *Dial.* 113–17; Aph. *Dem.* 11,6; Lact. *D. I.* IV,17; Max. *C. Jud.* 4; Isid. *C. Jud.* II,16.

118. Nov. *Carn. Jud.* 3.

119. Nov. *Carn. Jud.* 3; *Ep.* Barn. 10,1–11; Lact. *D. I.* IV,17; Just. *Dial.* 20; Aug. *Adv. Jud.* 2; *Dial. S.-T.* (*PL* 20,1180); Isid. *C. Jud.* II,18.

120. Josh. 6:4; Aph. *Dem.* 13,12; cf. Ter. *Adv. Jud.* 4; Jak. Serug. *Hom. C. Jud.* III.

121. Diog. *Ep.* 4; Just. *Dial.* 23, etc.

122. *Ep.* Barn. 15,1–9; Just. *Dial.* 21; Iren. *Haer.* IV,6; Ter. *Adv. Jud.* 4; Ps.-Nys. *Test.* 13; Aug. *Adv. Jud.* 2; Aph. *Dem.* 13,13; Jak Serug, *Hom. C. Jud.* III; *Dial. S.-T.* (*PL* 20,1179); Isid. *C. Jud.* II,15; Prud. *Apo.* 504–07; John Dam. IV,23.

123. *Ep.* Barn. 15,8–9.

124. John Dam. IV,23.

125. *Ep.* Barn. 2,4; Just. *Dial.* 22; Iren. *Haer.* IV,17,18; Ter. *Adv. Jud.* 5; Cyp. *Test.* I,16; Ps.-Nys. *Test.* 12; Chry. *Or. C. Jud.* IV,4; *PG* 48,876).

126. See chap. 1, above, p, 57.

127. See above, n. 77.

128. 1 Cor. 3:16–17.

129. *Ep.* Barn. 4,11; 16,1–10.

130. Lact. *D. I.* IV,14; Cyp. *Test.* I,15; Orig. *C. Cel.* VIII,19; Prud. *Apo.* 515–40.

131. Euseb. *Vita Con.* III,33; *H. E.* X,4,3. Cf. *Dial. G.-H.* (*PG* 86,731).

132. Ter. *Adv. Jud.* 3,6; Just. *Dial.* 33; Lact. *D. I.* IV,14; Aug.

Adv. Jud. 13; Aug. *C. D.* XVI,22; XVII,17; Eph. *Rhy. C. Jud.* 12; Max. *C. Jud.* 7; *Dial. A.-Z.* (Conybeare, pp, 450–51).

133. Cf. *Did. Jak.* (*Pat. Orient.* 3, p. 617); Isid. *C. Jud.* II,27; Chry. *Or. C. Jud.* VII,2–3 (*PG* 48, 919).

134. Chry. *Or. C. Jud.* III,3 (*PG* 48, 866); Aug. *Adv. Jud.* 2.

135. Aph. *Dem.* 12; also Aug. *Adv. Jud.* 2; Prud. *Apo.* 346–62; Chry. *Or. C. Jud.* III,3 (*PG* 48,865), etc.

136. *Dial. J.-P.* (*PG* 5,1178–79). Typical patristic trinitarian exegesis of the O.T. is found in *Dial. A.-Z.* (Conybeare, *Expositor* 45, pp. 304ff.); Just. *Dial.* 56–65; Isid. *C. Jud.* I,1–4; *Dial. Z.-A.* bk. I passim; *Dial. S.-T.* (*PL* 20,1167ff.); *Did. Jak.* 58 (*Pat. Orient.* 13, pp. 10ff.); *Dial. T.-A.*, foll. 79–113.

137. Cf. Cyp. *Test.* II,9–30; Ps.-Nys. *Test.* 2–9; Isid. *C. Jud.* I,7–62; *St. Silv.* (*PG* 121,122–35).

138. Just. *Dial.* 92; Lact. *D. I.* IV, 17; Iren. *Haer.* IV, 7,4; Cyp. *Test.* I,4–5; Orig. *C. Cel.* II,5; Isid. *C. Jud.* II, 22–23, 28.

139. Just. *Dial.* 82; Ter. *Adv. Jud.* 8; 11; 13; Iren. *Haer.* II,32,4; V,6,1; Clem. *Strom.* I,21,135–36; IV,13,93; Euseb. *D. E.* IV,18,8.

140. Just. *Dial.* 112,117; Hipp. *Ref. Haer.* IX,13; Iren. *Haer.* IV, 12,1.

141. E.g., Prophyry and Celsus.

142. Most of the Church fathers are not reliable sources of Jewish midrashim, but there are exceptions: Justin and especially Origen, also Jerome. See the articles by S. Krauss (n. 38 above). Also W. Bacher, "The Church Father Origen and Rabbi Hoshaya," *JQR* 3 (1891), pp. 357–60, and G. Bardy, "Les traditions juives dans l'oeuvre d'Origène," *Revue Biblique* 24 (1925), pp. 217–52, and "S. Jérôme et ses maîtres hébreux," *Revue Bénédictine* 46 (1934), pp. 145–64.

143. Amos Hulen, "Dialogues with the Jews as Sources for Early Jewish Arguments Against Christianity," *JBL* 51 (1932), pp. 58ff. Perhaps the most believable Jewish disputant appears as Herbanus, in the "Dialogue of Archbishop Gregentius with the Jew Herbanus" (*PG* 86,621–784).

144. Salo Baron, *A Social and Religious History of the Jews* vol. 2, pp. 134–35. Also Sidney Hoenig, "Circumcision: The Covenant with Abraham," *JQR* (April, 1963), pp. 322–34.

145. Baron, *Social and Religious History* 2, pp. 134–35; see chap. 2, above, pp. 87–88.

146. M. Simon, *Verus Israel*, pp. 234–35; B. Helfgott, *The Doctrine of Election in Tannaitic Literature* (New York: King's Crown, 1954), p. 135; Baron, *Social and Religious History* 2, pp. 136–41; Wilken, *Judaism and the Early Christian Mind*, pp. 36–37 and passim.

147. Helfgott, *Election*, pp. 68–70, 130–31 and passim.

148. b. Men. 110a (R. Samuel b. Nahmani); cf. Neusner, *Aphrahat and Judaism*, p. 173, no. 90, and p. 174.

149. B. Bamberger, *Proselytism in the Talmudic Period* (New York: Ktav, 1968), pp. 156ff.

150. Helfgott, *Election*, p. 101.

151. Pesik. R. 21, pp. 99ff.; Tos. San. 13:2, p. 434; San. 105a; cf. Helfgott, *Election*, pp. 67ff. and 137.

152. Yeb 102b; Midrash Ha-gadol, Lev. 36:9; Hag. 5b; Kid. 36a; Ex. R. c. 3; cf. Helfgott, *Election*, 137–8.

153. Simon, *Verus Israel*, pp. 233–38.

154. j. Shabbat VI end, 8d; cf. Helfgott, *Election*, pp. 85–86.

155. Simon, *Verus Israel*, pp. 231–32.

156. Travers Herford, *Christianity in Talmud and Midrash* (London: Wms. & Norgate, 1903); cf. Simon, *Verus Israel*, pp. 219ff.; J. Neusner, *A History of the Jews in Babylonia* (New York: Humanities, 1966–70) vol. 5, pp. 20ff.

157. "When the Messiah is near, insolence multiplies and the Empire will pass into heresy," M. Sota 9.15 (R. Eliezer the Great); cf. Simon, *Verus Israel*, p. 223.

158. Bamberger, *Proselytism*, pp. 31f., 149–56; Helfgott, *Election*, pp. 62–63.

159. Midr. Ex. r. 46, sur 34.1; cf. Simon, *Verus Israel*, pp. 225–27.

160. Gen. r. 11,46; Pes. r. 116b, 117a; Num. r. 14,9; cf. Simon, *Verus Israel*, p. 226.

161. Gen. r. 11,6.

162. Helfgott, *Election*, pp. 136–41; Baron, *Social and Religious History* 2, pp. 130–41.

163. Neusner, *Jews in Babylonia* 3, pp. 354–58.

164. Orig. *Hom. in Jer.* 12,13; Jerome, *Comm. in Matt.* 33,6; cf. Simon, *Verus Israel*, pp. 373–82; Baron, *Social and Religious History* 2, pp. 188–89.

165. Simon, *Verus Israel*, pp. 391–93; Juster, *Les juifs dans l'empire romain* 1, pp. 277ff. Bamberger, *Proselytism*, pp. 134–40.

166. Aug. *Epp.* 56, 67, 117; Jerome *Ep.* 112,4; see R. E. Taylor, "Attitudes of the Fathers toward Practices of Jewish Christians," *Studia Patristica* 4 (1961), pp. 504–11.

167. Simon, *Verus Israel*, pp. 361–73.

168. Carl Kraeling, "The Jewish Community in Antioch," *JBL* 51 (1932), pp. 130ff. Also the introduction to C. Mervyn Maxwell, *Chrysostom's Homilies Against the Jews* (University of Chicago, Ph.D. thesis, 1966).

169. The Jewish community had recently been enheartened by the favor given them by Julian, which is doubtless why Chrysostom lays such stress on the hopelessness of their expectations of rebuilding the temple, which had been revived by Julian. Chrysostom's tale of miraculous defeat of this project is a myth based probably on

Gregory Nazianzus: See M. Adler, "The Emperor Julian and the Jews," *JQR* (old series) 5, (1892–93), pp. 591–651.
170. Cf. *Or. C. Jud.* VI, 6–7 (*PG* 48, 913–14); I,5 (*PG* 48,851).
171. Citing Deut. 32:15; Hos. 4:16; Jer. 31:18; and Luke 19:27.
172. Kraeling, see above, n. 166.

NOTES TO CHAPTER FOUR

1. S. L. Greenslade, *Church and State from Constantine to Theodosius* (London: SCM, 1954).
2. J. Juster, *Les juifs dans l'empire romain* (Paris: P. Geuthner, 1914) vol. 2, pp. 291–326.
3. James S. Seaver, *The Persecution of the Jews in the Roman Empire* (University of Kansas, 1952), p. 56. The original ms. of this thesis (Cornell, 1947) is more extensive and contains both the Latin and Mr. Seaver's English translation of the legal texts. See also James Parkes, *The Conflict of the Church and the Synagogue* (London: Socino, 1934), p. 199.
4. *CTh.* 16,9,1 (21/10/335); also *Constitutio Sirmondianis*, no. 4 (21/10/335).
5. The laws promulgated against Jewish ownership of Christian slaves between 335 and 423 are found in *CTh.* 16,9, 1–5; Clyde Pharr, *The Theodosian Code and Novels and the Sirmondian Constitutions* (Princeton: University, 1952), pp. 471–72.
6. Solomon Katz, *The Jews in the Visigothic and Frankish Kingdoms of Spain and Gaul* (Cambridge, Mass., 1937), pp. 96–103.
7. This dispute arose in Carolingian times, with secular rulers either forbidding conversion or defending compensation to Jews for converted slaves, while the Church insisted that conversion freed the slave. In the high Middle Ages, the Church granted a token compensation, while secular rulers supported the claim of the Jews for a full market value. See Solomon Grayzel, *The Church and the Jews in the Thirteenth Century* (New York: Hermon, 1966), pp. 23–24.
8. *Can. Apost.,* 71: Seaver, *Persecution of the Jews,* p. 36; also Parkes, *Church and Synagogue,* p. 176.
9. *CTh.* 16,8,1 (13/8/339), which forbade under pain of death either conversion to Judaism or efforts to make a convert return to Judaism. Also *CTh.* 16,8,26 (9/4/423).
10. *CTh.* 16,8,7 (3/7/353).
11. *CTh.* 16,7,3 (21/5/383).
12. *CTh.* 16,8,23 (24/9/416).
13. *CTh.* 9,45,2; repeated in *CJ.* 1,12,1. Honorius' law of 416 was dropped in the Justinian Code.
14. Grayzel, *Church and the Jews,* pp. 13–15; see Document 12

(p. 101) in this volume: "Innocent III to the Archbishop of Arles," Sept./Oct., 1201.

15. *CTh.* 16,8,5 (21/10/335); also n. 9 above. Also *CTh.* 16,8,28 (7/4/426).

16. *CTh.* 16,8,6 (13/8/339).

17. *CTh.* 3,7,2 and 9,7,5 (14/3/388).

18. Council of Elvira: canon 16 and canon 78: Mansi II, 8, and 18; also the Arabian collection of the canons of Nicea, canon 13: Mansi II, 969. See Seaver, *Persecution of the Jews*, pp. 25–28. This legislation was continually repeated by conciliar legislators in the following centuries.

19. *CTh.* 16,8,16 (22/4/404); and *CTh.* 16,8,24 (10/3/418).

20. *Constitutio Sirmondianis*, no. 6 (9/7/425); and *CTh.* 16,8,22 (20/10/415); Novella 3 (31/1/439).

21. Ferrandus, *Brevatio Canonum*, Title 196 (*PL* 67, 959). Parkes believes that the inclusion of this law in the ecclesiastical canons must mean that it was present in imperial legislation: *Church and Synagogue*, p. 233. Also Seaver, *Persecution of the Jews*, p. 68. Also *CJ.* (28/7/531).

22. Novella 3 (31/1/438).

23. *CTh.* 16,8,14 (11/4/399); also *CTh.* 16,8,17 (25/7/404); and *CTh.* 16,8,29 (30/5/429).

24. *CTh.* 16,8,22 (10/20/415).

25. See Michael Adler, "The Emperor Julian and the Jews," *JQR* (old series) 5 (1892/3), pp. 591–651. Also M. S. Ginzburg, "Fiscus Judaicus," *JQR* 21 (1930/1), pp. 281–91. This tax continued to be exacted sporadically in Byzantine times; Andrew Sharf, *Byzantine Jewry from Justinian to the Fourth Crusade* (London: Routledge and Kegan Paul, 1971), pp. 189–200.

26. *CTh.* 16,8,3 (11/12/321); and *CTh.* 16,8,2 (29/11/330).

27. *CTh.* 12,1,99 (18/4/383). This law was rescinded on 1/7/397 (*CTh.* 16,8,13) and superseded by a law that restored to the Jewish clergy the same exemptions as the Christian clergy. But this decree was reversed two years later: *CTh.* 12,1,165 (28/12/399).

28. *CTh.* 16,8,25 (15/2/423); and *CTh.* 16,8,27 (8/6/423); Novella 3 (31/3/439).

29. *CTh.* 16,8,18 (29/5/408).

30. Preserved in the Codex Justinianus 1,9,7 (Theodosius I [30/12/393]).

31. *CTh.* 2,1,10 (3/2/398).

32. *CTh.* 15,5,5 (1/2/425).

33. See A. W. W. Dale, *The Council of Elvira* (London: Macmillan, 1882). The anti-Judaic canons of this council are translated in Jacob R. Marcus, *The Jew in the Medieval World* (New York: Atheneum, 1972), pp. 101–3.

34. Seaver, *Persecution of the Jews*, pp. 25–28.

35. Parkes, *Church and Synagogue*, pp. 174–76.

36. Ibid., p. 304. Various baptismal abjurations for the Jewish convert are printed by Parkes in Appendix 3 of this volume, pp. 394–400.

37. Assemani, *Cod. Lit.*, I, p. 105; Parkes, *Church and Synagogue*, p. 397.

38. *CTh.* 16,8,9 (29/9/393); *CTh.* 16,8,12 (17/6/397); *CTh.* 16,8,20 (26/7/412); *CTh.* 16,8,21 (6/8/412) (repeated in 418 and 420 C.E.); *CTh.* 16,8,25 (15/2/423); *CTh.* 16,8,26 (9/4/423).

39. *CTh.* 16,8,8 (17/4/392); and *CTh.* 16,8,10 (28/2/396).

40. Seaver, *Persecution of the Jews*, p. 45 and n. 145.

41. Parkes, *Church and Synagogue*, pp. 233, 236, 238.

42. Ambrose, *Epp.* 40 and 41; F. H. Dudden, *The Life and Times of St. Ambrose the Great* (Oxford: Clarendon, 1935), vol. 2, pp. 371–80.

43. Evagrius, *Hist. Eccl.* I, 13; Seaver, *Persecution of the Jews*, p. 76; Parkes, *Church and Synagogue*, p. 238.

44. Socrates, *Hist. Eccl.* VII,13. See also Robert L. Wilken, *Judaism and the Early Christian Mind* (New Haven: Yale, 1971), chaps. 2 and 3.

45. The bishop's own account of this incident is preserved: Severus, *Epistola ad omnem ecclesiam de virtutibus ad Judaeorum conversionem in Minorcensi insula factis in praesentia reliquarum Sancti Stephani* (*PL* 20, 731–46); Seaver, *Persecution of the Jews*, p. 70.

46. Carl Kraeling, "The Jewish Community at Antioch," *JBL* 51 (1932), pp. 130ff.

47. *CTh.* 16,8,1 (13/8/339).

48. Seaver, *Persecution of the Jews*, p. 54.

49. See the summary of Theodosian laws printed in Marcus, *Jew in the Medieval World*, pp. 4–6.

50. Parkes, *Church and Synagogue*, pp. 245–55.

51. Sharf, *Byzantine Jewry*, pp. 19–41.

52. Novella 146: English translation in Parkes, *Church and Synagogue*, pp. 392–93. See also Sharf, *Byzantine Jewry*, p. 24.

53. *Corpus Iuris Civilis* 3, pp. 277–79; see Sharf, *Byzantine Jewry*, p. 21 and note.

54. *CTh.* 16,8,9 (29/9/393). "It is sufficiently established that the sect of the Jews is forbidden by no law, since we are gravely disturbed that their assemblies have been forbidden in certain places." This law was not included in the Justinian Code. Instead, Justinian lumped Jews together with pagans and heretics as groups without civil standing (*CJ.* 1,5,12). See Parkes, *Church and Synagogue*, p. 249.

55. Sharf, *Byzantine Jewry*, chaps. 3–5.

56. Ibid., p. 184 and passim.

57. Parkes, *Church and Synagogue,* pp. 206–9.

58. Solomon Katz, "Pope Gregory The Great and the Jews," *JQR* 24, no. 2 (Oct. 1933), pp. 113–36.

59. Gregory the Great to Cyprian, bk. 5, Ep. 8.

60. Parkes, *Church and Synagogue,* p. 220. See, for example, Gregory the Great, *On Job* iii, 1, and *On Ezekiel* I, Hom. 12.

61. Gregory the Great, bk. 8, Ep. 25.

62. Grayzel, *Church and the Jews,* pp. 9–12.

63. See Katz, *Jews in the Visigothic and Frankish Kingdoms.* Also Salo Baron, *Social and Religious History of the Jews,* 3, pp. 33–46, and A. K. Ziegler, *Church and State in Visigothic Spain* (New York: Columbia University, 1930).

64. Katz, ibid., pp. 11–22.

65. Sharf, *Byzantine Jewry,* pp. 99–101, 143, 166, 168. Also S. D. Goitein, *Jews and Arabs: Their Contacts Through the Ages* (New York: Schocken, 1955), passim.

66. Yitzhak Baer, *A History of the Jews in Christian Spain,* vol. 2 (From the Fourteenth Century to the Expulsion), (Philadelphia: Jewish Publication Society, 1966); see also Cecil Roth, *A History of the Marranos* (Philadelphia: Jewish Publication Society, 1947).

67. Katz, *Jews in the Visigothic and Frankish Kingdoms,* pp. 22–26.

68. James Parkes, *The Jew in the Medieval Community* (London: Soncino, 1938), pp. 158–60; a charter of Louis the Pious to Domatus is printed in Appendix 1 to this volume.

69. Ibid., p. 56; a Christian account of the conversion of Bodo, court chaplain to Louis the Pious, attributed to Prudentius, bishop of Troyes, is found in *The Annals of the Cloister of St. Bertin;* see Marcus, *Jew in the Medieval World,* pp. 353–54.

70. Andreas, archbishop of Bari (a prominent center of Talmudic studies in the ninth and tenth centuries), converted to Judaism in the early tenth century. See Sharf, *Byzantine Jewry,* pp. 122–24. An account of his conversion is found in "Fragment from the Chronicle of 'Obadyah, the Norman Proselyte: from the Kaufmann Geniza," edited by A. Scheiber, *JJS* 5 (1954), pp. 32–35.

71. See especially the letters and treatises of Agobard, ninth-century bishop of Lyons, who struggled to reassert anti-Judaic laws and practices at a time of neglect of these traditions. Writing to the bishop of Narbonne, who had so forgotten ancient hatreds as to commonly dine with Jews, contrary to ancient canonical regulations, Agobard writes: "It seems to me to be unworthy of our faith that the sons of light should associate with the children of darkness and that the Church of Christ, which ought to present itself for the kisses of the celestial spouse without blemish and without wrinkle, is disgraced by contact with the defiled and repudiated Synagogue" (*Ep.* 9). For editions of the texts of Agobard's letters and his

treatises on the baptism of slaves of the Jews and on the "insolence of the Jews," see Parkes, *The Jew*, p. 21.

72. Leon Poliakov, *The History of Anti-Semitism*, vol. 1 *From the Time of Christ to the Court Jews* (New York: Vanguard, 1965), pp. 33, 53ff.

73. Descriptions of the Crusade pogroms, especially that of the first Crusade, are found in Poliakov, *History of Anti-Semitism*, vol. 1, pp. 41–72. Also Parkes, *Jew in the Medieval Community*, pp. 59–92. Marcus, *Jew in the Medieval World*, provides several eye-witness documents for the first Crusade; pp. 115–20.

74. "We have set out to march on a long road against the enemies of God in the East, and, behold, before our eyes are the Jews, His worst foes. To ignore them is preposterous" (i.e., to put the cart before the horse) (Guiberti, *de vita sua* II, v). See Parkes, *Jew in the Medieval Community*, pp. 65–66.

75. The economic theory of anti-Semitism, according to which each major wave of repression corresponded to the expropriation of a major area of the economy pioneered by Jews, was developed by William Roscher, "The Status of the Jew in the Middle Ages from the Standpoint of Commercial Policy," *Historia Judaica* 6 (1944), pp. 13–26 (trans. Solomon Grayzel). Frederick Schweitzer, in his one-volume *History of the Jews Since the First Century* A.D. (New York: Macmillan, 1971), follows a version of this thesis, pp. 165–84. Guido Kisch criticizes the thesis on the grounds that it cannot explain the character of fanaticism of medieval anti-Semitism which must be viewed from the psychology of theological negation: *The Jews in Medieval Germany: A Study of their Legal and Social Status* (University of Chicago Press, 1949), pp. 320–22.

76. For medieval Jewish martyr theology, see especially Jacob Katz, *Exclusiveness and Tolerance* (New York: Schocken, 1969; reprint), pp. 82–92.

77. Poliakov, *History of Anti-Semitism*, vol. 1, pp. 50–64.

78. An analysis of the effect of the King's Peace on redefining Jewish legal status is found in G. Kisch, *Jews in Medieval Germany* (New York, Ktav, 1970), pp. 107–28.

79. Ibid., pp. 129–52.

80. This is the explanation given by Parkes, *Jew in the Medieval Community*, pp. 102–8.

81. Kisch demonstrates this fact to disprove the Nazi racial theory, which tried to prove that Jews had always been regarded in medieval Germany as "strangers" in an ethnic, racial, and nationalist sense: *Jews in Medieval Germany*, pp. 335–41.

82. Grayzel, *The Church and the Jews*, p. 25, and documents 14, 15, 29, 69, and 104; also conciliar decrees: documents 3, 16, 25, and 33.

83. See Wolfgang S. Seiferth, *Synagogue and Church in the Middle*

Ages: Two Symbols in Art and Literature (New York: Frederick Ungar, 1970).

84. Grayzel, *Church and the Jews*, pp. 10–11. Kisch, *Jews in Medieval Germany*, pp. 145–52.

85. Poliakov, *History of Anti-Semitism*, p. 65. Also Grayzel, *Church and the Jews*, pp. 59–71.

86. Poliakov, *History of Anti-Semitism*, pp. 33–36.

87. Ibid., pp. 29–34.

88. Marcus, *Jew in the Medieval World*, prints several contemporary documents on the burning of the Talmud of 1239–48; two letters from Odo, the French papal legate charged with the investigation, to the Pope, and a chronicler's account of the fate of a French bishop who tried to prevent the burning of the Talmud, pp. 142–50.

89. For the role of the Church in shaping the image of medieval usury, see Parkes, *Jew in the Medieval Community*, pp. 273–306.

90. Ibid., pp. 307–38. Also Kisch, *Jews in Medieval Germany*, pp. 327–29; and Grayzel, *Church and the Jews*, pp. 41–49.

91. Parkes, *Jew in the Medieval Community*, pp. 339–82.

92. Contemporary documents on the accusations against the Jews at the time of the Black Death are found in Marcus, *Jew in the Medieval World*, pp. 43–48.

93. Poliakov, *History of Anti-Semitism*, pp. 123–54. Also Joshua Trachtenberg, *The Devil and the Jews* (New Haven: Yale University, 1932); and Salo Baron, "Demonic Alien," *Social and Religious History of the Jews*, vol. 9, pp. 122ff.

94. For a summary of these developments, see Schweitzer, *History of the Jews*, pp. 185–280.

95. See D. C. Smith, *Protestant Attitudes Toward Jewish Emancipation in Prussia* (New Haven: Yale University, Ph.D. thesis, 1971), esp. chap. 3.

96. Poliakov, *History of Anti-Semitism*, pp. 202–9.

97. Jacob Katz, *Out of the Ghetto: The Social Background of Jewish Emancipation: 1770–1870*, (Harvard University Press, 1973), pp. 11–27.

98. Selma Stern, *The Court Jew: A Contribution to the History of Absolutism in Central Europe* (Philadelphia: Jewish Publication Society, 1950). Also F. L. Carsten, "The Court Jews: A Prelude to Emancipation," *Year Book III*, publication of the Leo Baeck Institute of Jews from Germany (London, 1958), pp. 140–56.

99. See Norman Cohn, *Warrant for Genocide: The Myth of the Jewish World Conspiracy and the Protocols of the Elders of Zion* (New York: Harper & Row, 1969); also Hannah Arendt, *Anti-Semitism: Origins of Totalitarianism*, pt. 1, (New York: Harcourt Brace, 1951), pp. 12ff.

100. Jacob Katz, *Tradition and Crisis, Jewish Society at the End of the Middle Ages* (New York: Schocken, 1961).

101. Katz, *Out of the Ghetto*, pp. 57–79. Smith, *Protestant Attitudes*, chap. 2 and passim.

102. Katz, *Out of the Ghetto*, pp. 124–41; also Katz, *Exclusivism and Tolerance*, pp. 156ff. and passim.

103. Smith, *Protestant Attitudes*, pp. 143–44 and passim; also Jean Paul Sartre, *Anti-Semite and Jew* (New York: Schocken, 1948).

104. Arendt, *Anti-Semitism*, pp. 52–53.

105. Smith, *Protestant Attitudes*, pp. 74ff.; also Nathan Rotenstreich, *The Recurring Pattern: Studies in Anti-Judaism in Modern Thought* (London: Weidenfeld and Nicolson, 1963): on Kant, Hegel and Toynbee.

106. Eva Fleischner, *The View of Judaism in German Theology since 1945* (Milwaukee: Marquette University, Ph.D. thesis, 1971), citing especially H. Rost, *Gedanken und Wahrheiten zur Judenfrage* (Trier, 1907), p. 41.

107. George Mosse, *The Crisis of German Ideology: Intellectual Origins of the Third Reich* (New York: Grosset and Dunlap, 1964) pp. 88–107.

108. Ibid., pp. 126ff. and passim.

109. James Parkes, *Anti-Semitism* (Chicago: Quadrangle Books, 1963) pp. 20–44; also P. G. J. Pulzer, *The Rise of Political Anti-Semitism in Germany and Austria* (New York: Wiley and Sons, 1964); and Paul W. Massing, *Rehearsal for Destruction. A Study of Political Anti-Semitism in Imperial Germany* (New York: Harper Bros., 1949).

110. Parkes, *Anti-Semitism*, pp. 87–103.

111. Schweitzer, *History of the Jews*, p. 222.

112. Karl Barth, *The German Church Conflict* (London: Lutterworth, 1965), see pp. 16–17: "Fundamentals of the Church's Opposition: 1933."

113. Dietrich Bonhoeffer, *No Rusty Swords: Letters, Lectures and Notes: 1928–36*, from *Collected Works*, vol. 1, ed. and intro. by E. H. Robertson (New York: Harper and Row, 1965), pp. 226–27. Also *Ethics*, E. Bethge, ed., (New York: Macmillan, 1963), pp. 89–90.

114. Mosse, *Crisis of Germany Ideology*, chap. 17.

Index of Scripture Passages

Index of Modern Authors